Peacemaking in Rwanda

 *A project of the International Peace Academy*

PEACEMAKING IN RWANDA

THE DYNAMICS OF FAILURE

Bruce D. Jones

boulder
london

Published in the United States of America in 2001 by
Lynne Rienner Publishers, Inc.
1800 30th Street, Boulder, Colorado 80301
www.rienner.com

and in the United Kingdom by
Lynne Rienner Publishers, Inc.
3 Henrietta Street, Covent Garden, London WC2E 8LU

© 2001 by the International Peace Academy, Inc. All rights reserved by the publisher

Library of Congress Cataloging-in-Publication Data
Jones, Bruce D.
  Peacemaking in Rwanda : the dynamics of failure / Bruce D. Jones.
    p. cm.
  Includes bibliographical references and index.
  ISBN 1-55587-994-2 (alk. paper)
    1. Genocide—Rwanda—Prevention. 2. Conflict management—Rwanda. 3. United Nations—Peacekeeping forces—Rwanda. 4. Rwanda—Ethnic relations. I. Title.
DT450.435.J66 2001
341.5'84—dc21   2001019383

British Cataloguing in Publication Data
A Cataloguing in Publication record for this book
is available from the British Library.

Printed and bound in the United States of America

∞ The paper used in this publication meets the requirements
of the American National Standard for Permanence of
Paper for Printed Library Materials Z39.48-1984.

5 4 3 2 1

Contents

Acknowledgments		vii
1	Introduction: The Rwandan Civil War in Context	1
2	War and Genocide: History of the Rwandan Conflict	15
3	Early Peacemaking Efforts: Regional Prenegotiation	53
4	The Arusha Negotiations: Mediation and Facilitation	69
5	UN Peacekeeping and the Collapse of Arusha: Implementation Efforts	103
6	Genocide, Crisis, and the Renewal of War: The Consequences of Failure	135
7	The Dynamics of Peacemaking in Rwanda: Conclusions and Implications	157

List of Acronyms 179
Bibliography 181
Index 199
About the Book 209

Acknowledgments

This study could not have been written without the help and support of a tremendous number of people, to whom I would like to express my gratitude.

At the London School of Economics and Political Science (LSE), Mark Hoffman was unstinting with his time, insight, and friendship; the book could not have been completed without his support. Other LSE colleagues and friends, including Michael Banks, Emery Brusset, Christopher Coker, Dominique Jacquin-Berdal, Bice Maiguascha, Desiree McGraw, and Zoe Stephenson, deserve thanks for help along the way. Particular thanks to James Mayall and Susan Woodward, who read and commented on the final text and whose writings taught me much about international politics. Also in London, Andy Carl and David Lord of Conciliation Resources gave me that most valuable commodity—space—and let me be a fly on the wall as they practiced what others preach. A special thanks is due to Beverly Neufeld, who suffered through my first drafts, tolerated my too frequent presence on her spare sofa, and was the best possible friend throughout. My debt to Alexander Costy is almost as great as our friendship.

Many other colleagues made invaluable contributions to the project. I was fortunate to work closely with Astri Suhrke and Howard Adelman, whose boundless curiosity and passion continue to be a source of inspiration. Astri also arranged for a visit to the Chr. Michelsen Institute (CMI), where the penultimate draft of the book was written, and has been a valued colleague and coauthor over the past half-decade. Thanks also to Gunnar Sorbø and Arve Ofstad of CMI for making my visit possible and productive. Stephen John Stedman shared with me his encyclopedic knowledge of international peacemaking efforts, made possible my fellowship at Stanford University's Center for International Security and Cooperation, and has been an important intellectual collaborator and friend ever since. At Stanford, I also profited from the support of David Holloway, Scott Sagan, and particularly Lynn Eden, the friendship of Page Fortna and Ade Adebajo, and the opportunity to collaborate with Charles Tilly. In Toronto, Janice Stein piqued my interest in the humanitarian dimensions of the international response to crises and became a frequent source of advice and support, including putting me in contact with CARE Canada. At CARE, I am grateful to Michael Bryans, John Watson, and Nancy Gordon for their support in past and present collaborations. At the United Nations in New York, Martin Griffiths, Ed Tsui, and especially Martin Barber created a working environment that allowed me to complete this project while on staff at the Office for the Coordination of Humanitarian Affairs, and were the very best of colleagues. I also owe a continuing debt of gratitude to Shepard Forman of New York University's Center on International Cooperation, for his friendship and guidance.

Other people who gave of their time, expertise, and contacts, commented on drafts, or in many other ways facilitated elements of this project include: Taisier Ali, Kathi Austin, Omar Bakhet, Jean-Cristophe Beliard, Mark Bradbury, John Borton, Michael Brown, Kathleen Campbell, Rebecca Dale, Danielle de Lame, Antonio Donini, Michael Doyle, Mark Duffield, Carol Fuller, Lindsey Hilsum, Randolph Kent, Sue Lautze, Anne Mackintosh, Joanna Macrae, Robert Matthews, Catherine Newbury, Norah Niland, Eugenia Pisa-Lopez, Johann Poittier, Jude Rand, Nicola Reindorp, Barnett Rubin, Wilson Rutayisire, Jack Snyder, Nick Stockton, Rowland Roome, Necla Tschirgi, Barbara Walter, and I. William Zartman. Many thanks to all of them. Thanks also to two anonymous reviewers of the manuscript, whose comments helped shape the final draft.

Karin Wermester proofread the penultimate draft and undertook the Herculean task of sorting out my footnotes and bibliography, for which I am endlessly grateful.

This book would not have been possible without the financial support of the Social Sciences and Humanities Research Council of Canada, the Association of Commonwealth Universities, the London School of Economics, the Academic Council of the United Nations System, and the Carnegie Commission for Preventing Deadly Conflict.

I am particularly grateful to David Malone, president of the International Peace Academy (IPA), for supporting the publication of this book and for much else besides. I was fortunate to spend two years in New York when his intellect and energy, and that of his IPA colleagues, made it a more exciting place to be. I am equally grateful to Lynne Rienner and her colleagues for agreeing to publish this work.

There is no part of this book that does not bear the traces of my family's support. I hope the final product reflects some part of the humanity and editorial acuity of my father, Terry Jones; the patience, insight, and expert proofreading of my mother, Dawn Jones; and the warmth and writer's instinct of my sister, Kari Jones, who edited many drafts. Along with Michael Pardy and Rowan, they sheltered me, literally and otherwise, when the darkness of Rwanda was overwhelming, and they kept me going.

It should be clearly stated that the views expressed in this book are not necessarily those of the United Nations. I am, of course, solely responsible for the final contents of this book, as well as any errors or inaccuracies contained therein.

—Bruce D. Jones

1

Introduction: The Rwandan Civil War in Context

It is difficult to overstate the scale or brutality of the Rwandan genocide of 1994. Between 6 April and 17 July, the Rwandan state engaged in an act of mass carnage against its own population, targeting a minority ethnic group and political opponents. In a mere fourteen weeks, several hundred thousand people—perhaps as many as a million—were gunned down, beaten to death, or literally hacked to pieces by machete, often after being raped, tortured, and forced to watch or participate in the execution of family members. Apart from the killing, almost 4 million people were displaced from their homes—more than 50 percent of the prewar Rwandan population—with 2.3 million of those fleeing the country altogether. The result was the greatest humanitarian crisis of this generation.

The Rwandan genocide was horrific even by the standards of a century repeatedly marred by mass political and ethnic slaughters: of Armenians at the onset of the century; of Jews during World War II; of Cambodians at the height of the Cold War. In the final decade of the twentieth century, mass genocide found its most brutally efficient expression to date in Rwanda.

In early April 1994, the *Times* of London carried a report about a development in a little-known war in Central Africa, reprinted here in its entirety:

> The leaders of Rwanda and Burundi were killed last night when their plane was shot down by a rocket, according to UN officials, as it approached the airport at the Rwandan capital of Kigali.[1]

Behind this bare-bones report, one of modern history's most intensely violent acts was unfolding.

Translating the numbers from the Rwandan horror into a Western context helps illustrate the scale of what occurred during those monstrous months. The percentage of the Rwandan population killed in a single day of genocide exceeded by at least a factor of ten the percentage of the U.S. population killed throughout the entire Vietnam War. The intensity in the rate of killing was shocking even by the bloody standards of the twentieth century. In European mythology, the Battle of Paschaendale looms large in the history of senseless slaughter, with its 35,000 killed in a single day. Scaled to the size of the population, the daily death rate in Rwanda exceeded that of Paschaendale by at least a factor of three, repeated day in and day out for more than ninety days.

The extraordinary irony is that this slaughter escalated out of a civil war so low in intensity that it escaped the radar of international conflict monitoring. For the four years prior to the genocide, Rwanda had been engaged but not engulfed in a civil war that each year tallied a mere few hundred battle casualties and some few hundred civilian deaths. Indeed, the number of war deaths was so low as to make the fighting correspond to what is listed by the Stockholm International Peace Research Institute as a dispute.[2] Yet out of this dispute grew a genocide of horrific magnitude and intensity.

Such was the scale of carnage in Rwanda, and so little known was the civil war preceding it, that it quickly became conventional wisdom that nothing had been done to prevent the genocide. For years afterward, newspaper editorials berated the international community for having failed to act in Rwanda. Focusing their attention on the period immediately prior to the genocide itself, even informed participants in the conflict resolution field tended to argue that the international community was insufficiently engaged in Rwanda. Within two years of the genocide, this perception was so pervasive that Thomas Weiss, a leading humanitarian scholar, would characterize weak conflict resolution efforts as exhibiting "Rwanda-like diplomatic timidity."[3] Indeed, the independent investigation conducted by the United Nations (UN) castigated the international community for inaction.[4]

Yet even the most cursory examination of the international presence in Rwanda reveals that there was a meaningful effort under way long prior to the genocide to mitigate and contain the Rwandan civil war. These efforts were not designed specifically to prevent a genocide, but they were designed to prevent an escalation of the crisis and to lay the groundwork for peace. Indeed, efforts to find a peaceful resolution to the Rwandan war began within days of its outbreak and continued almost unbroken for the following three and a half years. The construction of a basic outline of the peace process in Rwanda reveals a series of intersecting peace negotiations involving both regional and international actors. These were sustained through 1990 and 1991 and then, following a brief interruption, ran almost continuously from March 1992 until August 1993, when a peace agreement was signed in Arusha, Tanzania.

Furthermore, Rwanda was the site of a host of other peacemaking activities by national, regional, and international actors, both state and nonstate. These activities were designed to monitor the conflict, mitigate its consequences, manage its negotiation, prevent its escalation, and secure its resolution. Apart from formal and informal diplomatic processes, no fewer than five neutral military missions were sent to Rwanda to aid in the conflict management processes. Some of these were innovative, including the first ever military deployment by the Organization of African Unity (OAU) in a member state's internal conflict, and the first ever on-the-ground collaboration between the OAU and a UN peacekeeping operation. There were also unilateral military interventions in Rwanda. Although some of these were partisan, others, such as France's Operation Turquoise, purportedly had humanitarian objectives.

The Failure of International Peacemaking Efforts

Thus, at first glance the reality of peacemaking efforts in Rwanda appears directly contrary to the conventional wisdom that has developed. International conflict management efforts to deal with the civil war were substantial, not less than wide-ranging, and innovative at least in parts. They were also, of course, an absolute failure. Conventional wisdom would have Rwanda be a story of the failure to take action; it is in fact a story about the failure of actions taken.[5]

Herein lies the puzzle: How could multiple conflict resolution efforts by the international community fall so wide of the mark and produce so little? How, and why, did conflict management efforts in Rwanda fail? How could one of the century's most violent acts have escalated out of a low-intensity conflict that was the subject of wide-ranging preventive and peacemaking efforts?

It is the central purpose of this book to explain this seeming paradox, to identify the dynamics of the failure of the international and regional conflict management efforts to prevent this massive escalation of violence. The second purpose is to extrapolate the implications—analytical, theoretical, and practical—of this failure, as well as draw lessons for future peacemaking endeavors.

As I will show, from the outset the prospects for successful resolution of the Rwandan civil war were diminished by the inflexibility of the rebel movement and, more significantly, by the presence of powerful actors within the Rwandan government committed to a program of hostility to peace. These actors, however, were neither monolithic nor all-powerful; their existence did not predetermine Rwanda's fate. But efforts by others to respond to extremists in Rwanda were incoherent and insufficient and, in the end, played into their hands.

There were several successes in the Rwandan peace process, but also several flaws—none of them fatal in and of themselves, but fatally compounding one another. Prenegotiation efforts successfully constructed a political mediation process, involving all key actors. But they also complicated those negotiations by bringing new actors into the process whose presence undercut the position of key moderates within the Rwandan regime. Likewise, the negotiation process itself succeeded in producing a comprehensive peace agreement that addressed all the major issues at stake in the war and charted a course for transition to democratic government and the rule of law. But it isolated powerful figures within the government, actors who then saw common cause with extremist forces seeking to overturn the peace and launch their genocidal alternative. The UN peacekeeping effort that followed the signing of a peace accord was ill-coordinated with the mediation process and, therefore, based on false premises. For this reason, and because of the minimal strategic relevance of Rwanda to the major powers, the peacekeeping effort was wholly insufficient to implement the peace.

These failures cascaded, resulting in the collapse of peace efforts in the face of a concerted—and brutal—challenge by extremist opponents of peace. Extremist forces followed a clear and deliberate strategy to undermine the peace process and, as an alternative, laid the foundation for genocide. By contrast, third-party strategies were poorly coordinated, so the results were diffuse and often contradictory. Extremist forces were able to maneuver among different third parties and turn conflict resolution processes to their rhetorical and political advantage. The failure of the peace process in Rwanda has multiple dimensions, but it can be understood in part as a function of the inconsistency and overall incoherence of its component parts.

Most postmortems on the Rwandan peace efforts blame the weakness of the UN peacekeeping operation. Had the UN operation been more substantial, the argument goes, the flaws of earlier negotiations would not have mattered and the genocide could have been halted. Although logically sound, this position is analytically and politically unhelpful. A decade's experience of peacekeeping in internal wars shows that the challenge of keeping and/or enforcing a contested peace is daunting. As Howard Adelman has compellingly argued, peacemaking efforts must be grounded in both realistic analyses of conflict dynamics *and* realistic assessments of the capacities and capabilities of the diplomatic and international organizations involved in the response. It is far too easy to treat peacekeeping operations as a form of deus ex machina that can compensate for the failings of other forms of peacemaking. Instead, this book treats the array of official and unofficial peacemaking efforts in the Rwandan conflict, involving political, diplomatic, humanitarian, and peacekeeping actors, and explores the implications of their collective failure.

The core paradox of conflict resolution in Rwanda—the relative sophistication and breadth of the management efforts undertaken, contrasted with the terrible depth of their failure—gives these implications resonance. Indeed, a leading scholar of international conflict management, I. William Zartman, began a recent account of international peacemaking with the following argument: "On the edge of the millennium, the methods of conflict have been more brutal and the methods of conflict resolution more sophisticated than ever before, leaving a tremendous gap."[6]

Nowhere more than in Rwanda have the methods of conflict been more brutal, or the methods of conflict resolution more apparently sophisticated. Understanding the nature of this gap between catastrophic results and ostensibly sophisticated efforts provides important clues on how to improve contemporary peacemaking.

These clues are relevant to the question of conflict prevention, which has become a clarion call for those seeking to strengthen international capacities for conflict management. The lesson of Rwanda, it is said, has been learned: early warning and early action is far less costly than late containment of crises. Correctly understood, however, Rwanda is not a tale that illustrates the need for early action. Rather, it is a cautionary tale about the limits of conflict prevention and the potentially disastrous consequences of peacemaking done poorly.

Moreover, Rwanda highlights structural problems in existing international systems for managing conflict, problems not easily overcome absent meaningful reform. The simple fact is that the international tools developed over fifty-plus years to foster peace and security—such as the 1948 Genocide Convention, conflict resolution mechanisms, and UN peacekeeping—failed to provide even a shred of protection to the hundreds of thousands of Rwandans who fell victim to the barbarism of their own government. From this reality emerge sobering lessons for those who seek to build an ambitious international regime of conflict prevention and management.

Context: Internal Wars in the 1990s

If the Rwandan genocide was among the bloodiest episodes of post–World War II history, the civil war from which it sprang was far from unique. Indeed, the Rwandan civil war shares with dozens of internal wars that have plagued recent decades several themes pertinent to the challenge of peacemaking.[7] As diplomats, aid workers, scholars, journalists, and others have studied and lived the wars of the 1980s and 1990s, two sets of challenges have become evident. The first relates to the complexities and contingencies of internal war itself; the second relates to the equal complexities of the organizations involved in response.

The complexity of internal war has multiple dimensions. For example, the so-called life-cycles of war, once thought to be predictable, have proved contingent and unpredictable. Real conflict situations have been shown to be characterized not by predictable cycles but by "chaos, irrationality and confusion" that "always makes a mockery of the best models."[8] Experience has also shown that parties to conflict, rather than being unitary or unified, frequently represent a "collection of constituencies" among which complete cohesion is likely to be short-lived.[9] An extreme example is found in the Somali civil war, which has for the past decade been characterized by shifting alliances based on the intricate dynamics of clan relations.[10]

Even in a less fluid environment, such as Northern Ireland, relations between different factions within the Unionist and Republican movements constitute a salient factor in the dynamics of the conflict and have posed major obstacles to resolution.[11]

Moreover, conflict occurs (and must be resolved) at different levels in society.[12] These levels may include the so-called top leadership, which encompasses political, military, and religious leadership of high visibility; middle-range leadership, which includes ethnic and religious leaders of lower visibility, academics and intellectuals, and leaders within particular sectors (such as prominent businessmen, doctors, etc.); and grassroots leadership, which includes leaders of indigenous nongovernmental organizations (NGOs), community developers, local health officials, and others. Specialists have theorized that successful conflict resolution requires connections between initiatives at these different levels.[13] This argument was given credence after the early successes of the Oslo process, in which an unofficial (and secret) dialogue between Israelis and Palestinians, begun at the academic level and facilitated by a team of Norwegian diplomats and academics, led first to unofficial dialogue between higher-level representatives of the two sides and eventually to formal, official dialogue between the Israeli government and the Palestine Liberation Organization.[14]

An additional element of the complexity of internal conflict is its subjective nature.[15] Although a conflict may have begun over an objective issue, the rising importance of subjective factors over time poses obstacles. Through the course of fighting, especially in conflicts of long duration, "civil wars often become total wars because the parties perceive that the character of their opponents is the cause of war."[16] In such circumstances, success will depend in part on the willingness of combatants to change their perceptions of their opponents—a very difficult challenge indeed. Along with totalistic perceptions, would-be peacemakers also contend with the security fears of parties. For example, in implementing a peace agreement in an internal war, it will usually be necessary to integrate two formerly opposing armies into a single national force, which entails the demobilization and partial disarmament of the parties.[17] This has frequently been a source of acute difficulty for mediators and peacekeepers, as the process of disarmament creates opportunities for each side to take advantage of the other, posing difficult issues of trust. In a recent instance, the question of decommissioning the armed wings of the parties in Northern Ireland has been among the thorniest challenges to implementation of the Good Friday Accords.[18]

To complicate matters, parties to conflict can make use of inflammatory rhetoric, often painting negative portraits of the opponent as a tool for political mobilization within their own ranks. U.S. characterizations of Iraq's Sadaam Hussein are a case in point. Of course, totalistic rhetoric can also be a negotiating tool. Parties will often claim that they will accept no outcome other than total victory.[19] The problem then becomes distinguishing rhetoric from strategy. Although good intelligence and analysis can help, rhetoric is often difficult to distinguish from the real perceptions and positions of parties.[20] It may therefore amplify the fears and risk perceptions of the opposing side. This can enormously complicate the search for peace.

Even more challenging are circumstances in which totalistic rhetoric expressed as aspirations for total victory actually *do* represent real positions. There are contexts where the leaders of rebel movements or governments are unwilling to negotiate a compromise settlement short of total victory, and where their intransigence does not seem warranted either by the justice of their cause or the costs of achieving victory. Sometimes, as with the Revolutionary United Front (RUF) in Sierra Leone, the reasons can be economic. RUF's leader, Fodeh Sankoh, has profited hugely from war and thus resisted serious peace efforts throughout the 1990s.[21] In other cases, the resistance to settlement can take pathological dimensions. An example is found in Angola, in the recurrent unwillingness of the rebel leader, Joseph Savimbi, to accept a variety of profitable settlements to the conflict. Although some have argued Savimbi, too, is seeking profits from war,[22] Jeff Herbst has noted that Savimbi might long ago have accepted a settlement, invested his profits to date in the markets, and be far richer today as a result.[23] Many familiar with the Angolan conflict have come to believe that Savimbi has an obsessive attachment to the goal of becoming president of Angola and, as long as that prospect remains even faintly attainable, will settle for nothing less.[24] Savimbi is an example of what Stephen Stedman calls a "spoiler"—a leader who will almost never negotiate a peaceful settlement to conflict.[25] Where such spoilers exist, they will enormously complicate the search for peace. Understanding the motivations of spoilers, and adapting peacemaking strategies to deal with them, is, according to Stedman, the sine qua non of effective peacemaking and implementation.[26]

Along with the complexity and contingency of war, there is growing evidence of the challenges posed by the organizational and political complexities of peacemaking actors themselves. As public attention to internal wars has mounted, so more and more actors, official and unofficial, have become engaged in responding to the political, humanitarian, development, and human rights aspects of them.

To illustrate, consider peacemaking efforts in the Sudan in the 1980s and 1990s. As characterized by Christopher Mitchell, a variety of actors took on a variety of peacemaking roles in Sudan.[27] These included facilitation of communication between parties; convening meetings; exploring options; reassuring parties about conflict resolution processes; decoupling internal parties from external patrons; unifying internal parties; training negotiating teams; fact finding; providing payoffs for success; monitoring progress; guaranteeing outcomes; enforcing deals; and reconciling the parties once peace on paper is achieved. So many roles are not likely to be played by any single actor. Rather, a range of "appropriate intermediaries"[28]—including official diplomats, church representatives, NGOs, UN agencies, peacekeepers, and others—may become involved. Whereas earlier conflict resolution processes were typically dominated by diplomatic mediation, both official and secret, contemporary conflict resolution involves a proliferation of actors and roles.[29] Complex crises, in short, have generated increasingly complex forms of response.

The range of peacemaking efforts now commonly in use, played by an equally wide range of external actors, creates a complex dynamic in its own right. The unavoidable impact of such efforts upon one another as well as the overall situation makes it critical to identify and manage the connections between individual efforts. The effects of efforts can constrain, or facilitate, new approaches. Further, individual interventions can overlap, occur simultaneously, or occur in parallel. Viewing individual efforts as part of an ongoing, cumulative process can thus help in understanding their impact.

In short, peacemaking interventions by third parties should be seen in what Mark Hoffman characterizes as an "interconnected framework":

> What is needed is a "thick" account of the whole of the third-party process which accurately captures and explains the dynamic connections between different third-party initiatives. . . . In any given

conflict it is the case that a full explanation of the long and complex process leading to a solution needs to incorporate the multiple levels at which third-party activity takes place and the nature of the interconnections between them.[30]

As he notes, when viewed as part of a whole, it is difficult to isolate "individual third-party *initiatives* [from] the larger third-party *process*."[31]

The importance of this approach has been stressed by several practitioners in recent cases, from Burundi to Bosnia, who have provided compelling accounts of the multiple connections—sometimes helpful, sometimes complicating—among the range of third-party actors involved in responding to conflict. The general sentiment is well captured by the title of a recent volume of practitioner accounts: *Herding Cats: Multiparty Mediation in a Complex World.*[32]

Connections between individual initiatives in an overall process can occur in one of two basic ways: accidentally; or deliberately, through efforts by any given third party to forge links to another, or through the efforts of some sort of "adaptive and co-ordinating component."[33] Theorists have argued that this coordination function can be addressed in several ways: through the development of a "peace inventory" (i.e., a database of who is doing what in the realm of peacebuilding); creation of a coordination commission; the utilization of "donor peace conferences"; creation of "strategic resource groups" that bring together experts, academics, and practitioners;[34] or through senior mediators, such as UN Special Representatives.[35] However, historically, such a coordinating element has frequently been absent. Mitchell records a "general impression to date . . . that role enactment in recent mediation processes has been almost totally *ad hoc*" and suggests that "this randomness may, of course, explain the low success rate of [conflict resolution] initiatives."[36]

As important if not more important than coordination between peacemaking initiatives is the question of strategy—that is, identification of a preferred set of outcomes and a means of achieving them.[37] Such a strategy must take into account obstacles and opportunities, including those arising from lack of cohesion among parties or the presence of spoilers. Furthermore, such a strategy should be common among major third parties or coordinated with them; having different third parties pursuing different strategies is likely to result in an incoherent framework for conflict resolution.[38] Moreover, such a strategy must take into account the roles and resources available to third parties. A strategy that relies on an unrealistic level of commitment or resources from the international community will run up against important limits and likely end poorly.

Finally, where third-party efforts involve the implementation of a peace agreement and guarantees to that effect, the seriousness of those guarantees will be a critical determinant of success. Several conflicts—including Rwanda—have entered their most deadly phase following the signing of a peace accord that included international guarantees.[39] Where such security guarantees are not serious, problems will occur. In practice, then, such guarantees are often largely symbolic and rarely result in any serious action in the face of a breakdown in the implementation of peace agreements; they are tantamount to a bluff. When such bluffs are called, the consequences can be dire. In Rwanda, those consequences were not borne by international third parties but by the victims of renewed, and vicious, warfare.

It is in this interaction between two sets of factors that the dynamics of failure in Rwanda can be identified. The complexities of peacemaking efforts in Rwanda intersected with the contingencies and uncertainties of the war itself, with unforeseen and ultimately tragic consequences.

Extrapolating those dynamics, and placing them in the context of recurrent challenges to peacemaking in internal wars, makes it possible to understand something of how and why peacemaking in Rwanda went so horribly wrong. It also makes it possible to begin the process of learning lessons from Rwanda, lessons that in turn suggest the nature and necessity of reforms in existing international systems for conflict prevention and peacemaking.

Notes

1. *The Times*, 6 April 1994: 1.

2. The Stockholm International Peace Research Institute (SIPRI) classifies as "disputes" conflicts resulting in under 1,000 battle deaths per year. *SIPRI Yearbook* (Stockholm: SIPRI, 1993).

3. Thomas G. Weiss, "Overcoming the Somalia Syndrome—'Operation Rekindle Hope'?" *Global Governance* 1 (1995): 171.

4. Ingvar Carlsson, Han Sung-Joo, and Rufus M. Kupolati, *Report of the Independent Inquiry into the Actions of the UN During the 1994 Genocide in Rwanda* (New York: United Nations, 15 December 1999).

5. This was the title of a joint paper by the author and Astri Suhrke. See Astri Suhrke and Bruce Jones, "Preventive Diplomacy in Rwanda: Failure to Act, or Failure of Actions?" in Bruce Jentleson (ed.), *Opportunities Missed, Opportunities Seized* (Lanham, Md.: Rowman and Littlefield, 2000).

6. I. William Zartman and J. Lewis Rasmussen, eds., *Peacemaking in International Conflict: Methods and Techniques* (Washington, DC: U.S. Institute for Peace Press, 1997), introduction, 3.

7. Whereas international wars were for a time the dominant form of warfare in the international system, by the mid-1970s their number had been overtaken by internal wars, and by the end of the 1990s internal wars accounted for the vast bulk of wars worldwide; see United Nations, *Annual Report on the Work of the Organisation* (New York: UN, 1999).

8. David Bloomfield, *Peacemaking Strategies in Northern Ireland: Building Complementarity in Conflict Management Theory* (Basingstoke, UK: MacMillan Press, 1997), 155.

9. Ibid. See also Vivienne Jabri, *Mediating Conflict: Decision-Making and Western Intervention in Namibia* (New York: St. Martin's Press, 1990).

10. The classic account of clan dynamics in Somalia is Ioan Lewis, *A Pastoral Democracy* (Oxford: Oxford University Press, 1961); for an account of clan dynamics in the causation of the Somali wars, see David Laitin, "Somalia: Civil War and International Intervention," in Barbara F. Walter and Jack Snyder (eds.), *Civil Wars, Insecurity, and Intervention* (New York: Columbia University Press, 1999), 146–180.

11. Bloomfield, *Peacemaking*. See also Brendan O'Leary, *The Politics of Antagonism: Understanding Northern Ireland* (London: Athlone Press, 1993).

12. John Paul Lederach, *Building Peace: Sustainable Reconciliation in Divided Societies* (Toyko: UN University Press, 1995).

13. Ibid.

14. For a range of views on the Oslo process, see Uri Savir, *The Process: 1100 Days That Changed the Middle East* (New York: Random House, 1998); Mahmoud Abbas (Abu Mazen), *Through Secret Channels* (Reading, UK: Garnet, 1995); and Jane Corbin, *Gaza First: The Secret Norway Channel to Peace Between Israel and the PLO* (London: Bloomsbury, 1994).

15. Ronald J. Fischer and Loraleigh Keashly, "The Potential Complementarity of Mediation and Consultation within a Contingency Model of Third-party Intervention," *Journal of Peace Research* 28, 1 (1991): 34. Also see Robert O. Matthews and Taisier Ali, "Introduction," in Matthews and Ali (eds.), *Civil Wars in Africa: Roots and Resolution* (Kingston: McGill-Queens University Press, 1999); and Jack Snyder and Barbara Walters, "Introduction," in Snyder and Walters (eds.), *Civil War*, 116–145. For a recent argument that "greed" and "grievance" (i.e., objective and subjective aspects) are both elements of causes of conflict, see Paul Collier and Anke Hoeffler, "Greed and Grievance as Causes of Civil War," paper presented at the conference Economics of Political Violence, Center of International Studies, Princeton University, 18–19 March 2000.

16. Stephan J. Stedman, "Negotiation and Mediation in Internal Conflict," in Michael E. Brown (ed.), *The International Dimensions of Internal Conflict* (Cambridge: MIT Press, 1996): 345.

17. Barbara F. Walter, "The Critical Barrier to Civil War Settlement," *International Organisation* 51, 3 (1997): 335–369. See also Stedman, "Negotiation and Mediation," 344.

18. See "The Blame Game: Northern Ireland's New Crisis: The Government Has Suspended Northern Ireland's Devolved Government. Let the Recriminations Begin," *The Economist*, 19 February 2000; and "Listening Mode in Ulster: The Participants in Northern Ireland's Peace Process Are Running Out of Ideas," *The Economist*, 22 April 2000.

19. Stedman, "Negotiation and Mediation," 349–350.

20. See Barbara Walter, "Designing Transitions from Civil War: Demobilisation, Democratisation, and Commitments to Peace," *International Security* 24, 1 (Summer 1999): 127–156.

21. David Keen, *The Privatisation of War: A Political Economy of Conflict in Sierra Leone* (London: James Currey, 1997); see also Mark Bradbury, *Rebels Without a Cause* (CARE UK: London, 1995).

22. An evolving literature on the political economy of warfare raises questions about other kinds of dynamics that may diminish leaders' interest in peaceful settlement of conflict. Scholars such as Mark Duffield, David Keen, and William Reno have identified some of the parallel economies that develop during wars leading to economic interests in the perpetuation of warfare. The best early example of this work is Keen, *Privatisation of War*. For a recent collection, see Mats Berdal and David M. Malone, eds., *Greed and Grievance: Economic Agendas in Civil Wars* (Boulder: Lynne Rienner Publishers, 2000).

23. Jeffrey Herbst, "The Organisation of Rebellion in Africa," paper presented at the conference Economics of Political Violence, Center of International Studies, Princeton University, 18–19 March 2000.

24. UN and Canadian government officials involved in the Security Council efforts on Angola sanctions, author interviews, New York, April 2000.

25. Stephen J. Stedman, "Spoiler Problems in Peace Processes," *International Security* 22, 2 (Fall 1997): 5–53.

26. Indeed, Stedman has argued (referencing in part works by this author) that the existence of spoilers is the major explanation for the collapse of the peace process in Rwanda. I recognize the salience of the spoiler problem but argue in the end that it is not a sufficient explanation.

27. Christopher R. Mitchell, "The Process and Stages of Mediation: Two Sudanese Cases," in David R. Smock (ed.), *Making War and Waging Peace: Foreign Intervention in Africa* (Washington, DC: U.S. Institute for Peace Press, 1993), 142.

28. Mitchell, "The Process and Stages."

29. See, for example, J. Bercovitch and J. Rubin, eds., *Mediation in International Relations: Multiple Approaches to Conflict Management* (New York: St. Martin's Press in association with the Society for the Psychological Study of Social Issues, 1992).

30. Mark Hoffman, "Third-party Mediation and Conflict Resolution in the Post-Cold War World," in John Baylis and Nick Rengger (eds.), *Dilemmas of World Politics: International Issues in a Changing World* (Oxford: Clarendon Press, 1992), 277.

31. Hoffman, "Third-party," 277.

32. Chester A. Crocker, Fen Osler Hampson, and Pamela R. Aall (eds.), *Herding Cats: Multiparty Mediation in a Complex World* (Washington, DC: U.S. Institute for Peace Press, 1999).

33. Hoffman, "Third Party Mediation," 228; see also Mitchell, "The Process and Stages," 157.

34. Lederach, *Building Peace*.

35. Chester Crocker, Fen Osler Hampson, and Pamela Aall, "Introduction" and "Multiparty Mediation and the Conflict Cycle," in Crocker et al., *Herding Cats*, 3–18 and 19–46. See also Michael Lund, *Preventing Violent Conflicts: A Strategy for Preventive Diplomacy* (Washington, DC: U.S. Institute for Peace Press, 1996).

36. Mitchell, "The Process and Stages," 158.

37. Stedman, "Negotiation and Mediation," 361–363.

38. For an elaboration of this argument, see Bruce D. Jones and Charlie Cater, *Civilians in War: 100 Years after the Hague Peace Conference* (New York: International Peace Academy, 2000).

39. In a major review of the implementation of peace agreements in the 1990s, the editors note that several of the worst humanitarian crises of the decade—including in Rwanda—have occurred after international actors, including the UN, did not respond to the collapse of peace agreements those same actors had brokered or guaranteed. Stephen Stedman, Don Rothchild, and Elizabeth Cousens (eds.), *Peace Implementation: Themes, Issues, and Challenges* (Forthcoming, 2001).

2

War and Genocide: History of the Rwandan Conflict

The genocide of 1994 was an apocalyptic event that shattered Rwandan society. Its roots lie in the twists and turns of Rwandan history since the colonial era, in particular the formation of two political groupings that would meet in war in 1990: the Young Turk movement of Tutsi Rwandans in exile; and a clan-based Hutu oligarchy that controlled the Rwandan state under President Juvénal Habyarimana—the so-called *akazu*. Understanding the political history of these two groups, and the dynamics of their political and military struggle in the early 1990s, helps explain the genocide and is the first step toward explaining the failure of international peacemaking efforts to prevent its occurrence.

Backdrop to War: Some Themes from Rwandan History

The civil war in Rwanda began on 1 October 1990 with an invasion from southern Uganda of the Rwandese Patriotic Front (RPF) rebel movement. The next three years saw sporadic fighting between the RPF and the Rwandan army, interrupted by a series of partially observed cease-fires. In April 1994, the launching of a genocide by Rwandan extremists brought about the collapse of a long-running cease-fire and brought the two sides back to war. Three months of fighting saw the RPF rout the former Rwandan army, but not before hundreds of thousands of Rwandans perished in a genocide conducted by Rwandan government forces.

In many respects, both the war and genocide were conducted in ethnic terms. The membership of the RPF was predominantly Tutsi, whereas the government of Rwanda (we will sometimes use the acronym "GoR" in reference to the Rwandan government) was dominated by Hutu. (A third ethnic group, the Twa, represented only 1 percent of the prewar population and was never a significant factor in the war.) The genocide was targeted principally against the Tutsi, although a large number of Hutus were also killed, especially at the onset. Was this ethnic war? An outburst of ancient enmities? Journalistic accounts of the genocide painted it as an all-out war: Hutu against Tutsi.

Reality, of course, was more complex. To gain an initial understanding of the war, we need to answer two questions: Who were the combatants? Why were they fighting in 1990? A brief account of key developments in Rwanda's state and social history lays the groundwork for an analysis of the evolution of the combatants and the nature of their competition. It also provides evidence of a recurrent theme, namely, elite manipulation of social cleavages—including but not limited to ethnicity—for the purpose of political competition.[1] The methods of political mobilization used by both Hutu and Tutsi elites, from the colonial era onward, included the use of targeted violence spanning the range from assassination through limited massacres to war and ultimately genocide.[2] Both the civil war and the genocide are well accounted for by this elite-manipulation dynamic. Insufficient understanding of this aspect of the Rwandan conflict was part of the reason for the failure of international conflict resolution efforts.

Elite Competition and the Creation of Ethnicity:
Historical Roots of Conflict

A recurrent theme in the literature on underdevelopment in Africa and the weakness of the African state traces the source to the impact of colonial rule on the process of state formation.[3] One early focus of this literature was the impact of colonial boundaries on the formation of national identity, especially problems associated with mapping a series of prior ethnic, tribal, or clan identities onto the outlines of newly formed, bounded states.[4] In this literature, the creation of borders is seen as the defining legacy of European colonization.

Rwanda is not a case that supports this argument. During the periods of first German (1897–1919) and then Belgian (1919–1962) colonial rule, and into independence, Rwanda's borders went largely unchanged. In the first part of the nineteenth century, and for an uncertain period before, Rwanda had been divided between a kingdom that dominated central Rwanda and a series of smaller kingdoms in the west and the north that maintained a degree of autonomy.[5] During the late 1800s and early 1900s, the central kingdom, first under King Rwabugiri, succeeded in bringing these satellite kingdoms under more direct control. European colonists encountering Rwanda met with a political system whose boundaries roughly conformed to the borders of the colonial and the modern Rwandan state. Nevertheless, European interaction with Rwandan society was important, not for its impact on borders but for its impact on social relations within those borders.

The expansion and consolidation of the central kingdom corresponded roughly with the arrival of the first Europeans in Rwanda, German explorers and anthropologists who documented their first encounters with the Rwandan tribes.[6] Although historians agree that German contact with Rwanda was cursory and superficial, the first moment of German-Rwandan contact laid the seed of what was to prove a powerful and explosive interaction. Exploring Rwanda and the surrounding regions through the lens of European social thought, the German explorers and early colonial representatives were the first exponents of the application to Rwanda of an anthropological/social argument known as the Hamitic thesis, which was used throughout the colonial period to explain the domination of certain African groups over others, and thus to justify European comprador (intermediary) arrangements with some of those groups for the consolidation of their colonial presence.[7] Rooted in racist understandings of the inherent superiority of white European races, the Hamitic thesis attempted to explain Europe's encounter with sophisticated tribal kingdoms and peoples in their various incursions into Africa. The thesis argued that the Hamites, a race of people that included the Egyptians, had spread through parts of Africa, carrying with them their greater sophistication than the Negroid races of equatorial Africa. Thus, one could explain what to European eyes seemed the relative sophistication of, for example, the Oromos by arguing that these people were in fact descendants of the pseudo-European race that inhabited the Nile.

Similar reasoning was used in the case of Rwandan peoples. Germany's first encounter with Rwanda was of a sophisticated kingdom and peoples, with a developed court system, including a rich language specific to its functions.[8] Seeming to dominate this system were a tall, light-skinned people—the Tutsi—who appeared to dominate a shorter, darker people—the Hutu. In the imagination of the German explorers, here was graphic evidence of the truth of the Nilotic people: this tall, light people had migrated to Rwanda and imposed their dominance on the lesser, Negroid Hutu. Further evidence was found in the type of cattle owned by the Tutsi masters of the Rwandan feudal system: a long-horned cattle found in use by a variety of Hamitic clans. Thus was born a powerful myth: that the tall Tutsi had immigrated into Rwanda some centuries earlier, bringing with them their long-horned cattle and imposing their natural superiority over the Hutu peoples.

The reality suggests that social relations were far more complex than this German caricature. The idea that the Tutsi were the superior race in Rwanda, ruling over the agriculturist Hutu through a feudal system of client relations, was much oversimplified. According to historians such as Catherine and David Newbury, and anthropologists such as Johan Pottier, the terms *Hutu* and *Tutsi* in pre-independence Rwanda referred to a complex set of social relations that had some of the elements of class, caste, and social status.[9] Critically, they were not fixed categories but fluid ones, varying through time and location depending on such factors as wealth, military prowess, family, control over a precious commodity, or occupation of a prestigious social position. There was mobility among the "classes": Hutu could become Tutsi and vice versa, although the precise conditions that led to a change in status are unclear in the historical literature. Moreover, ruling status in the Rwandan kingdom was not simply a function of ethnicity but of clan. The dominant clans of late-nineteenth-century Rwanda, among them the Abeega and Abanyiginya, each contained Tutsi, Hutu, and Twa members. The hierarchy of power in Rwanda was a function of the intersection between clan lineage, ethnicity, and social function.[10]

After World War I, colonial authority over the Rwandan territory passed from Germany to Belgium. The Germans' system of rule in Rwanda thus came into contact with the oppressive system of rule that had developed in what was first known, ironically, as the Belgian Free State and then as the Belgian Congo.[11] The development of colonial systems of rule under Belgium would prove to be a critical moment in laying the groundwork for decades of civil tension and conflict in Rwanda.

When the Belgians began to establish control over Rwandan territory, they imposed on the country an intellectual and administrative simplification that equated "Tutsi" with "ruling class."[12] The Belgian colonists relied on Tutsis to fulfill the administration of the League of Nations mandate under which the Belgian presence was formally legitimized. The Belgians even went so far as to introduce a system of identity cards that specified ethnicity to aid the administrative system. The creation of this internal discrimination system, which allowed the Tutsi privileged access to the state, to jobs, and to the church, would have a profound impact by creating an ethnic hierarchy. Although this period was short-lived, the memory of Tutsi domination, and subsequent competition, would cycle through Rwandan history to the contemporary period. Although relations between Tutsi and Hutu would again become complex, this historical moment of dominant relations would remain embedded in the Rwandan consciousness.

The return to complex relations came with the end of World War II and the adoption within elements of Belgian society—notably the church—of new European ideas about democracy and egalitarianism.[13] In the Rwandan context, this led parts of the Belgian administrative structure to open doors to Hutus, giving them access to jobs, promotions, and access to an increasingly monetized economy, through schools and the church. The late 1940s and 1950s saw the development of an emerging modern elite among Hutu as well as Tutsi parts of Rwandan society.

Competition between these groups became intensified as pressure for democratic change mounted in Rwanda. The 1950s saw the beginning of a movement for decolonization and independent governance. In the late 1950s, this movement began to take on an ethnic character as political leaders, not for the last time, used ethnic identification to generate political mobilization against competing elites. This was particularly true of the Parmehutu, a movement of educated Hutu elites who circulated manifestos calling for Hutu freedom, not only from Belgian colonization but from Tutsi overlordship.[14]

The high point of ethnic tension in pre-independence Rwanda came in the late 1950s, when emergent Hutu elites, who had been given increased access to the church, and through it to social status, began to react against the dominance of the Tutsi and to use this dominance as a focal point for generating political support. The crucible of political competition forged a new, combative set of relations between Tutsi and Hutu elites that ultimately became violent. The mobilization of ethnic identities led to what most French scholars refer to as *les évenements* and Anglophone scholars call the Rwandan Revolution: a series of clashes, some violent, between Tutsi and Hutu elements in Rwanda over who would control decolonization and who would emerge dominant in an independent Rwandan state.[15] Writing about the similar ethnic relations in Burundi, René Lemarchand, a noted scholar of the region, has argued, "The Hutu-Tutsi conflict is a recent phenomenon, rooted in part in the process of social change introduced by the colonial state, in part by the rapid mobilization of ethnic identities under the pressure of electoral competition."[16]

In 1959 members of the Tutsi ruling elite reacted violently against the Hutu fomenters of revolution. Modern accounts of this period are politicized, described as the first phase in a thirty-year genocide by Hutu against Tutsi and the high point of Tutsi oppression. Modern historians by and large agree that use of violent tactics for political gain was common to both Tutsi and Hutu elites during the period. Most of the historical literature agrees that violence started when members of the dominant Tutsi party, the Union Nationale Rwandaise (UNAR), drew up plans to eliminate members of the emergent Hutu elite.[17] The UNAR plan to crush emergent Hutu opposition collapsed when it was not supported by the Belgian administrators, who at this time had begun to believe that their best hope for an easy exit from Rwanda lay with transferring allegiance and then power to the growing Hutu movement. The targets of this UNAR policy in turn reacted against the Tutsi elites, sparking the killings of thousands of Tutsis in Kigali and the countryside, and causing a mass outflux of Tutsis to neighboring Uganda, Tanzania, and Burundi. Tens of thousands of Tutsis, especially those affiliated with UNAR, ended up in Uganda. A two-way flow of violence continued on a moderate scale (by the now bloody Rwandan standard) until after independence, which was won in 1962 and saw the Parmehutu win elections giving them control over the newly independent state.

It is in this moment of ethnic competition, and the creation of a large exodus population in the neighboring countries, that we find one of the long-term roots of the Rwandan civil war in the 1990s. The civil war in 1990 would be launched by the descendants—familial and political—of this period of competition, and the memory of Tutsi dominance, however brief, would be a critical factor in the political mobilization toward genocide.

Young Turks Versus the Oligarchy: Proximate Causes of War

Three decades later, the two principal foes of the 1990 war were a Young Turk movement of second-generation Rwandan refugees in Uganda, leading the Rwandese Patriotic Front, and a clan-based oligarchy, the *akazu,* which came to dominate the Rwandan state after independence.

Several scholars have attempted to identify the causes of the Rwandan civil war and genocide by looking at the stresses on the social fabric of postindependence Rwanda, including economic collapse, the environment, land pressure, the hierarchical and oppressive nature of Rwandan culture, and others.[18] These stresses tell part of the story of the war, but this misses the obvious point that the war was started by a political group that not only was based but had lived for a generation in neighboring Uganda. Thus, it is more productive to look at the evolution of the two eventual opponents in the civil war, in both Rwanda and Uganda, up to the point of combat. In this history we see the interplay of elite politics with the changing Rwandan, regional, and international political, social, and economic contexts and find what may be called the proximate causes of the war; and in the dynamics of the war itself, we find the sources of the genocide.

Young Turks: The Rwandese Patriotic Front

The violent convulsions that accompanied Rwandan independence produced a flow of refugees into surrounding countries, including tens of thousands of Tutsis who fled to Uganda. There, known collectively as the 59ers, the Rwandan refugees joined a large population of Banyarwanda already living in Uganda. This population, which numbered several hundred thousand, composed a small number of Rwandan economic migrants from the 1920s and 1930s, of both Tutsi and Hutu derivation, as well as a larger population of indigenous Ugandan Banyarwanda. The story of the formation of the RPF, whose members were predominantly second-generation 59ers, is complex and includes the interaction of the 59ers with other Banyarwanda groups, and of the interaction of the Banyarwanda population as a whole with wider processes of Ugandan politics. The net result—summarized below—was the integration of a disproportionate number of 59ers into the military and security apparatus of the Ugandan government of the late 1980s under Yoweri Museveni and the creation of a problem as well as an opportunity.

The history of the 59ers in Uganda can be viewed in three phases.[19] The initial phase lasted from the late 1950s into the early 1980s when relations between the 59ers and the rest of the Banyarwanda, and between the Banyarwanda and other elements of Ugandan society, were relatively calm despite some underlying economic tensions. This period was interrupted by the brief period in the late 1960s when Uganda was ruled by Milton Obote. Obote, in another example of a political elite manipulating socioethnic tensions for the purpose of political gain, played up tensions between Banyarwanda and other ethnic groups in order to portray himself as the protector of the latter. The ascension to power by Idi Amin, so traumatic for many Ugandans, actually saw a return for the Banyarwanda to the relative calm of the pre-Obote era.

The second, more troubled, phase began in 1981 when Tanzania's invasion of Uganda to oust Idi Amin ended with the resumption of power by Milton Obote.[20] Once again, the Banyarwanda became targets of attacks by Obote. In response, a number of 59ers joined a guerrilla opposition movement known as the National Revolutionary Army (NRA), headed by Yoweri Museveni. Two 59ers who would later command the RPF were among the initial small guerrilla army commanded by Museveni. The guerrilla years saw as many as 60,000 Banyarwanda killed during fighting, especially in the notorious Lowero Triangle, where Obote challenged Idi Amin's record for brutality by killing hundreds of thousands of peasant farmers and villagers in a counterinsurgency campaign.[21] In classic guerrilla style—foreshadowing much of the more recent history of the region—the counterinsurgency attacks on the population boosted membership in Museveni's NRA, which eventually came to power in 1986.

The ascension to power of the NRA led to the third, most complex phase of Banyarwanda and 59er history in Uganda. This phase saw two interrelated developments: the integration into Museveni's security apparatus of a large number of Banyarwanda, most of them second-generation 59ers; and a growing split between this group and the rest of the Banyarwanda population. The integration into the security apparatus was a natural outcome of the critical role played by the Banyarwanda in Museveni's guerrilla years. The two early-joining officers mentioned above, Fred Rwigyema and Paul Kagame, rose, respectively, to the positions of deputy minister of defense and deputy chief of military intelligence. These positions were even more powerful than they sound, for in the politics of Museveni's National Revolutionary Movement (NRM) government, several Museveni opponents were given seats in the Cabinet; real power was controlled by deputies and key ministers loyal to Museveni. Rwigyema and Kagame were at the heart of a powerful network of Banyarwanda soldiers and security officials in the NRM.[22]

This position of power was both boon and challenge. By the late 1980s, the influence of the Banyarwanda was a topic of increasingly vocal criticism by Museveni's political opponents, who attempted to use Museveni's reliance on the Banyarwanda as a tool to isolate him from some of the ethnic communities with whom the Banyarwanda had tense relations.

Connected to these developments was a growing split between the second-generation 59ers and the wider Banyarwanda population. In 1979 the wider population had lent support to the Rwandan Alliance for National Unity (RANU), a diplomatic lobby organization that sought the legal right of return for Rwandan refugees. This right had been repeatedly denied by the Rwandan government. RANU proposed a compromise position. The premise of this position was that the majority of Rwandans would actually stay in Uganda, where economic life and opportunity were considerably better than in Rwanda, but nevertheless seek the legal right of return as an important symbolic gain.

For the second-generation 59ers, RANU was altogether too passive. Men like Fred Rwigyema, in positions of considerable power, influence, and security, began to explore more radical alternatives, including a military option of forced return. In 1987 a group of like-minded second-generation 59ers, the majority of whom had been born in Uganda and never even set foot in Rwanda, formed the Rwandese Patriotic Front. From the outset the RPF was a movement conceived at least in part to organize for a military return of the Rwandan refugee population.[23]

Although relations between Museveni and the RPF leadership were strong, by the end of the decade many of the old antagonisms between the Rwandans and their neighboring populations had reappeared. Evidence for this tension is found in, among other things, the fact that the topic of the Rwandan refugees was discussed as a problem in Uganda's senior legislative body, the National Ruling Council, in August 1990. The National Ruling Council, which was not fully controlled by Museveni, decided to remove remaining Rwandan nationals from the National Revolutionary Army and to bar Rwandans in Uganda from owning land.[24] Moreover, President Museveni, President Mobutu Sese Seko of Zaire, and President Habyarimana of Rwanda met in Kampala two weeks before the RPF invasion to discuss the issue and find a regional solution; it eluded them. A letter from the Ugandan government to the Human Rights Watch Arms Project suggests, in a remarkable euphemism, that the Rwandan refugees in Uganda had become convinced "that they did not have a bright future in Uganda."[25]

In an otherwise excellent overview of the history of Rwandan refugees in the context of the 1990–1994 war, Rachel van der Meeren suggests that the presence of a large number of Banyarwanda officers in the NRA had become embarrassing to Museveni.[26] This gives credence to Museveni's own account of the invasion, namely, that he knew nothing of it until being surprised by his own advisers recounting that the "Banyarwanda boys are deserting." Such an account does not wash, being at odds with the then widespread belief that Museveni at least passively supported the RPF invasion, a view later confirmed by U.S. intelligence sources (see Chapter 4). As argued below, it would appear less that Museveni was embarrassed by his Banyarwanda officers, more so that he worked with them. It would seem, then, that Museveni facilitated the armed repatriation of the Rwandan refugees, both to repay the support of the RPF leadership and to solve an internal Ugandan problem.

Creation of an Oligarchy: The Akazu

The timing of the invasion was propitious. In 1990 Rwanda was undergoing a process of rapid economic, social, and political decay that had substantially weakened the position of what amounted to a ruling oligarchy. This internal crisis stemmed from the intersection of a changing international political economy with the evolution of power structures in Rwanda since independence.

The evolution of Rwanda after independence can also be characterized as having three phases. The first began with independence in 1962 and lasted for the duration of the First Rwandan Republic, until 1973. The second commenced with a 1973 coup and lasted until the mid-1980s. The period from the mid-1980s until the start of the RPF invasion can be characterized as the third, albeit brief, phase of Rwandan evolution.

A movement of Hutu elites mobilizing popular opinion won Rwanda's first elections upon independence. The Parmehutu movement was led by Gregoire Kayibanda, who in 1962 was installed as president of the First Republic. The first phase of Rwandan evolution corresponds to Kayibanda's tenure in power (1962–1973). His regime is characterized by most observers as being based among Hutu clans from southern Rwanda, and as having given preference to southern Hutus in terms of access to the state, jobs, and church positions.[27] In this, Kayibanda's regime was far from unusual in the context of postindependence Africa.

Of course, preference given to southern Hutu clans during the First Republic led to resentment among northern Hutu clans. Indeed, it was a movement of northern Hutu that deposed Kayibanda in what is referred to as a bloodless coup that took place in 1973 under the leadership of Júvenal Habyarimana.[28] The coup initiated the Second Republic—and the second phase of evolution of Rwandan politics and power structures.

Habyarimana's initial period of rule is noted among historians as one of calm, prosperity, and relative tolerance between socioethnic groups. Even such historians as Catherine Newbury, a longtime observer of Rwanda and later a sharp critic of the Habyarimana regime, acknowledges that in the first years of his rule Habyarimana used the state to attempt to level some of the imbalances between ethnic groups that characterized the Kayibanda era. For example, Habyarimana's party, the Mouvement Révolutionnaire National pour le Développement (MRND), instituted such measures as a quota system that guaranteed Tutsis and southern Hutus roughly equal access to state jobs and economic opportunities. Also during the 1970s and well into the 1980s, Rwanda excelled at attracting aid from foreign donors and had a successful economy. This success was not surprising given its neighbors: between dictatorial Burundi to the south, genocidal Uganda to the north, corrupt Zaire to the west, and economically collapsing Tanzania to the east, in aid terms Rwanda was an island of comparative stability and prosperity in a sea of turbulence, bad policy, and conflict. Indeed, so successful was the Habyarimana regime at projecting an image of stability and prosperity that Rwanda became known—also partially for its topography—as the "Switzerland of Africa."

Today, we can see that this optimism masked a far different feature of real politics, one that would have profound relevance for the calamitous events of the 1990s. In reality, during this second phase the state was progressively being captured by a movement of northern clan members related by clan-family to Habyarimana. Whereas the standard picture of the Rwandan regime depicted it as a Hutu regime, this failed to capture the reality of pregenocide Rwandan politics. Even though the vast majority of those who held power in Rwanda before the genocide were Hutu, they were Hutu of particular clans—especially from the Bushiru region. As in precolonial times, the clan was a powerful factor in Rwandan political life. The Habyarimana regime was in fact a clan-based northern Hutu regime that was as discriminatory against Hutus from southern Rwanda as against Tutsis.[29]

After gaining power in a coup in 1973, the members of Habyarimana's regime consolidated both formal and informal control over the Rwandan state and through it the main channels of Rwanda's commercial, intellectual, and cultural life. In the arena of formal power, the Bushiru Hutu dominated the Rwandan state through the MRND, which President Habyarimana declared to be the only legal party. The relationship between the MRND and the state was similar to that of the old Communist Party of the Soviet Union (CPSU) to the Soviet government. Government became in effect a subset of the party, and security and success within the party were the sine qua non of political advance in Rwanda. Similar to the CPSU, the MRND ran what amounted to a system of nomenclatura through which key positions in the regional bureaucracy, the education sector, the army, the state enterprises, and the church were given to party members and supporters. One measure of success of the northern Hutu in working this system is that by 1980 some 80 percent of command positions in the armed forces were held by members of Habyarimana's clan.[30]

At the elite level, the inner circles of power, state enterprise, army command, regional prefectures, and church leadership were dominated by Habyarimana's clan family—indeed, so closely knit was this circle that it earned the nickname "little house" (i.e., the little house around Habyarimana), or *akazu*. Senior members of the *akazu* controlled the state banks and led the major enterprises, which were financed with concessionary state loans and received virtually all government contracts. Tourism and coffee, Rwanda's two foreign currency–earning industries, were dominated by *akazu* members. Critically, the *akazu* dominated the army, not only through all the major command posts of the regular army, the Forces Armées

Rwandaises (FAR),[31] but through total domination of the Presidential Guard, a praetorian guard that was Habyarimana's first line of defense and, as it proved, first line of attack.

The *akazu*'s domination of Rwandan political and economic life began to come under strain, however, in what can be seen as a third phase: the late 1980s, which saw an increase in social and political tension in Rwanda precipitated by economic decline and exacerbated by intersecting international pressures. By the late 1980s the country was socially strained, economically and environmentally destitute, and politically fractured. The years since independence had seen large population growth and the consequent exacerbation of problems regarding population density and the availability of arable land. Rwanda in the late 1980s was one of the poorest countries in the world, had the highest population density in the continent, and had experienced a decade's worth of declining land productivity. A short rainy season in 1989 also led in 1990 to widespread food shortages and, in some regions, famine. The situation rapidly deteriorated further in July 1989 as a result of a dramatic fall in world coffee prices, which came at the same time as a diminishing coffee yield in Rwanda following years of already low prices. A large drop in Rwanda's foreign export earnings resulted.[32]

Gérard Prunier, in his account of the growing internal crisis in Rwanda that preceded the RPF invasion, argues that "one can say that the political stability of the regime followed almost exactly the curve of those prices."[33] He notes a 40 percent reduction in the Rwandan budget as an indicator of the impact of the fall of coffee prices and traces the impact of that cut on social services, as well as opportunities for elites to enrich themselves. Missing from Prunier's account is the fact that the July 1989 decline in foreign earnings also triggered negotiations with the International Monetary Fund (IMF). These negotiations led to the drastic curtailment of budgetary spending. Thus, although it would be accurate to say that the strength of the regime followed the rise and fall of coffee prices, it is also the case that foreign intervention in the form of a structural adjustment program also helped weaken the regime at a critical moment.

Not surprisingly, Rwanda also experienced all of the social ills associated with the budget cuts, including high levels of unemployment, especially among youths. By early 1990 the unemployment had begun to manifest itself in student protests and other forms of political unrest. The combination of economic contraction, budgetary retraction, and political unrest meant that by mid-1990 the Habyarimana regime was much weakened.

The RPF attack in October 1990 thus had three impacts beyond the immediate military challenge: First, it exacerbated a rapid economic decline that would sap the Rwandan state of its already limited strength; second, it increased pressure on an already strained social order; and third, it further eroded the international public image of Rwanda and thereby attracted additional pressure for reform.

The war would also have other effects. Notably, it would isolate the *akazu* and further corrode their grip on power. This was dangerous. The *akazu* was a classic oligarchy, defined in clan terms, and, like all oligarchies, the maintenance of their own power became the central concern. The *akazu*'s defense of its power base would become a major factor in the Rwandan war and its escalation into genocide.

Rwanda in the 1990s: Invasion, War, and Genocide

If the timing of the war was propitious, it was not entirely accidental. Major-General Paul Kagame, military head of the RPF for all but the first few weeks of the invasion, has said that the timing of the invasion came from the failure of diplomatic efforts to resolve the question of the rights of refugees to return to Rwanda. More credibly, both "push" factors—the increasing tensions around the Banyarwanda population in Uganda—as well as "pull" factors—the mounting tension in Rwanda itself—appear to have been salient. The extent of tension in Rwanda and the disarray within government circles were certainly brought to the RPF's attention in August 1990 by the defection from Kigali, the capital of Rwanda, of Pasteur Bizimungu, a senior figure in government.[34]

The October 1990 RPF invasion occurred at the Uganda-Rwanda border crossing of Kagitumba. Some 1,500 soldiers of the RPF fought south from Kagitumba along the Gabiro Highway, winning a series of rapid victories against their government-force opponent, the FAR, which was caught in disarray. Within days, the RPF had captured Gabiro and was celebrating its victories by consuming vast quantities of looted pink champagne.[35] More important than the champagne they looted were the armored vehicles and weapons captured from FAR supply dumps in the northern province. They suffered one important loss when the military head of the RPF, Major Fred Rwigyema, took a bullet in the forehead on the first day of battle.[36]

The fact that the FAR was caught off-guard was in part a function of U.S. intelligence. In December 1989 Habyarimana had asked the U.S. Department of State to verify Rwandan intelligence reports of RPF mobilization along the Uganda border. Herman Cohen, then assistant secretary of state for African affairs, recalls that he consulted with the U.S. Central Intelligence Agency (CIA), which reported it had no intelligence on troop activity in southern Uganda, having "turned off" the CIA's monitoring presence there. Unwilling to reveal that U.S. intelligence was not watching events in the region, Cohen reported back to Habyarimana that the United States had no intelligence on troop activity, without clarifying why.[37] Evidently, Habyarimana took Cohen at his somewhat disingenuous word.

The bulk of the RPF troops that invaded in October had deserted their posts in Uganda's NRA, taking with them weapons, ammunitions, and trucks. Despite the close connections between Museveni and senior RPF commanders, Museveni denied knowledge of the RPF's plans. Most observers in the region disbelieved Museveni's protestations of innocence, not least because of the major role played by Rwandan nationals in the NRA. Many Ugandan observers felt that it would have been unlikely for Museveni not to have been aware of a planned invasion involving several of his most senior officers and a significant body of his troops. In point of fact, U.S. intelligence sources ("turned on" after Habyarimana's visit) later confirmed what many observers suspected: that the NRA was providing direct support to the RPF inside Uganda, including transporting arms from depots in Kigali to the border for RPF use, making Ugandan military hospitals accessible to RPF casualties, and keeping civilians clear from strategic crossings into Rwanda, which had previously been unguarded.[38]

Habyarimana, who at the moment of the invasion was addressing the United Nations in New York, recovered quickly. He flew directly to Europe to request military support from Belgium, with whom Rwanda had colonial ties, and France, with whom it enjoyed close relations. The Belgian government agreed to provide troops but, at parliament's insistence, had to limit the troops' task to protection of Belgian nationals; Belgian troops were in Rwanda only for a matter of days.

France was more forthcoming; President Francois Mitterrand intervened directly. This was in keeping with French postcolonial tradition in francophone Africa[39] and was in line with a 1975 defense agreement between Rwanda and France. On 5 October, France sent roughly 150 paratroopers from bases in the nearby Central African Republic to bolster Habyarimana's regime. Many have claimed that these troops engaged the RPF, but this has never been proven. What is known is that the troops backstopped the FAR in the capital, Kigali, securing the airport and other major sites, freeing the FAR from defensive tasks, and thereby enhancing their capacity to engage the RPF in the north.

Habyarimana also sought support from Zairian President Mobutu, who agreed to send 1,000 men from his paratroop division to fight in Rwanda. These troops conducted themselves with extreme indiscipline, looting, harassing, and raping Rwandan civilians. Within a few weeks, Habyarimana was in the awkward position of having to ask Mobutu to recall his troops.

Before they were recalled, however, the Zairian troops, along with the French troops, helped the FAR to turn the tables on the RPF. Reinforced in Kigali by 300 French troops, and with direct support from Zairian soldiers, the FAR engaged the RPF in the north. The FAR and the Zairians moved into the territory west of the Gabiro Highway, and a smaller force set an ambush for the RPF.[40] Some Western journalists contend that French pilots flew spotter planes that directed the ambush, although there is no evidence to prove this.[41] The ambush was successful, resulting in the deaths of two more senior RPF commanders, Major Paul Banyingana and Major Paul Bunyenyezi, and handing the RPF its first loss in battle. Disoriented by the loss of troops and leadership, the RPF retreated and by 1 November had been pushed back into Uganda. Radio Rwanda announced that the so-called October War was over and victory achieved.

Competition: The Course of War

But the war was far from over. The RPF's retreat into Uganda was tactical, not decisive. Indeed, from just across the border the RPF quickly regrouped under new leadership. Leadership was provided most importantly by Major Paul Kagame, a charismatic Tutsi in his thirties who had earned his leadership position through years of tough fighting. Kagame's first war was with the Tanzanian army when, in 1979, it invaded Uganda to depose Idi Amin. Later, after Obote proved a false friend to the Rwandans in Uganda, Kagame took up sides with what was then a small rebel movement—Museveni's NRA. The tough fighting of the NRA's legendary guerrilla struggle in the

Lowero Triangle of Uganda gave Kagame critical experience in the tactics of successful insurgency. The victory of the NRA in 1985, and Museveni's ascendancy to power in 1986, paid off for Kagame, who as previously noted became Museveni's deputy chief of military intelligence. In November 1990, he was recalled from a training program at Fort Leavenworth to take over the reins of the RPF.

After a brief period of regrouping in Uganda, the RPF divided into two groups. A smaller force crossed south into Rwanda and hid in the forests and marshes of Akagera National Park, destabilizing the eastern part of the country. A larger force took advantage of Ugandan support and stole along the Rwanda-Uganda border to the volcanic mountains of Virunga National Park, in northwestern Rwanda, famous for its other guerrilla occupants.

From the high vantage point of the Virunga Range, Kagame's RPF began a classic guerrilla campaign of hide-and-harass. By mid-1991 the RPF had limited the FAR's offensive options and disrupted economic activity in the north, thereby straining government revenues. A January 1991 attack on Ruhengiri succeeded in freeing sympathetic prisoners, capturing military hardware, and, most important, making a strong psychological imprint on the country.[42]

A cease-fire signed in March 1991 held barely long enough for the signatures to dry. Unable to dislodge the RPF from the northwest, the Rwandan government focused its attention on improving the rather decrepit state of the FAR. Its first initiative was to launch a massive recruitment process. The army was expanded, from roughly 5,000 men in 1990 to roughly 30,000 by the end of the following year, and still further to roughly 50,000 by mid-1992.[43] Many of the new recruits were young Hutu men from southern clans, who had previously had only limited access to the army. Also, almost immediately following the invasion, Kigali began purchasing weapons from suppliers in South Africa, France, and Eastern Europe.

Despite its enlarged army and rearmament program, the FAR's repeated efforts to dislodge the RPF from the Virungas were unsuccessful. As described by Colonel Tito Rutaremara, the RPF's third-ranked officer at the time, the FAR attempted to use artillery to destroy the RPF's positions in the mountains. The attacks were simply ducked by the RPF, who used the dense bamboo foliage of the mountains, as well as valleys and overhangs, to wait out the barrage.[44]

An important turning point came in November 1991. Immediately following the signing of a second cease-fire, the FAR launched a major artillery attack on the RPF's positions. They were a total failure. As recounted by RPF soldiers, this failure turned the psychological and military advantage decisively in their favor. Moving out from their positions in the mountains, the RPF launched a series of attacks not only to disrupt FAR movements but also, for the first time, to hold territory. During the first months of 1992, the RPF consolidated its position in the north, imposing the reality of its presence especially in the prefecture of Byumba, the breadbasket of Rwanda. The economic and financial impact on the Rwandan state of the destabilization of Byumba was perhaps more important than the simple military loss. In June 1992, the Rwandan government agreed to the launch of comprehensive political negotiations to lead toward a peace settlement (see Chapter 5).

Polarization: The Politics of War

The peace negotiations (considered in detail in the following chapters) began formally in July 1992. Between that time and February 1993, there was only sporadic fighting between the RPF and the FAR. The government of Rwanda was more consumed with fighting a variety of political battles in Kigali, where economic collapse and the RPF's success had combined to seriously weaken the Habyarimana regime. In April 1992, the Habyarimana government was forced to give way to pressure for multiparty politics and introduce a coalition government.[45] The momentum of the war gave way to momentum in the political negotiations, which were propelled forward by moderate members of the new coalition government.

At the same time, however, the *akazu* moved in defense of its eroding power base. The *akazu* reacted to the emergence of a new, formal opposition by formalizing its own network, in part through the creation of a pseudo-party, the Coalition pour la Défense de la République (CDR). The CDR brought together senior *akazu* members of the inner circle from both formal and informal realms of power: MRND ministers, army chiefs, religious leaders, and enterprise leaders (among them those who would later establish an important hate-radio station.)[46] The CDR's purpose was to stem the flow of power away from the ruling oligarchy. While negotiators talked, the CDR began to lay the groundwork for radical opposition to a negotiated settlement.

It is important to note that the membership and politics of the CDR and MRND overlapped but were not identical, the CDR bringing together the more radical members of the MRND and nonparty elites from a variety of walks of life and, therefore, being the more extreme of the two groupings. There were members of the MRND whose politics were quite different from those of the CDR.[47] For example, James Gasana, a longtime MRND politician who became minister of defense in the power-sharing government, opposed much of the CDR's politics. Gasana crossed swords with the CDR when, in 1993, he attempted to recall some weapons that had been distributed to so-called civilian defense groups. Gasana's chief of staff was Colonel Théoneste Bagasora, the senior army figure in the CDR; Bagasora threatened Gasana over the weapons recall, and Gasana was eventually forced into exile in Europe.

In any event, the power-sharing government engaged in peace talks with the RPF. In January 1993, after a seven-month cease-fire, the negotiations stalled. On 8 February, the RPF launched a major offensive from positions in northeastern Rwanda. This would prove the second decisive turning point in the war—again in the RPF's favor. Suddenly, the pattern of small skirmishes and guerrilla tactics changed. Within days of launching the attack, the RPF had fought to within twenty-three kilometers of Kigali. The offensive provoked further French intervention: two waves of paratroopers, totaling 600 new troops, were sent to Kigali to shore up the FAR's defenses. In the face of the added strength provided by France, and under intense diplomatic pressure to hold off from outright military victory, the RPF halted its offensive. Subsequent negotiations saw the RPF return to its pre-offensive lines, with the territory they gained during the offensive being designated a demilitarized zone (DMZ), monitored by UN and OAU observer troops (more details on this period are found in Chapter 5).

The offensive had four effects. First, it revealed that the expansion of the FAR had done little to enhance its effectiveness: many of the thousands of additional soldiers recruited into the FAR proved to have no stomach for serious fighting. This was especially the case of those southern Hutus who were recruited (and, in some cases, impressed) into the FAR. Thousands of these troops deserted in the face of the RPF offensive. As the mother of one deserter put it, "When they saw the RPF's guns, they remembered they were southerners before they were Hutu."[48] Second, the success of the offensive demonstrated to all concerned that the RPF held the upper hand militarily; separate analyses by French and Tanzanian military intelligence came to the same conclusion: that the RPF could handily defeat the FAR, even with French backing.[49] Third, the defeat intensified the feeling of isolation and threat within the inner circles of the *akazu*, represented by the CDR. Fourth, the offensive intensified and complicated the struggle for the support of a critical political group in Kigali: moderate members of the Habyarimana regime.

The return to the negotiating table was accompanied by an expansion of the UN's so far peripheral involvement in the peacemaking process. In March 1993, the Departments of Political Affairs and Peacekeeping Operations sent a joint mission to Rwanda in order to bring the RPF back to the bargaining table.[50] The expansion of UN involvement represented an important shift in responsibility for the peace process, an increased international role that would diminish that of the OAU. One early effect was to supplant the OAU's Neutral Military Observer Group (NMOG) by a UN observer force, proposed by Museveni and deployed in the summer of 1993 as the UN Observer Mission to Uganda-Rwanda (UNOMUR; see Chapters 4 and 6). The deployment of UNOMUR laid the groundwork for the UN's eventual agreement to deploy the UN Assistance Mission in Rwanda (UNAMIR) to "secure" the transitional arrangements specified by the Arusha Peace Accords.

Political negotiations continued for another six months, resulting in August 1993 in the Arusha Accords, signed by the government of Rwanda, the RPF, and a series of external third parties. During this time, and for nine months following the signing of the peace accords, there was once again a general cessation of hostilities between the two armed forces. Once again, the two sides were differently preoccupied. According to former Reuters correspondent Aidan Hartley, who traveled with the RPF at various stages of the war, the focus of RPF activity during this phase was on rearmament and resupply through channels in Uganda.[51] Patrick Mazimpaka, a senior RPF negotiator, later confirmed that the RPF in this period was not counting on peace to hold but was preparing for the contingency of renewed war.[52]

In Kigali, the visible focus was once again on competition between political parties and factions. A variety of parties that gained representation under the peace settlement formed and broke coalitions, trying to outmaneuver the Habyarimana government, which fought back with its own series of alliance bids. A Canadian diplomat who visited Kigali during this period said that the city—from which the RPF was absent—seemed to be at war with itself, so vicious was the political fighting.

The essence of the political fight was for control over the moderate center, whose support for the Arusha peace deal was a necessary condition for implementation. From the *akazu*'s perspective, winning over Hutu moderates both within the ranks of the government and especially in the opposition parties was now the primary battle. A bitter political struggle ensued, whereby the *akazu* gained the upper hand. With control over the existing instruments of state, including the commercial sector, the *akazu* could wield promises of future benefit if the so-called moderates turned away from the Arusha deal. In at least one known case, political patronage was used to gain the support of a moderate politician for the anti-Arusha cause. In each of the opposition parties, a power faction was formed that represented in effect *akazu* recruits to the anti-Arusha faction. The factionalization of the opposition parties disrupted the delicate balance of power negotiated in Arusha. This delayed implementation of the formal peace deal and created further room and scope for the *akazu* to hatch its plans.

Escalation: Toward Genocide

If the visible political fight was vicious, the murky underside of the competition was downright malignant. While the public fight was on for control of the peace process, a shadow fight was forming to destroy the peace in its entirety. The second-track option—the radical fallback plan for defeating the RPF and ousting political opposition—was being geared up for a move onto the first track. A plan for genocide had been formed and was now being hatched.

Beyond simple planning, the *akazu* was also building the mechanical infrastructure for violent defense of its position. The centerpiece was the creation of a militia movement in late 1993.[53] The *impuzamugambi* (those who work together) and *interahamwe* (those with a single purpose) militias were formed under the direct control of the CDR and MRND, respectively, and financed illegally through the ruling MRND. Weapons were imported in violation of the Arusha Accords and distributed to "citizens"—the codeword for the militia groups. The militias trained in and around Kigali for their citizens' defense role. The *akazu* was gearing up for a major escalation.

The intellectual and philosophical groundwork for genocide had been laid early on. A number of intellectuals, politicians, and media personalities within the core of the *akazu* had spent the early part of the war disseminating propaganda about the dastardly nature of the

RPF.[54] Referring back to the brief period of Tutsi domination in Rwandan history, the *akazu* painted the RPF as the political inheritors of Tutsi domination, bent on returning Hutus to a condition of slavery and serfdom. The urgent need, therefore, was for a form of aggressive Hutu nationalism, one that would defeat the "cockroaches" before they could implement their oppressive plan.[55] As the civil war progressed, this rhetoric was ratcheted upward. The signing of the Arusha peace deal was the trigger for a major increase in the volume of the rhetoric, as well as its incendiary content. The radical hate-radio station Radio et Television Libre Mille Colines (RTLMC), created immediately prior to the signing of Arusha, notched up its own rhetoric, pumping out songs and talk shows that demonized the RPF, castigating those who negotiated or collaborated with the Tutsi, and calling for aggressive Hutu nationalism. The message was fear: any deal with the RPF would simply prove to be a Trojan horse, through which the RPF would impose oppressive slavery on the Hutu, stealing their land and threatening their lives and livelihoods.

In this program, the *akazu* was aided by Rwandan history and the fluid nature of Rwandan ethnicity, which was once again being used by elites to manipulate the past for purposes of political mobilization. The *akazu* was also aided by the repeated displacement many Hutus experienced as a result of the civil war. Moreover, events in Burundi gave credence to its radical portrayal of the RPF. In October 1993, a five-month-old experiment in democratic powersharing in Burundi collapsed when the Tutsi-dominated army launched what turned out to be an abortive coup that nevertheless generated a month of mass killings. The coup started with the assassination of the first Hutu president of Burundi, Melchior Ndadaye. Hutu civilians took their revenge for his assassination on Tutsi civilians, and in turn the Burundian army retaliated with bloody force. Later estimates would place the dead at between 35,000 and 50,000, split equally between the two ethnic groups,[56] but at the time in the region the killings were widely reported to be as high as 150,000 to 200,000.[57] The reality was bad enough and sent tens of thousands of Burundians fleeing the country. The fear that this prospect generated among the Hutu population was deliberately fueled by *akazu* members. As the process of negotiation brought Rwanda closer to some form of powersharing, the extremist ideologues deliberately exploited this fear to create space for their program of radical opposition.

By February 1994, the extremists in Kigali had put into motion a plan of assassination and disruption. (The elements of this plan were outlined to the United Nations by an informant in January 1994; reception to this fax, and the question of what the UN knew about the genocide, is addressed in Chapter 5.) Tension in Kigali, which had been mounting, reached a fevered pitch on 22 February with the killing of leading opposition member and key moderate Felicien Gatabazi. On 23 February Martin Bucyana, a key figure within the CDR, was killed by a spontaneous mob. On 24 February UN High Commissioner for Refugees (UNHCR) Special Representative Michel Moussali gave the most prescient international warning of what was to come, warning that Rwanda faced "a bloodbath of unparalleled proportions" unless action was taken to restore stability.[58]

In addition to targeted assassinations, the *akazu* organized logistics for a program of killing. In March 1994, orders went out from the central ministries to government offices throughout the country, ordering local administrators to have trucks and jeeps and other equipment on standby for "purposes of national defence."[59]

In early April, pro-Arusha forces tried to regain the initiative. A meeting was convened in Dar-es-Salaam between regional negotiators and President Habyarimana, a meeting designed to have regional political actors pressure Habyarimana to implement the Arusha peace deal. On 5 April, Habyarimana agreed to take steps to accelerate the timetable for peace.

On 6 April a series of confusing events threw Kigali into turmoil. First, Habyarimana and a handful of senior aides, as well as the president of Burundi, all returning from Tanzania, were shot down and killed as their airplane passed the Kanombe barracks, close to the Kigali airport. A series of roadblocks was established around the city, and an intense program of assassination—first of Hutu opposition politicians, journalists, human rights workers, and other civil society figures—began in the city.

The question of who shot down Habyarimana's plane remains unclear. In 1995 Filip Reyntjens provided compelling evidence to suggest that Habyarimana's plane was shot down by moderate forces who were seeking to eliminate hostile opposition to Arusha.[60] Then, in early 2000 a Rwandan intelligence official who had defected from Kigali suggested that Paul Kagame himself had been behind the killing. Whether it was the RPF or the moderate opposition (who were, at this point, in a tactical alliance), their momentum was quickly lost to countercoup forces lead by Colonel Bagasora. Galvanizing the forces opposed to peace, Colonel Bagasora led a two-pronged strike: a return to war with the RPF, and the launch of a mass genocide.

Genocide

Within forty-eight hours of the downing of Habyarimana's flight, an interim government had been formed under leading CDR figures. Among them was Colonel Bagasora, whose penchant for violence and doomsday rhetoric had earned him the nickname "Colonel of Death." In one negotiation session, Bagasora had threatened apocalypse if a peace deal was implemented in Rwanda. Now, the Colonel of Death was in charge of fulfilling his own prophecy.

In the first days of the killings, this interim government organized the execution of the Tutsi population of Kigali and wiped out the ranks of moderate politicians and civil society leaders, most of them Hutu. These were the "traitors" who had negotiated and made peace with the RPF. They were also the journalists, lawyers, human rights activists, church activists, and opposition intellectuals who supported the peace process. Moving throughout Kigali, the Presidential Guard wiped out this primary threat: Hutu who could make peace with the RPF. Over the next three months the *génocidaires* (those committed to the program of genocide), unchecked by any international force, systematically slaughtered Tutsi populations across the country. The primary tools for the killings were the Presidential Guard, the militias, and some loyal units of the FAR.

The FAR, of course, had two tasks: some units helped implement the genocide while others attempted to forestall the RPF's offensive. As had been seen in February 1993, the FAR's reliability was in question. Indeed, early reports suggested that there was fighting between the Presidential Guard and disloyal elements of the FAR. Although this is not certain, the loyalty of FAR units was no doubt a source of concern. However, the *akazu* had learned from past failures. When it deployed FAR units whose loyalty was in question, it then also deployed *interahamwe* units *behind* the FAR front units to ensure discipline. A cameraman who filmed alongside the FAR during its defense of Kanombe noted the bizarre spectacle of the *interahamwe* menacing the FAR to stay in position.[61]

While the weaker units attempted to contain the RPF, the more loyal units were put in motion to conduct the genocide. Along with the *interahamwe,* the FAR swept through the countryside, kicking into motion the elaborate logistical planning established by the central planners.

It is critical to be clear that the genocide was not spontaneous, not an eruption of ancient tribal hatreds, as it was quickly portrayed by the Western media. Rather, this was a planned, coordinated, directed, controlled attack by a small core. Indeed, Filip Reyntjens maintains that no more than two dozen senior figures controlled the genocide machine.[62] They were supported by senior military figures, *préfets,* and other senior members of the CDR.[63] Finally, they had the support of elements of the state machinery and arguably as many as 100,000 but possibly as few as 50,000 "henchmen"—essentially, a large section of the FAR plus the 15,000–20,000 militia members, all under the direct control of central authorities.[64] These henchmen had two tasks: implementing the genocide, and waging war against the RPF.

These killers quickly made recourse to wider "mobilization" to assist them in their plan. Rwandans who were part of neither the army nor the militias were impressed into service: forced to man barricades, forced to identify Tutsis, forced to participate in the killings. As the genocide progressed, the evidence suggests that popular participation was less directly forced.

Participation: Compliance or Coercion?

This has led some observers to focus on the wider popular dynamics of the genocide and to seek explanations in Rwandan society and culture, long-standing ethnic hatred, and similar factors. How could neighbor slaughter neighbor? How could family member give up family member? What can account for the transformation of Rwandan society into one rife with murderous hatred?

One argument that has been given wide credence concerns environmental stresses. This view holds that there was a crisis of arable land in Rwanda that led the wider Hutu population to see an interest in keeping the RPF out of Rwanda and its scarce land, thereby causing them to comply with or even participate in the genocide. A similar version is given by writers who connect the genocide, and conflict more generally, to poverty. Here the argument is that the serious and growing poverty of Rwandans created a perception of opportunity in the genocide, both to exclude economic competition (the RPF and the Tutsi returnees who would come with them) and to grab land and goods from the Tutsis being killed.

A far more powerful explanation for compliance and noncoerced participation, if indeed that did occur, can be found in the success of the propaganda effort run by the *akazu*. As noted earlier, the efforts by the *akazu* to demonize the RPF built upon deep themes of Rwandan history and made references (albeit grossly distorted) to real events of violence and oppression in Rwandan history. The essential message of this rhetoric was not, as has often been said, one of hate; rather, it was one of fear.

An important new argument with respect to the role of fear in the dynamics of mobilization has recently been made. Barry Wiengast has compellingly demonstrated that fear is a powerful tool for mobilization in instances of civil war in countries that have a history of past episodes of massacres and other forms of gross abuses.[65] Although his argument is based on a complex statistical model of so-called game theory, his core argument can be developed in simpler terms. Essentially, political entrepreneurs seeking to mobilize a population for a project of genocide or something similar have a very powerful tool in fear, especially fear of extreme consequences at the hands of the demonized other. Those consequences may not be certain, only a possibility, and we need not assume that the average Rwandan villager accepted wholeheartedly the *akazu*'s propaganda message. But there was always a possibility that the RPF was going to reimpose oppressive rule in Rwanda; after all, both sides had committed massacres during the war, and Rwandan history contained ample evidence of the feasibility of genocidal projects. (The fact that those projects were directed against Tutsi does not, in Weingast's argument, diminish their propaganda value: First, they established feasibility, irrespective of target; second, they established a potential revenge motivation for genocide attacks by Tutsi against Hutu.) Moreover, across the border in Burundi, a partial genocide had been committed just the past year. And if the *akazu* was right about the RPF, then the only rational option would be to rally around the *akazu* while the getting was good. However abhorrent the prospect of joining a genocide, the consequences of misjudging the issue were so extremely high, and so dangerous, that reason dictated acting as if the *akazu* were right.

Moreover, wide popular participation by the middle of the course of the genocide can more easily be explained by realizing that coercion can be both direct and indirect. Direct coercion in the first days and weeks of genocide, in particular swift and brutal reprisals against anyone resisting forced participation, quickly creates an environment where the options are, in essence, kill or be killed. Once a pattern of reprisals for nonparticipation is established, any form of participation is at least partially, and arguably largely, indirectly coerced.

Those who have suggested that there was large popular participation in the killings have argued that it would have been impossible for as few as 50,000 killers to achieve the death toll that occurred in Rwanda. But an analysis of the numbers does not bear this out. Taking a very high estimate of the death toll (say, a million people) and a low estimate of killers (say, 25,000), the numbers still show that it would be more than possible for the eventual death toll to have resulted over the course of a hundred-day campaign of genocide. A million killed in a hundred days gives us 10,000 people killed per day. If 25,000 killers were to achieve this figure, then each killer must have killed one person every two and a half days. Taking numbers at the high end, of 100,000 possible killers, the result is that each henchman would have killed only ten people during the hundred days of genocide, or one person every ten days. Shocking though it may be to realize, it is fully possible for 25,000 or even fewer killers to have killed several hundred thousand, even a million, people over the course of a hundred days (or even less).

Of course, this numerical analysis bears no resemblance to what occurred; it serves simply to establish feasibility. Rather, direct killing was concentrated among the *interahamwe* and *impuzamugambi* militias and the Presidential Guard, with elements of the FAR fighting off the RPF. Also, killing was concentrated in April and May, although some killing did continue until the end of the war in July. Popular participation was critical to the social environment of fear needed to implement the genocide, but it was probably incidental to the actual rates of killing. A combination of widespread fear, direct coercion, and indirect coercion can strongly account for popular participation and compliance with the genocide without relying on accounts of mass popular hatred, ancient enmity, or anything similar. What we might best call "coercive mobilization" led to a phenomenon that Jean-Pierre Chrétien has called "innocent murderers" and Prunier calls "victim killers."[66]

Return to War: The RPF Offensive

Quite distinct from the execution of the genocide were the actions of the RPF and FAR as they returned to war on the heels of Habyarimana's assassination. Immediately following the downing of his flight, the RPF launched a five-pronged offensive for control of Rwanda.[67]

First, part of a battalion stationed on the northern side of the DMZ, near the town of Byumba, literally ran along mountain trails and backroads, avoiding engagement with the FAR in order to reinforce the RPF battalion in Kigali, which it did within seventy-two hours.[68] There, the reinforced RPF battled for control of Kigali, parts of which it quickly gained and held.

Second, other RPF troops stationed north of Byumba engaged the FAR in that town, fighting the first major battle of the summer offensive. Here the RPF used to great effect a tactic that brought repeated victories against the larger, better-equipped forces of the FAR. The RPF all but surrounded the FAR forces at Byumba, launching a near continuous barrage of artillery and small weapons fire. When the FAR attempted to counterattack, the RPF retreated back into earlier positions, allowing the FAR to spend its energy and ammunition on the banana trees into which the RPF melted. The RPF then resumed the attack, leaving only a rearward exit for the FAR. Eventually, the FAR took the bait, at which point the RPF fell on the retreating column, decimating troops.

The RPF battalion that had successfully broken through FAR defenses at Byumba continued onto the Kanombe barracks on the eastern edge of Kigali, where a repeat of the same tactics eventually succeeded in breaking the FAR's hold on the remaining parts of Kigali. Meanwhile, a third battalion fought down from Gabiro through eastern Rwanda, capturing the southeastern town of Kibungo, then breaking for southern Kigali Province. By late May, these three RPF columns converged on the FAR in Kigali, again leaving it an exit to the west. When the FAR retreated into the trap, the RPF attacked the rear of the column. The RPF took Kigali on 4 July 1994 and declared "independence." At this stage it was joined by the fourth prong of the offensive, which swept southwest from the Virunga regions to engage the retreating FAR. Finally, the fifth prong of the offensive engaged the FAR at Ruhengiri, in the northwest, and, having successfully routed the FAR, joined the wider pursuit of the retreating columns toward the Zaire border.

At this stage the RPF offensive was set back by French intervention (see Chapter 5), which blocked its advance in the southwest, to where large sections of the FAR retreated. The intervention was France's Operation Turquoise, launched with UN Security Council authorization under Chapter 7 of the UN Charter in mid-June. The force of roughly 2,500 men, backed by artillery and Jaguar aircraft based out of Goma, Zaire, quickly seized southwestern Rwanda, blocking the RPF's advance into what was then termed the "Safe Humanitarian Zone," or Zone Turquoise. The RPF threatened to launch an attack on French forces in the zone. RPF delegates were invited to Paris to meet Foreign Minister Alain Juppé; Gérard Prunier, East Africa adviser to the Socialist Party in France and a onetime active ally of Museveni's NRA, was sent to Mulindi and Kigali to negotiate with the RPF.[69] Prunier's message was that Operation Turquoise would not interfere with the RPF's war outside Zone Turquoise and that the RPF could profitably stay clear of engaging the French.

The RPF took the option of avoiding a costly engagement with the French. A section of the FAR was thus eventually able to retreat into Zaire intact, with its full complement of military equipment. The RPF shifted its tactics and converged its five-pronged assault on the northwestern town of Ruhengiri. The same battle tactics were deployed, with the combined RPF divisions surrounding all but a rear exit from Ruhengiri. After a day of fighting, the FAR took the rear exit into Goma, Zaire, pushing in front of it a wall of human beings. Roughly 1.7 million people were pushed into refugee status in Zaire. On 17 July 1994, the RPF took Ruhengiri and declared the end of the civil war.

Large-scale killing did not stop with the declaration of the end of war. During the three months of the offensive against the FAR, and for at least a few weeks afterward, RPF troops also committed mass killings of civilians as they moved through Rwanda. Although estimates vary widely, most independent accounts of this period suggest that the killings were on the order of 60,000—some of them FAR, militia members, and other henchmen of the genocide, but at least tens of thousands of Hutu civilians were slaughtered either during the genocide or in its immediate aftermath.

Conclusion

Apart from the killings by the RPF, most sources estimate killings conducted by the Rwandan regime as falling between 500,000 and

1 million. In the period immediately after the genocide, the bulk of estimates fell at the higher end of the spectrum. Based on analyses of pregenocide census data, counts of refugee populations, and estimates of deaths, informed estimates of 800,000–900,000 deaths were chosen by Studies II and III of the Joint Evaluation, as well as by Gérard Prunier, in his *The Rwanda Crisis*.[70] More recently, Alison des Forges, in *Leave None to Tell the Story,* concludes that these early figures overestimated the percentage of Tutsi in the overall Rwandan population; she shows that more conservative figures lead to estimates that the overall death toll was closer to 500,000. She concludes that at least 500,000 were killed.[71] Given uncertainties about who identified themselves as Tutsi in the 1991 census, it is likely that we will never know precisely how many were killed during the summer of 1994. Of course, even the low end of these numbers is staggeringly large.

It is this massive slaughter that stands as the critical, disastrous outcome of the Rwandan civil war. And it is the failure of international conflict resolution efforts to prevent this tragic outcome that is the central analytical concern of this book.

This brief history of political turbulence in Rwanda reveals a clear pattern in the causation of violence and war, which can usefully be noted.[72] From the historical roots to the proximate causes of conflict in 1990, to the social transformations in Rwandan society and the cataclysmic genocide of 1994, the common thread is bloody manipulation of social categories by elite groups seeking narrow political advantage through political mobilization, as well as the direct recourse to violence by elites, also for political gain. Belgian elites manipulated Rwandan social categories to further their program of colonial rule; southern Hutus played up the unity of Hutu identity in pre-independence Rwanda to gain control of the state; Tutsi elites sought in the 1950s to use violence to postpone a democratic threat to their power, and they resorted to violence again in 1990 to fulfill their political agenda; northern Hutu elites, most brutally, manipulated ethnic fears and identities in Rwanda in the 1990s to lay the groundwork for the genocide.

Social categories can be manipulated only so far. The relevant categories in Rwanda—Hutu and Tutsi, northerner and southerner—were sufficiently fluid to allow for integration when relevant and were sufficiently distinct to allow for isolation when productive. Elites cannot make social history out of their imagination but must work within the constraints of existing social categories and established social histories if they are to turn and twist these to their advantage. A two-decade-long period of hierarchical rule becomes a several-hundred-year history of enslavement; northern Hutu exclusivism becomes pan-Hutu inclusivism when the Tutsi exist as a common threat. Social conditions, such as poverty, environmental degradation, land and population density, economic collapse—all are fuel for history's fires. Those fires must be lit, however, and nourished. History serves as raw material for profound political battles of memory and mobilization. It is in the course of that mobilization, and in the manipulation of the memory of Tutsi domination, that we find the common causal pattern of struggle, conflict, war, and genocide in Rwanda.

* * *

We can identify several themes that spring from the contingencies and complexities of war, and several points from the historical summary above that illuminate generic themes regarding the challenges to peacemaking.

First, it is evident that the Rwandan war did not conform to any neat pattern or cycle of escalation and de-escalation. Tracing battle deaths, one would see a pattern of sharp escalation in 1990, a moderate level held throughout 1991, a decline into 1992, a brief peak in early 1993, slowing almost to a halt until April 1994, and then an escalation so steep as to be off the curve. On the flip side of this point, however, it does seem clear that at the political level there was a steady buildup of tension and isolation that could be described in terms of political escalation. As we shall see in later chapters, too little attention to political escalation was a salient factor in weakening international peacemaking efforts.

Second, the Rwandan conflict continued to exhibit the characteristic of a lack of cohesiveness among parties. The fractured nature of Kigali politics in particular makes it clear that there were not just two sides to the war but rather a spectrum of political opinions relating to the RPF invasion and the peace process, ranging from compliant support to outright hostility. Again, a limited understanding of the fractures and complexities in Kigali politics would prove to be a salient factor in international peacemaking.

Third, the polarization in Kigali politics reveals the important role played in the war by totalistic rhetoric and perceptions. Clearly, the totalistic perceptions of the RPF were very widely held in Rwanda and were a factor in the politics of the war and in the mobilization of fear and coerced compliance with the genocide. However, it is critical to note that at least to a certain extent these totalistic perceptions were not inherent features of the war but rather deliberate creations of the *akazu*'s propaganda machine. That is to say, totalistic perceptions and rhetoric were not merely features of war and part of its mechanics; they were *tools* of war. The same is true of security fears; clearly, episodes such as the killings in Burundi led to or reinforced security fears inherent in the war. Once again, however, they were also deliberately manipulated and amplified by the *akazu*; as with totalistic rhetoric, they were not just features of war; they, too, were tools of war.

Finally, an important political force in Rwanda—the inner core of the *akazu*—opposed peaceful outcomes from the onset. These were "spoilers." At the inner core of the *akazu,* there is no evidence of there ever having been any willingness to consider a negotiated settlement with the RPF. However, the remaining chapters will provide evidence that the presence of spoilers in Rwanda was not an insurmountable obstacle to peacemaking efforts.

The strategy of the architects of genocide can thus be summarized as comprising the elements of demonization, polarization, and escalation. The demonization of the RPF began early in the war. As war moved into the political arena, extremists fought to win over the moderate center, polarizing politics in Kigali in a manner that complicated the possibility of powersharing and forced moderates into a difficult and dangerous choice (to put it simplistically) between the CDR and the RPF. Finally, they escalated the war, moving quickly to kill off those moderates who would not join their effort and thereby tearing down any possibility of negotiated peace.

Demonization, polarization, escalation. And against these strategies, what role was played by international peacemakers? Where and why did peacemaking efforts fail to control or at least contain the dynamics of escalation? Chapters 3, 4, and 5—which constitute the heart of the analysis—tackle these questions. Looking first at prenegotiation efforts to open up a space for political dialogue, then at the formal mediation process, and finally at the peace implementation and peacekeeping processes, these three chapters explore an entire range of third-party interventions that collectively failed to provide a coherent strategy for responding to extremist opposition. This failure meant the global community was unable to prevent Rwandan extremists from launching their mass genocide.

Notes

1. See the recent edited volume by Matthews and Ali, *Civil Wars in Africa*, to which the author contributed a chapter on Rwanda. It takes as its common theme the role of elite manipulation of social cleavage as the triggering cause of civil war.

2. Such factors as Rwandan culture, poverty, and environmental stress, which some Rwandan observers have argued were causes of the war and genocide, do not provide sufficient accounts of the actions and strategies of warring parties, although in some instances they had facilitating or amplifying effects. For competing causal accounts of the war, see, inter alia, Valerie Percival and Thomas Homer-Dixon, "Environmental Scarcity and Violent Conflict: The Case of Rwanda," *Journal of Environment and Development* 5, 3 (September 1996): 49–70; Scott Grosse, "The Roots of Conflict and State Failure in Rwanda: The Political Exacerbation of Social Cleavages in a Context of Growing Resource Scarcity," Department of Population Planning and International Health, University of Michigan, unpublished paper, 15 November 1994; Peter Uvin, "Tragedy in Rwanda: The Political Ecology of Conflict" *Environment* 38, 3 (1996): 7–15; and Catherine André and Jean-Phillipe Platteau, *Working Paper, Faculté des sciences économiques et sociales:* "Land Relations Under Unbearable Stress: Rwanda Caught in the Malthusian trap" (Namur: FUNDP, January 1996).

3. For a good review, see Mohammed Ayoob, "State Making, State Breaking, and State Failure," in Chester A. Crocker, Fen Osler Hampson, and Pamela R. Aall (eds.), *Managing Global Chaos: Sources of and Responses to International Conflict* (Washington, DC: U.S. Institute for Peace, 1996), 37–51.

4. See esp. Anthony D. Smith, *State and Nation in the Third World* (New York: St. Martin's Press, 1983).

5. Catharine Newbury, *The Cohesion of Oppression: Clientship and Ethnicity in Rwanda, 1860–1960* (New York: Columbia University Press, 1988); and David Newbury, *Kings and Clans: Ijwwi Island and the Lake Kivu Rift, 1780–1840* (Madison: University of Wisconsin Press, 1991).

6. The classic English-language account of this period is given by Sir Harry Johnston, *The Uganda Protectorate*, vols. 1–2 (London: Hutchinson, 1902).

7. See John Hanning Speke, *Journal of the Discovery of the Source of the Nile* (London, 1863). Gérard Prunier has a good account of the debates

surrounding this early literature of Rwanda; see Chapter 1 in Gérard Prunier, *The Rwanda Crisis: History of a Genocide* (New York: Columbia University Press, 1995).

8. See esp., D. Newbury, *Kings and Clans*.

9. C. Newbury, *The Cohesion of Oppression*, and D. Newbury, *Kings and Clans*; see also Johann Pottier, "The 'Self' in Self-Repatriation: Closing Down Mugunga Camp, Eastern Zaire," in R. Black and K. Kosher (eds.), *The End of the Refugee Cycle* (Oxford: Berghahn, 1999).

10. The concept of ethnicity in Rwanda corresponds to that provided by constructivist accounts of ethnicity—i.e., the notion of ethnicity being a social feature constructed through people's interactions over time. This is contrasted to a primordialist account of ethnicity, which sees ethnicity as a fixed, ethnographical feature given by birth. Rwanda was one of the early case studies that gave strength to the constructivist account. See Leroy Vail, ed., *The Creation of Tribalism in Southern Africa* (London: James Currey, 1988).

11. For an account of King Leopold's role in the brutal colonization of what became at independence the state of Zaire, see, inter alia, Thomas Pakenham's magisterial account of the period, *The Scramble for Africa, 1876–1912* (New York: Random House, 1991).

12. C. Newbury, *Cohesion of Oppression*; see also Prunier, *The Rwanda Crisis*.

13. Much of this section draws on conversations held with Danielle de Lame, London, March 1994; we collaborated on an evaluation of emergency assistance to Rwanda. I am indebted to her patient attempts to explain to a novice the rich complexities of Rwandan social history, with which she is deeply acquainted. I hope I have not too far distorted the subtleties of her argument.

14. C. Newbury, *The Cohesion of Oppression*.

15. Ibid.

16. René Lemarchand, "Burundi in Comparative Perspective: Dimensions of Ethnic Strife," in John McGarry and Brendan O'Leary (eds.), *The Politics of Ethnic Conflict Regulation: Case Studies of Protracted Ethnic Conflicts* (London: Routledge, 1993), 153.

17. C. Newbury, *Cohesion of Oppression;* and Prunier, *The Rwanda Crisis*.

18. Percival and Homer-Dixon, "Environmental Scarcity"; André and Platteau, "Land Relations."

19. This account relies primarily on Rachel Van der Meeren, "Three Decades in Exile: Rwandan Refugees, 1960–1990," *Journal of Refugee Studies* 9 (1996): 252–267; Catherine Watson, *Background to an Invasion* (Washington, DC: U.S. Committee for Refugees, 1992); and Ogenga Ottunnu, "Rwandese Refugees and Immigrants in Uganda" and "An Historical Analysis of the Invasion by the Rwandese Patriotic Army (RPA)," both in Howard Adelman and Astri Suhrke (eds.), *The Path of a Genocide: The Rwanda Crisis from Uganda to Zaire* (New Brunswick, NJ: Transaction Publishers, 1999), 3–30 and 31–50.

20. Excellent accounts of this period are to be found in Van der Meeren, "Three Decades"; and Watson, *Background*.
21. Van der Meeren, "Three Decades."
22. Watson, *Background*.
23. Founding members of the RPF, author interviews, Kigali, June 1996.
24. Watson, *Background*.
25. Document supplied by Human Rights Watch Arms Project, Washington, DC.
26. Van der Meeren, "Three Decades."
27. See esp. Catherine Newbury, "Rwanda—Recent Debates over Governance and Rural Development," in Göran Hydén and Michael Bratton (eds.), *Governance and Politics in Africa* (Boulder: Lynne Rienner Publishers, 1992), 193–220.
28. The coup may have been bloodless in its implementation, but members of the Kayibanda regime were executed following Habyarimana's ascension to power.
29. C. Newbury, "Rwanda."
30. *Africa Research Bulletin*, No. 10512 (March 1992).
31. The French acronym is used in this report because the English acronym, RGF—for Rwandese Government Forces—is too easily confused with RPF.
32. On the impact of the coffee crisis and other developmental issues, see esp. Peter Uvin, *Aiding Violence: The Development Enterprise in Rwanda* (West Hartford, CT: Kumarian Press, 1998).
33. Prunier, *The Rwanda Crisis*, 84.
34. Pasteur Bizimungu would later become president of Rwanda under the first RPF-led government.
35. Reuters Rebel Correspondent for East Africa, Aidan Hartley, traveled down the Gabiro highway with the RPF, capturing on film the RPF's victory antics. Aidan Hartley, author interview, Nairobi, June 1996.
36. Rumors that Rwigyema was killed by rivals are denied by the RPF leadership and are discounted by Prunier in *The Rwanda Crisis*, 95.
37. Herman Cohen, former Assistant Secretary of State for African Affairs, U.S. Department of State, author interview, Washington, DC, June 1995; also, U.S. Department of State, confidential author interview, Washington, DC, June 1995.
38. Cohen, author interview. Access to information for CIA documents relating to this subject was refused.
39. Alain Rouvez, "French, British, and Belgian Involvement," in David Smock (ed.), *Making War and Waging Peace: Foreign Intervention in Africa* (Washington, DC: U.S. Institute for Peace, 1993), 27–51.
40. Colonel Tito Rutaremara, former Vice President, RPF, author interview, Kigali, July 1996.
41. Hartley, author interview, Nairobi, June 1996.
42. Colonel Rutaremara and Major Wilson Rutayisire, RPF, author interviews, Kigali, July 1996. Also, Watson, *Background*.

43. Prunier, *The Rwanda Crisis*, 113.

44. In June 1996, the author hiked with the RPF to the old bases in the Virungas. A long, steep hike up a bamboo-entangled face led to a series of well-hidden plateaus, where the RPF had encamped. It was evident how difficult it would be for any army to find, let alone dislodge, the RPF from these positions.

45. A nominal coalition government was appointed in December 1991 but contained only one member not from the ruling party.

46. See Joan Kakwenzire and Dixon Kamukama, "The Development and Consolidation of Extremist Forces in Rwanda," in Adelman and Suhrke (eds.), *The Path of a Genocide*, 61–92.

47. The relationship between the CDR and the MRND would be similar to that of the Christian Coalition in the Republican Party in the United States or the anti-Europe faction in the Tory Party in the United Kingdom: a key faction but not representative of the entire sphere of the party, and with powerful opponents in other factions of the party; and therefore able to shape, but not fully control, the political agenda. See Prunier, *The Rwanda Crisis;* and Jacques Bihozagara et al., "Analyses de la situation Rwandaise," in André Guichaoua, *Les crises politiques au Burundi et au Rwanda, 1993–1994* (Lille: Université des Sciences et Technologies de Lille, 1995), 185–210.

48. Former employee of the Rwandan Ministry of Transportation, confidential author interview, Washington, DC, December 1995.

49. Confidential author interviews, Dar-es-Salaam, December 1993; and Carol Fuller, Africa Bureau, U.S. Department of State, author interview, Washington, DC, December 1994. Reports from both the U.S. and Canadian embassies in Dar-es-Salaam confirm that Tanzanian government sources believed the RPF capable of defeating the FAR outright, even with French backing.

50. UN Department of Political Affairs, *Mission Report* (New York: March 1993).

51. Hartley, author interview.

52. Confidential author interview, Kigali, 3 July 1996.

53. See Kakwenzire and Kamukama, "Development and Consolidation."

54. Ibid.

55. A good source on the propaganda is Alison des Forges, *Leave None to Tell the Story* (New York: Human Rights Watch, 1999), 65–95.

56. See Commission Internationale d'Enquette sur les Violations des Droits de l'Homme au Burundi depuis le 21 octobre 1993, *Rapport Final* (New York and Paris: Commission Internationale d'Enquette, July 1994). Similar estimates were also given in reports by Burundi-based officials of the U.S. Office of Foreign Disaster Assistance, shown to the author in December 1995.

57. The author was in Tanzania during the period of the killings; figures of 150,000 and upward were used repeatedly in discussions with diplomats and others involved in the Arusha negotiations.

58. Moussali's comments were reported in a cable from a Western embassy to their headquarters (confidential document).

59. A copy of one such order (dated March 1994) was shown to the author by an official of the Rwandan embassy in Washington, DC, 18 December 1995.

60. Filip Reyntjens, *Trois jours qui ont fait basculer l'histoire* (Bruxelles: CEDAF, 1995).

61. Confidential author interview, Nairobi, June 1996.

62. Reytnjens, *Trois jours.*

63. See, inter alia, Des Forges, *Leave None to Tell the Story,* 199–201. The RPF's assessment of who was involved is given in an RPF document entitled, "Those Most Responsible for the Genocide," a copy of which was read by the author at the UN Rwanda Emergency Office archives, UN Integrated Regional Information Network, Nairobi.

64. In a United States Institute of Peace conference in Washington in December 1996, Gérard Prunier asserted the figure of 100,000; the lower figure of 50,000 was derived by the author in 1996 from estimates of the size of the militias added to estimates of FAR units not deployed to frontline battle with the RPF; see Adelman and Suhrke with Jones, *Study II of the Joint Evaluation.* See also Des Forges, *Leave None to Tell the Story,* 15–16, and Prunier, *The Rwanda Crisis,* 261–265.

65. Rui J.P. de Figueiredo Jr. and Barry R. Weingast, "The Rationality of Fear: Political Opportunism and Ethnic Conflict," in Barbara F. Walter and Jack Snyder (eds.), *Civil Wars, Insecurity, and Intervention* (New York: Columbia University Press, 1999), 261–302.

66. Jean-Pierre Chrétien is quoted in Prunier, *The Rwanda Crisis,* 247.

67. This account of the offensive developed through author interviews with RPF officials in Kigali, as well as author interviews with journalists who witnessed some of the battles.

68. Running from a base in Byumba, loaded with supplies, the reinforcements traversed forty kilometers of mountainous terrain in less than three days, a remarkable military feat.

69. Gérard Prunier, "Operation Turquoise: A Humanitarian Escape from a Political Dead End," in Adelman and Suhrke (eds.), *The Path of a Genocide,* 281–306. See also Gérard Prunier, "Operation Turquoise," presentation to the Rwanda Evaluation conference, U.S. Committee for Refugees, Washington, DC, 18 December 1996; and Prunier, *The Rwanda Crisis,* 281–295.

70. Two other instances of mass killing in the second half of the twentieth century approach the speed and scope of the Rwanda slaughter: ethnic and political genocide in Indonesia in 1964—the so-called communist killings; and the slaughter of Chinese by Japanese soldiers in December 1937–January 1938, referred to as the "rape of Nanking." Both these events saw more than 500,000 people killed in a matter of weeks. In terms of intensity, however, we should recall that both of these countries had vastly larger populations than did Rwanda.

71. Des Forges, *Leave None to Tell the Story,* 15–16.

72. For a useful review of the various approaches to the causation of war and their policy implications, see Chester A. Crocker, Fen Osler Hampson, and Pamela R. Aall, eds., *Managing Global Chaos: Sources of and Responses to International Conflict* (Washington, DC: United States Institute for Peace, 1996).

3

Early Peacemaking Efforts: Regional Prenegotiation

When war broke out in Rwanda in 1990, the U.S. National Intelligence Officer assigned to monitor developments later acknowledged that his first task was to locate Rwanda on an atlas.[1] The obscurity of Rwanda—long before it dominated the international media in the brutal summer of 1994—contributed to the conventional wisdom that nothing was done to prevent the terrible outcome. This obscurity masked from general awareness a period of energy and creativity by local, regional, and, to a lesser extent, international actors all seeking to contain and resolve the conflict.

Regional Peacemaking Efforts

The onset of the war was accompanied almost immediately by peacemaking efforts. In the days following the invasion, the Belgian government dispatched a peace mission to Rwanda composed of the prime minister, the foreign minister, and the defense minister. This trio met with President Habyarimana (who would be assassinated in April 1994) in Nairobi on 14 October and, over the next three days, held talks in Kenya, Uganda, and Tanzania, as well as with the Organization of African Unity. Although it is unclear whether this was the initial objective of the peace mission, it served to generate the start of a regional process. A summit held three days later at Mwanza, Tanzania, resulted in the Mwanza Communiqué, which formalized the involvement of

Rwanda's neighbors in the peace process, laid the basis for further discussions, and shifted the locus of talks to the OAU.[2]

As the RPF settled into a pattern of guerrilla warfare, a series of regional monitoring missions and mediation efforts were deployed to Rwanda to oversee developments. Indeed, Rwanda became a laboratory wherein subregional and regional interstate organizations tested their capacity to engage in conflict management. The results were largely negative, in that both their military and mediation efforts would prove ineffective in containing fighting. However, those interventions laid the groundwork for wider, international processes.[3]

The regional mediation process comprised two tracks: a series of official summit meetings between the heads of the member states of the subregional grouping, the Communité Économique des Pays des Grands Lacs (Economic Community of Countries of the Great Lakes Region; CEPGL); and broader meetings that brought the CEPGL members into contact with Ugandan, Tanzanian, OAU, and local UN officials. At a pair of such meetings held in late October in Gbadolite, Zaire, President Mobutu Sese Seko was appointed OAU mediator for the peace process. This appointment reflected Mobutu's role as *primus inter pares* in the CEPGL and subregional power broker. It was, however, controversial from the outset, especially given the fact that Zaire had sent troops to Kigali to support Habyarimana earlier that month.[4] The initial Gbadolite meetings also saw the CEPGL countries plus Uganda agree to establish a monitoring force for Rwanda, the Military Observer Group (MOG), under the observation of the OAU's Liberation Committee.

Following the Gbadolite talks, a working meeting of the CEPGL was held in Goma on 20–22 November, to which both Uganda and the RPF were invited. At this summit, President Museveni of Uganda was asked to organize a regional summit on the question of refugees in cooperation with President Ali Hassan Mwinyi of Tanzania.[5] The moves toward the conference began with a meeting of regional foreign ministers in Kinshasa, Zaire, on 17–19 January 1991, at which the OAU and UN High Commissioner for Refugees were represented.[6] At this meeting, Habyarimana confirmed that Mwinyi would host the conference, and a date for it was set. Then, immediately prior to the opening of the conference, Habyarimana attempted to gain the initiative by calling on all refugees to return, a futile gesture given both the situation in Rwanda and the troubled history of refugee diplomacy in the region.

Notwithstanding Habyarimana's grandstanding, the conference held in Dar-es-Salaam on 19 February was successful, at least on paper, resulting as it did in the Dar-es-Salaam Declaration on Rwandese Refugees Problem, which committed the government of Rwanda to finding a "definitive and durable solution" to the refugee problem.[7] This declaration became a prenegotiation text for the Arusha process and formed the core of the eventual Arusha protocol on refugees.

Another important development occurred at this juncture. In a preconference meeting between Mwinyi, Museveni, and Habyarimana, the latter was persuaded to sign the Zanzibar Communiqué, which restated a commitment, originally made in the Mwanza Communiqué, to finding a peaceful solution to the conflict through achieving a cease-fire agreement and through the regional conference on refugees.[8] The new twist was a commitment by Habyarimana to conduct a dialogue with the internal opposition.

The flurry of summitry had, to this point, done little to stop the fighting between the FAR and the RPF. Indeed, after the FAR succeeded in pushing the RPF into Uganda in October, the RPF attacked again in November, and heavy fighting ensued. By the time of the Zanzibar Communiqué, however, some substance was added to the summitry, and the process moved from general principles toward the negotiation of a real cease-fire. The first of these was signed on 29 March 1991, in N'Sele, Zaire (the N'Sele Cease-fire Agreement Between the Government of the Republic of Rwanda and the Rwandese Patriotic Front), the first formal cease-fire of the civil war. The N'Sele text established the terms of the cease-fire and set part of the agenda for continuing talks. It also revisited the makeup of the MOG, which was to police the cease-fire.

The MOG was now to be composed of five officers from each of the CEPGL countries and five officers each from Uganda and the RPF.[9] The participation of Ugandan troops was presumed to balance that of Zairians and Burundians and thereby ensure neutrality. However, the cease-fire did not last long enough for the force to be deployed. Ironically, one of the causes of the breakdown in the cease-fire was disputes over how the MOG would be implemented in practice. Before the MOG had a chance to deploy, the FAR broke the cease-fire by shelling RPF positions in northeastern Rwanda. Fighting continued for some months, although there was little movement on the ground: government forces took heavy losses, but the RPF did not advance much farther into Rwandan territory.

Having once failed to implement a cease-fire, negotiating a second would prove a more difficult task. Moves toward a second cease-fire saw, for the first time, a meaningful role for nonregional actors. The United States lent its weight to the peace talks in a meeting, organized by Irvin Hicks, the deputy assistant secretary for Africa, between GoR (that is, the government of Rwanda) and RPF representatives in Harare. The Hicks meeting did not produce anything concrete in the way of agreements, but it kept the spirit of negotiation alive and arguably laid the groundwork for a second round of cease-fire negotiations in Gbadolite.

The Gbadolite talks, held in September 1991, proved difficult to manage. The RPF refused to attend several sessions, despite the presence of Ugandan supporters. Nevertheless, two things were achieved. First, the Gbadolite meeting reissued the N'Sele cease-fire in amended form and reconfirmed the participants' commitment to peaceful resolution of the crisis.[10] Second, the Gbadolite cease-fire arrangement called for a revised observer group, with a more balanced composition, under the auspices of a nascent conflict resolution mechanism at the OAU (the first time the mechanism had been used, and the first time the OAU had deployed forces in a civil conflict of a member state).[11] The lead of the force was given to Nigeria, with the senior Zairian consigned to the role of deputy commander. The force comprised Nigerian and Zairian troops, with RPF and FAR representation. In later negotiations, the composition was further revised to add troops from Senegal and Zimbabwe and to remove the Zairian presence. The MOG did manage to deploy, although not before the FAR took advantage of delays to launch its November 1991 offensive in the Virungas.[12]

Just as the shifting composition of the MOG signaled a growing frustration with the lack of constructive contributions from neighboring countries, so the mediation process at this juncture reflected a similar exasperation, especially with the role played by Mobutu. Indeed, more significant than the content of the Gbadolite cease-fire was the fact that the meeting led to a displacement of Mobutu from the mediation role. According to diplomatic sources, all the parties recognized at this stage the inappropriateness (and incompetence) of Mobutu in this role.[13] Mobutu retained the formal title of "mediator" but was, from this point on, to have little role in the peace process. The need to bypass Mobutu's mediator position shifted the locus of the peace process to the OAU, minimizing the role played by the

CEPGL and increasing the participation of nonregional states and actors. Indeed, by the end of 1991 the regional mediation process had stalled. What kept the process alive, and moved it into a new phase, was quasiofficial mediation by both the U.S. State Department and the French Ministry of Foreign Affairs.[14]

The Shift to International Efforts

Starting in the fall of 1991, the foreign affairs ministries of both France and the United States held a series of unofficial meetings with parties to the war or their backers, designed to get the regional peace process back on track. The French and U.S. meetings with Rwandan participants ran in parallel, although each side kept the other informed of developments through working-level contacts.

At the Quai d'Orsay (French Foreign Ministry), the French foreign ministry's director for Africa and the Maghreb, Dijoud, tried to convene a 23–25 October 1991 meeting in Paris.[15] Major-General Paul Kagame, military head of the RPF, failed to show; the meeting was canceled as a result. A second attempt, on 14–15 January 1992, succeeded in bringing together Ambassador Kanyarushoke for the GoR and Pasteur Bizimungu for the RPF. At the meeting, Dijoud remarked to the RPF that there were two logics, the logic of peace and the logic of war: *Vous continuez à attaquer votre pays, votre pays se défend* (If you continue to attack your country, your country will defend itself). He challenged the RPF to halt its attacks on Rwanda and called on the GoR to listen more attentively to the RPF.[16]

In Washington, D.C., this same period witnessed a series of talks and initiatives from the Africa bureau of the U.S. State Department. The first of these was a working-level contact between RPF representatives in Washington and the State Department's desk officer for Rwanda, Carol Fuller. These talks eventually led to the involvement of Assistant Secretary of State for Africa Herman Cohen. First, Cohen called an interagency meeting to discuss the situation in Rwanda; this forum would meet over the next two years to coordinate U.S. efforts in Rwanda.[17] Having received the support of other relevant agencies to deepen U.S. involvement in the process, Cohen traveled to Kampala on 8 May 1992 and met with Museveni. At the meeting, Cohen not only offered U.S. technical assistance for the negotiations but also cajoled Museveni into buying in to the negotiation process.

Cohen's argument was that Uganda could not only solve its internal problems by helping the RPF negotiate powersharing in Rwanda; it could thereby deal a blow to Habyarimana, for whom Museveni had a long-standing animosity. Cohen then followed this visit with a two-day stop in Kigali, where he also offered U.S. technical support for negotiations.[18] By Christopher Mitchell's classification, Cohen's role was a combination of "explorer," "reassurer," and "enskiller" (see Chapter 1).

Independent of one another, the U.S. and French explorer and reassurer roles advanced the course of negotiations but made no formal breakthrough. However, upon his return from Rwanda, Cohen was asked by Dijoud to attend a meeting at the Quai d'Orsay with Ugandan Foreign Minister Ssemogerere. Cohen took the opportunity of talking to Ssemogerere, a political opponent of Museveni's, to convey a tough message. Citing Ugandan military support for the RPF, Cohen threatened to cut America's foreign assistance to Uganda if it did not pressure the RPF to participate in political negotiations toward a peace settlement.[19] Cohen would later acknowledge that he had no authorization to make such a threat; evidently, it worked.

This coming-together of forces would prove significant. Indeed, the critical meeting prior to the Arusha talks was one hosted at the Quai d'Orsay by Dijoud, at which Cohen was again present. It was at this session, on 6–8 June 1992, that the RPF and GoR finally agreed to hold comprehensive political negotiations under Tanzanian mediation and to meet in July to launch that process. It was not just the presence of U.S. and French mediators that shifted the talks into a new phase, however; several adjacent processes had been in the works, and had had some impact.

Adjacent Processes

If the focal points of activity in 1991 and 1992 were regional efforts to negotiate a lasting cease-fire and informal international prenegotiation talks, it is nevertheless the case that a series of other processes was occurring in Rwanda which either directly or indirectly impacted on those two main processes.

First, a series of "second-track" and "multitrack" negotiations was held during this period, involving both nonstate and quasistate actors. Second, there were two related adjacent international pressures that influenced events on the road to negotiation: Some international donors to Rwanda sought to place political (and especially human rights) conditionalities on their assistance to Rwanda in order to push the government into a more pacific stance.[20] These and other donors, both through aid conditionality and diplomatic suasion, pressured the Rwandan government to accept democratic reforms toward multiparty democracy. This last issue in particular had a critical—and not entirely positive—impact on the road to mediation.

Second-Track Efforts

Second-track, or unofficial, initiatives formed part of the move toward Arusha. The second track had several elements: unofficial contacts between members of the RPF's diaspora support network and Rwandan government officials in embassies overseas; a Rwandan church-based initiative; and efforts by the Vatican to support the church's initiatives.[21]

Regarding the first, little detail has been forthcoming, although some diplomats admit some knowledge of the meetings. What is known is that several members of the Rwandan diaspora began to hold secret talks with Rwandan diplomats and businessmen who had contacts with moderates among the MRND and the *akazu*. In Europe, Jacques Bihozagara, later to become minister for youth and sport in the first postwar RPF government, held a series of discrete meetings with diaspora groups in Brussels and Paris during 1991 and 1992.[22] On the other side of the Atlantic, Claude Dusaidi, RPF representative for North America (and later the cabinet chief for Minister of Defense Paul Kagame), held informal meetings with members of the diaspora, as well as informal, working-level meetings with the U.S. State Department. These latter meetings were significant in that they began to generate the State Department involvement in the Paris talks mentioned above. By and large, diplomats and Rwandan officials familiar with the European and North American talks suggest that their contribution was largely to improve the "atmosphere" by widening and deepening the contact between the Rwandan combatants. No specific outcome appears to have resulted from this process, although the importance of "atmosphere" in terms of facilitating moves toward formal negotiations should not be underestimated.

More substantial was the role played by the Rwandan church, especially under the aegis of Bishop Thadée Nsengiyumva. These efforts began as a process internal to the Catholic Church, which, according to church sources, had largely failed to address the issue of ethnicity in its own ranks prior to the onset of the war. Ethnic tensions within the church were considerable, especially because promotion to the rank of bishop was seen as closed except to Hutu from the northern clans. The war amplified these tensions and also led to initial efforts to address the issue both within the church and, by extension, in Rwandan society. The opening move came from the diocese of Kabgaye, where a pastoral letter written by the clergy addressed the theme *convertez-nous de vivre ensemble* (convert ourselves to living together).[23] The letter was politically charged yet prompted action from some of the higher ranks in the church.

In particular, Bishop Thadée Nsengiyumva began to exercise leadership on the issue. He convened a conference of bishops, bringing together both Catholic and Protestant bishops to address the issue of ethnic competition in the church and in Rwandan society. Also, critically, Nsengiyumva began in secret to initiate contact with the RPF through church officials in Burundi—contacts later placed at the disposal of Rwanda's then minister for foreign affairs and cooperation, Boniface Ngulinzira.

Nsengiyumva was prodded and supported in his efforts by the Vatican, which in 1992 began to lend its weight to the search for peace.[24] Indeed, throughout the war the Vatican played an important role in bringing together diplomatic actors and supporting moderate forces in the government and in surrounding circles of power, especially the church. Critical to these efforts was Monsignor Guiseppe Bertollo, who was assigned as papal nuncio in Rwanda in 1991 when it became evident to Rome that senior figures in the Rwandan church were caught up in the same politics of ethnic competitiveness that was increasingly gripping Rwanda. Bertollo sought to move the peace process forward in part by supporting Nsengiyumva's efforts. A critical juncture came in early May 1992, when secret meetings between Rwandan church leaders and the RPF were held in Bujumbura under the aegis of the papal nuncio in Burundi.[25] Using information gained in these talks, Bishop Nsengiyumva managed to convince newly appointed Foreign Minister Boniface Ngulinzira of Rwanda to make contact with Bertollo. This in turn led to a trip by Ngulinzira to the Vatican, where he was encouraged to play an active role in generating dialogue between the two sides. This bore fruit on 23 May 1992, when Ngulinzira met with the RPF in Kinihira, Rwanda, and won its agreement to attend Dijoud's Paris meeting the following month. That meeting, which launched the Arusha process, thus represented the coming-together not only of U.S. and French efforts but also those of second-track players, notably the Rwandan church and the Vatican. This episode underscores the importance of connections between third-party efforts on different tracks or at different levels.

This episode raises another, critical point: one of the key roles of these second-track efforts was in facilitating communication between the RPF, external governments, and internal opposition groups. Indeed, Foreign Minister Ngulinzira, whose presence in Kinihira was an important step toward Arusha, was a member of an opposition party, not of the ruling MRND. The role of opposition parties in the peace process was critical. The story of their connection to international peacemaking efforts begins in a second process adjacent to the formal negotiations, namely, international diplomatic and developmental pressure.

International Suasion and Conditionality:
Multiparty Politics and Human Rights

During the civil war period, and especially prior to the launch of formal mediation at Arusha, international diplomatic actors played a variety of roles that may be described as prenegotiation. The role of the Quai d'Orsay and the U.S. State Department in picking up the flagging momentum of the regional mediation effort has already been discussed. In 1991 and even into 1992, however, at least U.S. policy was driven by bureaucratic, not political actors, never reaching the level even of secretary of state, let alone the White House. For most of the Western powers, government policy toward Rwanda was shaped by the nature of their prewar relations, that is, it revolved around international development assistance, of which Rwanda was a heavily dependent recipient.

It has been previously noted that the Rwandan economy was heavily reliant on international aid flows and that during the 1970s and 1980s Rwanda had indeed been one of the success stories of the aid community. When war broke out, several donor governments sought to use the leverage provided by their aid role to shift the position of the Rwandan government, especially as it related to such grave human rights abuses as mass arrests and large-scale killings of the Tutsi. The donor governments attempted, in effect, to play a role opposite to that of the enhancer role depicted by Mitchell; rather than using aid resources to enhance the payoff associated with peace, these governments were using their resources as a source of leverage and pressure. They can perhaps be referred to as having acted as "inducers" to introduce an additional role.

Although the collective weight of the donor community was potentially considerable, a lack of coordination among the actors minimized the impact of conditionality and pressure.[26] Inconsistent and sporadic, human rights conditionality clearly did little to shift the GoR's tactics. Financial pressure brought to bear (e.g., by one government restricting aid flow) was counteracted (e.g., by another government expanding it); despite numerous violations, conditionalities never resulted in aid cuts. There was little that was consistent, and little that was effective, in this realm—an early example of the weakening of international peacemaking efforts by a lack of coordination between key actors.

There was, however, one very important exception, namely, the consistent pressure put on the Habyarimana government to move in the direction of multiparty democracy. In this realm, concerted pressure achieved an important result and had a direct impact on the peace process, albeit one that was arguably hollow.

Indeed, pressure toward democratization had begun before the start of the civil war. In particular, France had begun to place pressure on its Franco-African client states to adopt more democratic forms of governance, a theme it expounded at length at the 1989 Franco-African summit at Baule, France.[27] This pressure was sufficient to lead the Habyarimana government to announce in early 1990 that it was going to review its constitution with a view to making democratic changes. This constitutional review was quickly shelved when the RPF invaded in 1990.[28] However, within a few months, renewed international pressure was forcing the Habyarimana regime to pay some attention to the issue, changing the law to authorize multiple political parties and even, in November 1991, announcing the creation of the first multiparty government in Rwanda. The multiparty element of the government was barely credible, however; only one cabinet member came from a party other than the MRND.

Western governments, in particular the United States, kept up the pressure. Part of the reason was an analysis performed by the French military attaché to Rwanda, Lieutenant-Colonel Galinie, which was shared with the U.S. Embassy in Kigali.[29] The analysis suggested the existence of three circles of power in Kigali. In the inner circle was

Habyarimana, his immediate family, and their closest associates—people like Archbishop Vincent Nsengiyumva and Habyarimana's wife and brothers-in-law. Surrounding this inner circle, argued Galinie, was a second circle of power: lesser ministers, cabinet directors, generals, bishops, prefects, and the like whose power rested on the continued authority of the inner core. These two circles of power, Galinie argued, were unlikely, without pressure, to engage in serious negotiations toward a peaceful settlement, as they had everything to lose. However, there was also, Galinie asserted, a third circle of power that was more moderate and open to negotiation. This comprised a large number of second-level army officers, especially senior colonels, as well as political activists, civil society directors, some academics, and lower-level church officials. Many of these were Hutu from less-privileged clans or regions. This group was, in essence, blocked from attaining real power by the stranglehold on power held by the two innermost circles. This third circle, Galinie reasoned, would have cause to negotiate. During 1990 and 1991, as international pressure eased the restrictions on political activity in Kigali, this third circle had increasingly formed itself into internal opposition parties such as the Mouvement Démocratique Républicain (MDR), the Parti Libéral (PL), the Parti Chrétien Démocratique (PCD), and the Parti Socialiste Démocratique (PSD). (The MDR in particular was seen as a revitalization of the old southern Hutu party, Parmehutu, which had held power in Rwanda before the Habyarimana coup.) From the U.S. perspective, the implications of Galinie's analysis were clear: if the first two circles of power would resist direct negotiations with the RPF, they could instead be pressured to open the regime to multiparty democracy, and then the opposition parties could be relied upon to lead the way to formal negotiations.

This analysis proved accurate, and the policy was effective initially. Through the first months of 1992, the Western governments kept up the pressure for democratization. The combination of international pressure and internal pressure, applied largely by civic and human rights groups in Kigali, managed to pry open the Rwandan regime. In April 1992, Habyarimana gave in and announced the formation of the second coalition government, this one involving meaningful powersharing for the multiple opposition parties that had grown up during the war years. Roughly a third of the seats in the April 1992 government were held by opposition politicians, including, as noted, the position of foreign minister.[30]

As anticipated, the very first act of the coalition government, through the person of the foreign minister, was to approve formal peace talks with the RPF. This launched the major peacemaking process in Rwanda, a process formally known as the Arusha Political Negotiations.

Themes: Complexities of Peacemaking

During this initial prenegotiation phase, it is already possible to identify several dimensions of the complexity of peacemaking, as outlined in the Introduction. One is the wide range of peacemaking roles played by third parties. We can see, for example, the role of *explorer* in Belgium's preliminary talks, held between the Rwandan government and regional counterparts. Both the OAU and CEPGL contributed to the role of *convenor* in hosting subregional and regional summits during the early days of the peace process. In the initial stages, we can also describe the U.S. and French efforts to determine the feasibility of international talks between the Rwandan government and the RPF as *explorer, reassurer,* and *enskiller* roles. In the U.S. effort to pressure Uganda into pressuring the RPF to agree to talks, we can see something akin to Mitchell's "delinker" role: the U.S. role in this regard was not to delink Ugandan support from the RPF but to attempt to take Ugandan military backing out of the equation by trying to shift Uganda's links to the RPF into the political realm. Finally, in the deployment of the MOG, first by the CEPGL and later by the OAU, we see the *monitor* role being played. Additionally, in roles not foreseen by Mitchell, the Vatican can be seen as having acted as a *neutral messenger,* whereas the role of Western donor governments has been described as that of *inducers.*

It is also worth noting that a few third-party actors in Rwanda played more than one role: the United States was delinker as well as explorer; the OAU and the CEPGL were both monitor and convenor. Thus, although it is certainly relevant and valid to emphasize the variety of actors and multiple roles that composed the peace process, it is important not to lose sight of the capacity of a given third party to play a variety of roles at different stages—and even at the same stage.

The second general theme is that of connections between initiatives. During this phase, Belgium's explorer role in the first weeks of the war clearly facilitated the launch of the regional summit process.

Although it is likely that regional summitry would have taken place even without Belgium's role, it is doubtful that it would have been up and running so soon after the RPF invasion. In turn, the regional summitry and mediation process helped pave the way for later French and U.S. informal talks at the international level. There is both a positive and a negative sense to this. On the one hand, it was clearly the limited success of the regional summitry process that led to the increasing involvement of the U.S. and French diplomatic communities, and this can be seen as a negative interconnection. On the other hand, regional summitry also produced a series of partial agreements and partial cease-fires upon which the U.S. and French efforts would build.

Furthermore, links between second-track efforts and adjacent processes in the bilateral realm were important in creating the necessary conditions for agreement to proceed with formal political negotiations at the international level. This is true of the second-track efforts that led to Foreign Minister Ngulinzira meeting with the RPF prior to the Paris meeting in June 1992. It is also true, perhaps in a more profound sense, of the pressure placed on the Habyarimana government to open its regime to multiparty politics. The creation of a power-sharing government in April 1992, itself partially a result of bilateral pressure, was an essential (if not ultimately positive) step toward the agreement for formal negotiations.

There were other, more subtle interconnections. Although it is difficult to state with any certainty, it does seem likely that the poor performance of the MOG monitoring function over time reduced the credibility of first the CEPGL and then the OAU as convenors of the summitry process. This did not result in these actors being abandoned altogether as third parties in the process, but the lack of success in the regional mediation process—often because of disputes over the MOG—led to a shift toward UN involvement. As will become clear later, the weakness of the connections between regional mediators and the UN would open up an important gap in peacemaking efforts.

This latter point relates to a third theme, namely, the question of a coordinating element for peacemaking initiatives. Clearly there was no such coordinating element in Rwanda during this phase, a fact that conforms to Mitchell's somewhat pessimistic prognostications on the tendency for third-party roles to be deployed ad hoc. Still, considering the way in which both the U.S. State Department and the

Quai d'Orsay weighed in with exploratory talks just as the regional process was beginning to flag, it can be argued that during this stage there was in fact an appropriate sequencing of third-party roles. The explanation is relatively simple and comes from the good communications and relations enjoyed among the diplomatic communities in Africa at the working level, as well as the good collaboration between Cohen and Dijoud. But these good relations were spontaneous, unplanned, and not controlled. Does this suggest that the concern of the interconnected process framework for having a coordinating element is misplaced? The evidence is inconclusive, for this phase of events was relatively straightforward and reflected relatively few third parties and third-party roles. At later stages, the question of coordination would become more important.

For the moment, then, it suffices to note that the major success of early prenegotiation efforts—generating more formal political negotiations—actually planted the seed of later difficulties. Bringing the opposition parties into the government created a more complex set of parties to the negotiations and, in important ways, constrained the hands of international mediators. The dynamics of the Arusha negotiations would prove critical to the overall peacemaking effort in Rwanda.

Notes

1. Confidential author interview, Washington, DC, May 1995.

2. *Mwanza Communiqué* (Mwanza: Government of Tanzania, 17 October 1990): 1.

3. The timeline contained herein was developed, except where otherwise noted, through reference to *Africa Research Bulletin;* documents obtained from Western embassies in Dar-es-Salaam in December 1993 and January 1994; interviews with U.S., French, Canadian, and Tanzanian officials in Dar-es-Salaam, Ottawa, London, and Washington; interviews with Rwandan officials; and from the texts of the accords themselves, which are unpublished but not restricted.

4. Lieutenant Cameron, NGO Liaison Officer, RPF, author interview, Washington, DC, December 1995.

5. *Gbadolite Communiqué,* Gbadolite, Zaire (26 October 1990): 1; *Goma Communiqué,* Goma, Zaire (20 November 1990): 1.

6. By this point in time, fighting had displaced tens of thousands of Rwandans; CARE Rwanda, *Internal Reports,* Kigali, 1991. Also, the question of the refugee population in Uganda was a critical one in the conflict.

7. *Dar-es-Salaam Declaration on Rwandese Refugees Problem*, Dar-es-Salaam, Tanzania (19 February 1991): 1, Art.5.

8. *Zanzibar Communiqué*, Zanzibar, Tanzania (17 February 1991): 1.

9. *Ceasefire Agreement Between the Government of the Republic of Rwanda and the Rwandese Patriotic Front* (N'Sele, Zaire, 22 March 1991).

10. *The Gbadolite Ceasefire Between the Government of Rwanda and the Rwandese Patriotic Front* (Gbadolite, Zaire: 7 September 1991): 1–2.

11. For further details, see Amare Tekle, "The Organisation for African Unity and Conflict Prevention, Management and Resolution," paper prepared for Study II of the Joint Evaluation, Addis Ababa, Ethiopia, December 1995.

12. *The Gbadolite Ceasefire*; also, Rutaremara, author interview.

13. Ambassador Ami Mpungwe, former Tanzanian ambassador to the Arusha process, author interview, Bergen, Norway, September 1995; author interviews, Canadian and U.S. officials, Dar-es-Salaam, Tanzania, December 1993.

14. In the case of the State Department in particular, although the mediation effort involved U.S. government officials, it was bureaucratic officials who were involved, and they operated largely without oversight from responsible elected officials. For example, U.S. Assistant-Secretary of State for African Affairs Herman Cohen acknowledged that only once had he mentioned the talks to Secretary of State James Baker, who had simply agreed that Cohen should carry on. The issue was never raised in the Cabinet or in the White House. Cohen, author interview.

15. Official of the French embassy to the United States, author interview, Washington, DC, June 1995.

16. Front Patriotique Rwandais, "Compte rendu de la réunion du 14–15 janvier 1992 entre la délégation du gouvernement rwandais et celle du F.P.R." (RPF Territory, Rwanda, 14–15 January, 1992): 3.

17. Fuller, author interview.

18. This account, and the analysis that follows, relies in part on: Fuller, author interview; Charles Snyder, Political-Military Adviser to the Assistant Secretary of State for Africa, author interview, Washington, DC, May 1995; and Cohen, author interview. Also, official documents of the Canadian High Commission in Tanzania, October 1990 to July 1992, accessed under the Official Secrets Act of Canada.

19. Cohen, author interview.

20. The question of aid conditionality is treated in Adelman and Suhrke with Jones, *Study II of the Joint Evaluation*, 31–33.

21. Inter alia, confidential author interview, Rome, April 1995; and Christian Aid Representative, address, International Alert, Open Forum on Rwanda, London, UK, 27 January 1995.

22. Confidential author interview, Kigali, July 1996.

23. Letter supplied by Monsignor Bertollo, former papal nuncio in Rwanda; author interview with Astri Suhrke, Rome, April 1995.

24. Monsignor Bertollo, former papal nuncio in Rwanda, author interview with Astri Suhrke, Rome, April 1995.

25. Vatican official, confidential author interview, April 1995.

26. On the inconsistency and, to a certain extent, hypocrisy in donor conditionality toward Rwanda, see esp. Howard Adelman, "Canadian Policy in Rwanda," in Adelman and Suhrke (eds.), *The Path of a Genocide,* 185–208.

27. Embassy of France to the United States, confidential author interview, Washington, DC, November 1995.

28. For details on the constitutional discussions surrounding this process, see James K. Gasana, "La guerre, la paix et la démocratie au Rwanda" and "La mise en place des nouvelles autoritées rwandaises," in André Guichaoua (ed.), *Les crises politiques au Burundi et au Rwanda 1993–1994* (Paris: Kartala, 1995): 211–238 and 722–730.

29. The author was not allowed to see the cable from the U.S. Embassy in Kigali, which reported Lieutenant-Colonel Galinie's analysis, but the text of the cable was read to the author by a U.S. diplomat in Washington, DC, State Department, June 1995.

30. Lists of the members of the first and second coalition governments are provided in the annex of Guichaoua (ed.), *Les crises politiques.*

4

The Arusha Negotiations: Mediation and Facilitation

The Arusha peace process, launched in June 1992, is an extraordinary story of a sophisticated conflict resolution process gone disastrously wrong. The process itself was deliberate, inclusive, communicative, informed by a cogent analysis, and supported by a range of internal and external parties, many of whom cooperated beyond what might have been expected. The end result was celebrated in the region and by some participants as the framework for a "new order" in Rwanda: a comprehensive agreement that went beyond the traditional *settlement* of conflict and made real inroads into *resolving* some of the underlying tensions that had sparked the civil war. And yet, nine months after the Arusha signing, extremist forces in Kigali would implement their own bloody version of the new order. Did Arusha fall victim to its own success? Did the agreements contain inherent flaws that spawned this violence? Was it irrelevant? Or was any potential peace agreement bound to be subject to attack from spoilers—the internal forces over which it had no control? And can answers to these key questions be found in an analysis of the Arusha process itself (its participants; its conceptual foundations; the issues and process of negotiation; and its final content)? Or were problems in the connections (or their absence) between Arusha and other third-party initiatives responsible for the overall failure of peacemaking efforts?

Arusha: Foundations and Participants

The Arusha process is striking because it was a partially intentional, partially unintentional hybrid of traditional formal mediation processes and more innovative approaches to facilitating communication and problem-solving between the parties.

The starting point for the conceptual underpinnings of the Arusha process was a shared analysis, informed by a common negotiating history, among Tanzanian, French, and U.S. officials who were instrumental. The analysis was grounded on the comparative historical experience of conflict resolution processes in other parts of Africa, in which some key participants in the early stages of Arusha had been involved.[1] For example, officials such as Ami Mpungwe, Tanzania's principal facilitator for the Arusha talks, Herman Cohen, who helped launch them, and Charles Snyder and John Byerly, members of Cohen's conflict resolution team, had all been involved in conflict resolution processes in Namibia and Angola; indeed, Mpungwe was brought back from Namibia in February 1992 just as the run-up to Arusha began to gather steam.

These and other participants in the peace talks drew on a roughly shared pool of experiences from Cambodia, Liberia, Namibia, Angola, and Mozambique. Critically, many were also informed of the process of political change in South Africa, whose parallel developments would provide stark contrast to Rwanda. These reference points permeated the negotiation process. This was at least partially the result of a deliberate effort; strikingly, some of the early negotiators traveled to Zimbabwe and Nicaragua to compare notes with previous negotiation experiences.[2]

The shared analysis, and the conceptual foundations of Arusha, were not just drawn from the realm of common experience, however. Unusual though it is, it appears that the Arusha process was at least informed by, and in part designed around, the academic literature relating to social conflict and the need to address such conflicts through communicative processes. In particular, Ambassador Mpungwe had made it clear that he was familiar with some of the writings and concepts relating to social conflict (especially the concept of protracted social conflict); he had learned, both from that literature and from his experience in Namibia and from his observation of the peace process in South Africa, that a sustainable resolution to conflict in Rwanda would not come from high-level summitry. In his terms, he understood that the Arusha process, to have any chance of changing things in Rwanda, would have to give the two sides themselves a chance to communicate effectively and to change their attitudes and perceptions of one another, to forge agreements that would meet the security and political needs of both sides.[3] He thus convinced President Mwinyi that Tanzania would have to sponsor, rather than summitry, sustained face-to-face talks and take an active role in facilitating dialogue.

After the opening set of Arusha talks, which were presided over by President Mwinyi, Ambassador Mpungwe was given a fairly free hand to design the Arusha process. He did so with three principles in mind. First, the structure of the process should be designed to facilitate communication between the two parties. Second, the process should last for a long time to allow for changing perceptions as well as negotiation of a detailed text. Third, his own role, and that of his negotiation team, was not to hammer out a deal between the two but to facilitate dialogue and communication, channel input from the "observers," and create an environment in which the parties to the process could reach a mutually acceptable agreement. Moreover, Mpungwe's desired outcome was clear: not just a settlement that would freeze the conflict for a brief period but a political *resolution* to the conflict and its (perceived) underlying causes, one that would be durable and even a model for African internal conflict.[4]

In these three realms, the design of the Arusha process certainly conforms more closely to the conceptions of peace processes found in conflict resolution literature than in the more traditional negotiation/mediation literature. Moreover, some of the objectives and principles of the Tanzanian role are very similar in character to the role of an academic facilitator in a problem-solving process. There were, of course, important differences, the two principal ones being that the talks were not confidential in the manner of a facilitated problem-solving session, and that they were official, not unofficial. (However, it will be shown that an adjunct process designed by the Americans and Tanzanians together, known as the Joint Military-Political Commission [JMPC], provided a forum that although officially authorized operated in a manner similar to an unofficial, second-track process.) Thus, the Arusha process was an anomaly: an official, first-track, facilitative process of dialogue toward resolution, not settlement, of the Rwandan civil war. (In this, unbeknown to its architects, the Arusha process shared some of the features of such notable international negotiations taking place in parallel, such as the Oslo negotiations for Palestinian-Israeli peace.)

As for composition, the Arusha talks had two formal delegations: the GoR and the RPF. It also had several "observer" delegations whose active role warrants their consideration as participants in the talks.⁵ Finally, it had a "facilitator."

Rwandan Delegations

Clearly the most important teams at the Arusha talks were those of the GoR and the RPF. Some important insights into the Arusha process can be gained by examining the differences between the two delegations, as characterized by Western and regional participants and observers. A first distinction that recurs in discussion with these participants is that the RPF was extremely disciplined and effective, whereas the GoR delegation was divided, undisciplined, and ineffective as a negotiating team. The reasons for this are not hard to find. First, the RPF had an enormous amount to gain from the Arusha talks and sent a strong team that included the general secretary of the RPF, Dr. Théogène Rudasingwa, Pasteur Bizimungu, who would later become president of the republic, and Dr. Patrick Mazimpaka, vice chair of the RPF. Of these, Rudasingwa was seen as being the eyes and ears of Paul Kagame at the talks, Mazimpaka as the principal negotiator. The chain of command, through Rudasingwa back to the military and political leadership of the RPF, was clear.

The government of Rwanda, in contrast, was represented by members of at least three different political parties or groups, including the opposition MDR and PL, and the most extreme hard-line group, the CDR. The team members were Foreign Minister Boniface Ngulinzira (a member of the MDR); Landoald Ndasingwa, minister of labor and social affairs (also of the MDR); Colonel Bagasora (of the CDR);⁶ Ambassador Kanyarushoki (Rwanda's ambassador to Uganda for ten years and a close confidant of Habyarimana's); and occasionally Dismas Nsengiyaremye, prime minister in a coalition government. Separate chains of command were at play in this team, with Ngulinzira and Ndasingwa taking their orders from the prime minister, Ambassador Kanyarushoki dealing directly with President Habyarimana, and Colonel Bagasora forging a link to hard-line elements in Kigali. Indeed, Foreign Minister Ngulinzira, a member of MDR, is reported to have said that it was easier to negotiate with the RPF than with his own delegation.⁷ These wide divisions were reflected in a fractious negotiation team, as well as in the inability to keep team positions secret: observer team members would occasionally have GoR official negotiating papers, stamped "Secret," faxed to them via an unknown number in Brussels. This inability to maintain secret positions weakened their negotiating strength in Arusha.

This weak-versus-strong split was reflected even in the technological capacities of the delegations. According to participants, the RPF delegation was well equipped with cellular telecommunications equipment, allowing team members to communicate easily, and privately, with Kampala and RPF headquarters. The GoR delegation, by contrast, had no such equipment and was often placed in the position of having to communicate with Kigali via the public payphone in the lobby of the Mount Meru Hotel!

Some commentators have argued a second distinction between the two delegations, namely, the high level of RPF commitment to the process, which is said to contrast to the insincerity of the GoR's participation. This distinction, however, does not withstand the evidence. First, as shown above, the government delegation was led by two people—Ngulinzira and Ndasingwa—who stood enormously to gain from the Arusha process. And as Filip Reyntjens notes, the Arusha process won concessions from the government that the opposition parties could only have dreamed of a year earlier.[8]

As to the sincerity of the RPF, no questions have been raised. The seniority, discipline, and effectiveness of the delegation signaled the deadly seriousness with which the RPF viewed the Arusha process. But it is important to note that the RPF, according to several Western participants, gained important leverage over time from the sense given by the delegation that, although they were serious about negotiations, they were also prepared to return to the battlefield if they could not achieve what they wanted in talks. Having spent their lives in exile and ten years in armed camps in the bush (first with the NRA then with the RPF), they could afford a few more years' fighting more than they could afford to lose in the peace process. This was in stark contrast to the GoR position: Two years of war had savaged what was already an economy in deep retraction; domestic pressures for change were mounting; international pressure for change, from Western donors and from the international financial institutions, was equally intense; and the government was on its last legs and could ill afford a long, drawn-out peace process or a return to fighting. Thus, not only did the composition and capacity of the two teams reflect a power disparity, but their positions did as well.

This strength/weakness distinction can be seen as a critical variable in explaining the Arusha process, both for understanding the agreements reached and for understanding what would follow the signing of the Arusha peace deal. In essence, it seems that important elements of Arusha represented victories for the RPF rather than mutually acceptable settlements and, as such, were defeats for elements in the Habyarimana regime. The dynamic that led to the genocide involved precisely those extremist elements that lost in Arusha and that rejected the transition bargain it represented. The question of what responsibility the RPF has for the collapse of the process—having been so intransigent on key points—is one to which we shall return.

Observers

The six African states involved in Arusha were Uganda, Burundi, Senegal, Zimbabwe, Nigeria, and Zaire. Uganda was essentially a *guarantor* of the RPF; according to RPF negotiators, Uganda's presence at Arusha was a necessary precondition of RPF attendance.[9] Uganda was at times able to use this guarantor role to persuade the RPF to accept reasonable compromises. Senegal was involved because in 1992, when Arusha commenced, Senegal's Abdou Diouf held the chairmanship of the OAU. Both sides expressed admiration for the Senegalese delegate, Ambassador Louis "Papa" Fall, who was praised by several Western participants for his capacity, in the colloquialism of a U.S. negotiator, "to kick butt in two languages" (a reference to his rhetorical skills, not Senegal's clout).[10] Along with the Tanzanian facilitator, the Senegalese team was perceived to have played an effective *honest broker* role and to have been critical to reaching the final compromises of Arusha.[11] Burundi, as a neighboring state with the same tribal mix as Rwanda, was generally seen as supportive of the RPF but did not have much impact on the talks. And Zaire, having badly mishandled the regional peace process, was notable in Arusha largely by its absence. In addition to these states, Zimbabwe and Nigeria played a role through their participation in the military observer groups, and were signatories to the Arusha declaration, but they played minor roles in the talks themselves.

Although details of their roles are sketchy, the OAU and UN delegations appear to have balanced each other's presence and role in the Arusha negotiations. The GoR delegation did not fully trust the OAU;[12] equally, the RPF did not trust the United Nations, given France's membership in the UN Security Council. With assistance from the Tanzanian, Senegalese, and U.S. delegations, however, it proved possible for the OAU and UN to cooperate on negotiations over and management of two monitoring forces deployed in Rwanda: the OAU NMOG and the UNOMUR.[13] Additionally, various UN observers contributed technical expertise. UNDP's deputy representative in Tanzania was present at times. More frequently, UNHCR had a representative at the talks who contributed legal and technical expertise on the tricky question of refugee resettlement, one of the major issues of the war. As the talks moved into their final stages, the UN Department of Political Affairs (DPA) became more deeply involved, especially because DPA had played a role in getting the talks back on track after they had been derailed following the February 1993 offensive.

As for Western governments, the two former colonial powers, Belgium and Germany, were both represented in the talks. Their representatives, Conte Michel d'Aviola and Hans Peter Repnik, respectively, are credited by other participants with minor but useful roles in the talks. Far more significant were the roles played by the United States and France, both worth developing in some detail.

When members of the U.S. delegation to Arusha were asked what their interest was in getting involved, their unanimous answer was a simple end to the conflict. As one U.S. diplomat put it, "We didn't have a dog in that fight."[14] The United States had exactly one foreign direct investment in Rwanda, a minimal presence, and in general no special interest in the country. Later commentators have raised the question of Anglo-French competition as a source of U.S. foreign policy in Rwanda; this is dismissed as nonsense by U.S. diplomats. The evidence does suggest that U.S. policy was largely motivated by a concern to secure peaceful conditions throughout Africa, a standing concern of the State Department since the end of the Cold War.[15]

Representing neither a former colonial power nor a regional power, the U.S. delegation was trusted to a certain degree by both the RPF and the GoR delegations. A strong U.S. team of diplomats in the region and mediators from Washington worked closely with Tanzania to push negotiations forward. Enjoying good ties with the RPF as a result of Kagame's period spent in training at Fort Leavenworth in the United States, and having solid diplomatic relations with the Habyarimana government, the delegation was able to present ideas to both sides, serve as a conduit for suggestions from the less clearly neutral delegations, and put pressure both on the Rwandan delegations and on the other observer teams when their positions seemed unreasonable or unclear.[16] The United States also played the very important role as enskiller, that is, a party that aids the negotiation or mediation process by building skills among warring parties for political dialogue. Two individuals were assigned: Charles Snyder worked with the GoR delegation to help members prepare their negotiating books; John Byerly worked with the RPF on negotiating tactics. Later in the process, the joke would be that Byerly had done too good a job, given the RPF's superior skills.

As for France, much has been written about its dark role in supporting the Habyarimana regime and thus in fostering genocide, training those who executed the genocide, and denying legitimacy to the new regime. To what extent is this an accurate portrayal of French involvement?

First off, French policy in Africa is notoriously complex. Various elements of the French state have separate and often competing interests in Africa that far exceed any corresponding interest held by other Western foreign policy units. These include the Quai d'Orsay; the Elysée Palace, including the president himself and his special adviser for African affairs (a position staffed in 1991 by President Mitterand's son, Jean-Christophe, who had close personal ties with Habyarimana); the defense ministry; the Ministry of Cooperation; and the French Secret Services. All were active in Rwanda. French policy in Rwanda was thus at the very least confusing and arguably even contradictory.

In aggregate, it would appear that the effects of French actions in Rwanda were negative, especially because supportive signals from elements of the French state seem to have lent comfort to hard-line elements in Kigali, leading them to believe that they could get away with paying lip service to Arusha while conniving to secure their position and power.[17] However, there is both primary evidence and analytic argument for seeing the French role in Arusha in more positive terms.

Although overall French policy in Rwanda reflected the competing interests of the state elements just mentioned, French policy for the Arusha process specifically was dominated by the Quai d'Orsay. This was partially an accident of geography: because the talks were held in Tanzania, they were principally staffed by the French embassy in Dar-es-Salaam, rather than the Kigali embassy. Unlike the embassy in Rwanda, which reported to the Ministry of Cooperation (due to Rwanda's inclusion in special aid programs normally reserved for former colonies), the embassy in Dar-es-Salaam reported directly to the Quai.

According to senior Quai d'Orsay officials, their analysis of the civil war rested in large part on a French military intelligence report from 1990 suggesting that the RPF was capable of beating the Rwandan government forces in outright warfare.[18] The conclusion drawn was that the Arusha process, which represented a sharing of power between the pro-French Habyarimana regime and the perceived anti-French RPF, was the cheapest and most effective way to maintain French power and access in Rwanda, given the options of either outright RPF victory or large-scale military support to the Habyarimana regime. This analysis was reinforced by the RPF's February 1993 offensive, which saw RPF forces advance to within twenty-three kilometers of Kigali. Although France sent reinforcements to Rwanda to ensure that the Habyarimana regime did not collapse, the RPF battle victories confirmed the analysis.[19] The Quai d'Orsay was, in short, pro-Arusha, not out of humanitarian concerns or because of pro-RPF sympathies but because Arusha was the best solution in terms of French interests. In any event, they were pro-Arusha.

France's relative sympathy was enhanced by a second fluke of fate, namely, the illness that overtook France's ambassador to Tanzania, leaving the Arusha talks principally in the hands of the young chargé d'affaires in Tanzania, Jean-Christophe Beliard. Beliard, fluent in several regional languages and married to an African woman, was considered by diplomats in Dar-es-Salaam to be considerably more attuned to the realities of modern African politics than was his (older) ambassador.[20] Although Beliard was perhaps not trusted by the RPF in his official capacity, he appears to have enjoyed good personal relations with their delegates and with U.S. and other observer teams, as well as with the Tanzanian facilitator, through whom he occasionally fed ideas and solutions.[21] He also had a good working relationship with Lieutenant-Colonel Anthony Marley, a middle-ranking member of the U.S. team at Arusha. The trio of Beliard, Marley, and Mpungwe is credited by other participants with creativity and skill in managing the facilitative aspects of the Arusha process.

Notwithstanding the pro-Arusha policy of the Quai d'Orsay, it is quite clear that the French perceived their role in Arusha as lending support to the GoR and ensuring that negotiations did not jeopardize too much the interests of the Habyarimana regime. Accounts of the Arusha process are replete with stories of the French supporting the GoR when others were pushing for concessions, although participants will also talk of France having persuaded the GoR delegation to accept reasonable positions when it was otherwise unlikely to do so. This could be portrayed as yet another example of French support for a nasty regime, and in a sense that is what it was. But those who excoriate France for its role in Arusha also make the argument that the central flaw of Arusha was that it went too far, exceeding what was acceptable to hard-liners in Kigali and thus helping plant the seeds of genocide.[22] The two arguments are incompatible: France's role was to stop the agreement from going farther than was acceptable to Habyarimana, as distinct from moderates in what was by then a coalition government. Moreover, French policy was often identical to that of a more evidently neutral delegation: the Americans. And in retrospect there is reason to wish that the French had been more successful in supporting the government delegation.

The Facilitator

In June 1992, when the Arusha talks were agreed to at the Dijoud meeting in Paris, Tanzania's President Mwinyi was appointed facilitator to the talks, which were officially held under OAU authority. Mwinyi by and large delegated this role to Ambassador Ami Mpungwe—director for external relations–Africa and the Middle East—in the Tanzanian foreign ministry.

Three essential points need to be underscored regarding Tanzania's role in Arusha. First, Tanzania devoted high-level attention and dedicated some of its best diplomats to the Arusha talks and, in so doing, succeeded in facilitating an effective peace process, one in which Tanzania was judged to have played an honest broker role.[23] The second thing is that Tanzania's motivation for becoming involved in a long and costly facilitation process combined a mix of self-interest, regional concerns, and humanitarian concerns. The self-interest had largely to do with Tanzanian concern that conflict in Rwanda or Burundi would result—as it had previously—in large refugee camps on the Tanzanian border, a situation Tanzania was ill-equipped to handle. Tanzania's regional concern historically has been stable governments in neighboring countries; thus Tanzania sought a tenable solution to the political crisis in Rwanda. This goal was compatible with the Tanzania's humanitarian concerns, namely, a simple desire to secure a peaceful outcome in Rwanda. This leads to the third point: Tanzania was the only neighboring country generally perceived to be neutral in the Rwandan civil war.[24]

Tanzania's principal negotiator, Ambassador Mpungwe, was critical to the success of the negotiations, forging agreements through backroom diplomacy, nursing consensus, and serving as a conduit for ideas and solutions generated by the observer teams. Both Paul Kagame and Théogène Rudasingwa (general secretary of the RPF and one of its delegates) have publicly commended the Tanzanian role.[25] Diplomatic observers in Dar-es-Salaam give Ambassador Mpungwe much credit for the success—on paper—of the Arusha Accords.

Issues and Timelines

The formal Arusha talks lasted thirteen months and in that time shifted between Arusha and Kigali/Kampala as the two sides reached agreement, then deadlock, and then agreement again on a series of agenda items.[26] As characterized by a French participant at Arusha, the agenda for discussion was set by Tanzania (which facilitated the process) and covered the issues of a cease-fire agreement, the rule of law, powersharing, the integration of armies, and the repatriation of refugees. The cease-fire, being an amended version of a twice-amended cease-fire that originated in N'Sele, was quickly reached. In the other areas, key issues stalled negotiations and at various points threatened the entire peace process.

The agreement to meet in Arusha came on 8 June 1992, and the two sides met there for the first time on 12 July 1992. On 14 July they announced a cease-fire scheduled to come into effect on 31 July, as well as a start to peace negotiations by 10 August with a deadline of 10 October. Fighting in northern Rwanda on 29 July seemed to threaten that timetable, but the cease-fire did in fact come into effect as planned and held until the 10 October deadline. Also agreed to was yet another restructuring of the NMOG. The failure of the observer group to deploy effectively led to a reworking that removed from the force any officers from neighboring countries and replaced them with officers from Senegal, Zimbabwe, Nigeria, and Mali.

Significantly, this first round of Arusha talks also called for the creation of the Joint Political-Military Commission, to be established in Addis Ababa at the OAU headquarters.[27] The JPMC was composed of five representatives of the Rwandan government and five representatives of the RPF and included parallel observers from states observing the Arusha talks, as well as those that had contributed to NMOG as it was restructured by the Arusha cease-fire of 12 July 1992. Its mandate was to "ensure the follow-up of the implementation of the cease-fire agreement" and to "ensure the follow-up of the implementation of the peace agreement to be signed at the conclusion of the political negotiations."[28] As characterized by members of two Western observer teams, the JPMC served as a place to meet and talk but not negotiate, a place where complaints could be aired, where the NMOG could lodge complaints or accusations of violations, and in general where problems could be addressed without interfering with the process of negotiations. The JPMC thus effectively became a second channel through which the thorny issues of the Arusha process could be hammered out. Talks in November 1992 at Kibali, in northern Rwanda, under the chairmanship of the Nigerian commander of the NMOG, produced an agreement on the deployment of the NMOG forces along a neutral zone.[29]

This first phase of the Arusha talks led quickly to Arusha II, which on 17 August announced an agreement, the Protocol on the Rule of Law (signed on 18 August). The quick agreement on this protocol was made possible by an internal agreement among the delegates to leave some of the tricky issues—such as the composition of a transitional government—out of the protocol at this stage so as to focus discussion on broad principles. The outstanding items were referred to the end of the process.[30]

Arusha III ran from 7–18 September and saw Foreign Minister Ngulinzira of Rwanda table a series of conciliatory proposals. Agreements on powersharing, unification, and political cooperation were initialed but not signed, and the two sides returned to their respective bases for consultation.[31] It quickly emerged that Ngulinzira had acted without Habyarimana's support. However, subsequent negotiations inside Kigali, between Habyarimana and the opposition parties, produced an agreement on instructions for the delegates, who returned for the Arusha IV round of talks on 6 October. By 12 October the delegates had reached agreement on the issues of the nature of presidential power under the Broad-Based Transitional Government (BBTG).[32] It was agreed that the BBTG would last for no more than twenty-two months and would be followed by free elections to determine the government of the country. The system of authority was to be parliamentary in large measure rather than presidential; the RPF insisted that power reside in a council of ministers (effectively a cabinet) rather than with the president and presidential advisers. The powers of the president were diminished to those of a ceremonial head of state who did not even have the power to name his own government. His authority, such as it was, was secondary to that of the prime minister. A protocol to this effect was signed and issued on 30 October.[33]

This protocol also created the Transitional National Assembly (TNA) to replace the Conseil National du Développement (CND), which from the moment of the signing of the Arusha Accord was prohibited from passing new laws. Between the BBTG and the TNA existed a fairly typical parliamentary relationship, wherein the president of the republic could dissolve the assembly, but equally the assembly could censure the BBTG. The TNA also had the unusual power of being able to elect the president and vice president of the supreme court. It was, thus, a powerful institution. However, the protocol did not resolve the fundamental issue of seats in the TNA, that is, the question of who would control power in this institution or the distribution of cabinet posts in the BBTG.

Arusha V commenced on 25 November, with the agenda focused on the difficult topic of the precise composition of the transitional institutions whose frameworks had been agreed upon.[34] These discussions, which had taken three months of background negotiations to conclude, formed the first of the major sticking points in the Arusha process and would come back to bedevil the process of implementation. Two issues were at the heart of discussions. First, the RPF objected to a GoR proposal that included the CDR in the government. The RPF accused the CDR of being an extremist wing of the government party and, as such, ineligible for the role of a political party (technically, the RPF was correct on this point). However, the government delegation insisted on the CDR's inclusion (the role of the CDR in Habyarimana's power base was significant enough to ensure this insistence) and was backed in this demand by the French. According to one of its members, the French delegation argued that it was better to have the CDR in government, where it could be controlled, than on the outside where it could wreak havoc.[35] Equally, the U.S. delegation argued that it was better to have the extremists "on the inside of the tent, pissing out, than on the outside of the tent, pissing in."[36] In the end, however, the RPF prevailed, and the CDR was excluded from the BBTG. A protocol signed on 22 December contained the following agreement about seats in the transitional government: MDR—four portfolios including prime minister and foreign minister; RPF—five portfolios including the vice prime minister and the minister of interior; MRND—five portfolios including defense and public works plus the presidency; PSD—three, including finance; PL—three, including justice; and the PCD—one portfolio. Seats in the assembly were divided among the major opposition parties: the MRND, RPF, MDR, PSD, and PL each had eleven seats; the PCD had four; and a dozen small parties obtained one seat each. As Reyntjens has noted, the composition of the parliament meant that agreement from at least four parties was required to reach a majority.

The exclusion of the CDR from the transitional government became a central element of the accords and was to be central in the implementation phase as well. Those critical of the French role in Rwanda will no doubt see their backing of CDR inclusion as evidence of French complicity in the events that followed. But this was also the position of a more clearly neutral negotiating team, namely, the Americans. According to the State Department's desk officer for Rwanda at the time of negotiations, an interagency meeting on conflict resolution in Rwanda agreed as early as March 1992 to bring the extremists into government. Again, analogies were used; one U.S. official commented that the analysis was that "if you don't bring [the CDR] into the tent, they're going to burn the tent down."[37] The eventual exclusion of the CDR from power, and the subsequent denouncement of the Arusha Accords by the CDR, forms the beginning of the breakdown during the implementation period.

The CDR issue would resurface when participants reconvened on 5 January to tackle the question of the allocation of seats in the TNA. Agreement was quickly reached, and on 10 January the allocation of seats was announced: MRND—eleven seats; RPF—eleven seats; MDR, PL, and PSD combined—eleven seats. Significantly, one seat was allocated to each of two political "parties" outside of the coalition government, the PCD and the CDR. Confusion was created when the CDR announced that it had no intention of taking up the seat.[38]

Within days of the signing of this agreement, CDR and MRND members were involved in demonstrations against the peace talks, especially in Ruhengiri and Gisenyi. The demonstrations were a precursor to violence: between 22 and 31 January, more than three hundred Tutsis in the north had been killed. This civil violence in turn led to a renewal of the civil war: on 8 February 1993 the RPF launched a major offensive, claiming it was occasioned by the "recent massacres." However, more was at issue than the recent killings; after all, similar killings on a similar scale had been conducted in Rwanda since the onset of the invasion. Perhaps a more realistic explanation can be found in tactical thinking about the next agenda item for the Arusha discussions: integration of the armed forces.[39] Negotiating strength on this issue was to turn out to be a precise function of fighting strength on the ground. It seems likely that the RPF launched the offensive at this point to prove its fighting strength and thus put it on firmer ground for these most important negotiations.

The offensive certainly did confirm their strength: within some weeks of fighting the RPF had doubled the amount of territory under its control.[40] The impact on the balance of strength was so significant that Rwanda had to ask France to send reinforcements to Rwanda to bolster the army, which France did in two waves, on 9 February (150 troops) and 20 February (250 troops). France latter justified the deployment by arguing that the RPF advance threatened Kigali. Tanzanian and French intelligence sources confirm that their conclusions at the time were that the RPF could overrun the FAR were it not for the presence of the French troops in Kigali, and this intelligence would form the backdrop to the subsequent round of negotiations.[41] This perception evidently filtered to Habyarimana, for he personally called for a return to the Arusha process on 23 February. This next and final round would prove decisive.

That final round of negotiations addressed two sets of issues: refugees and security, including the composition of a neutral military force, the integration of the armed forces into a single national army, and the composition of the army command structure. The refugee issue was settled quickly, as the framework for agreement had already been laid by the Dar-es-Salaam Declaration on the Rwandese Refugees Problem. That declaration was for all intents and purposes simply reformulated in the framework of Arusha to form the Protocol on the Repatriation of Rwandese Refugees and Resettlement of Displaced Persons, agreement to which was announced on 9 June 1993.[42] The security issues were more complex.

The issue of the composition of a neutral military force was fairly easily handled through effective third-party mediation. Political divisions over whether the force should be composed by the OAU or the United Nations were settled by the OAU's announcement at the JPMC that it could not meet the requirements specified by the two sides.[43] On 6 April 1993 the GoR and RPF agreed to ask the United Nations to compose a Neutral International Force (NIF) to oversee the final agreement.

As in many other civil war negotiations, one of the most difficult issues was integrating the two armies into a single national army, as well as the percentage split of army command positions.[44] These issues took months of negotiations and on two occasions threatened to collapse the entire process. The GoR started off the negotiating on this issue by suggesting a 15 percent share of armed command for the RPF to reflect the percentage of Tutsis in Rwanda. The RPF rejected this outright, both because the figure was too low and because the rationale used for arriving at it contradicted the RPF platform of fighting for democracy for all Rwandans. The RPF counteroffer was a 50-50 split, which the government delegation also rejected outright. However, the RPF stood firm and was supported by the Tanzanians, in an unusual breach from the latter's role as honest broker. Negotiations took the number to 25 percent, then 30 percent, then 35 percent, then 40 percent, and finally reached 50 percent. Then the even stickier issue of how far down the command chain this split should go caused more problems. An eventual agreement was brokered wherein the command level was to be split 50-50; the forces were to be drawn 60 percent from government forces and 40 percent from RPF forces. At senior levels, the RPF would be given the head of the gendarmerie, and the government was to keep the head of the armed forces. Both armies would be integrated into a 13,000-strong army supplemented by a 6,000 strong gendarmerie. The announcement of this agreement on 24 June seemed to presage an imminent signing of the peace package.

On 24 June the government's negotiating team took this tentative agreement back to Kigali, where it was rejected by Habyarimana. A U.S. participant observed at the time that the division of the army as it stood would never be accepted by hard-line factions in the army and threatened to collapse the talks.[45] Differences emerged in the ranks as to what constituted a command-level position. When the issue returned to Arusha, the RPF not only stood its ground but it upped the ante in anger over the government's reneging on the agreement; the RPF called for a 60-40 split weighted to it. After heavy intercession by the Tanzanian, French, and U.S. teams, the two sides agreed again on the original deal, with the clarification that "command level" extended all the way to field command positions. This represented a big new victory for the RPF in terms of its capacity to control the merged security forces.

* * *

What allowed the RPF to win this major victory in the negotiation process? To return to the point made earlier, the central issue was strength on the ground. Although the two sides appeared to be in a military stalemate when Arusha began, the February offensive proved decisively that the RPF had a considerable military advantage on the ground and was poised to continue scoring victories should the negotiations break down. It was, therefore, in a position of strength and could effectively dictate the terms of this final issue. In the end, this victory would prove to be disastrously misjudged.

Also, at this point we can see the important role of the observers. Interviews with Western delegates suggest that there had been, through the course of negotiations, a general shift in atmosphere that saw a growing frustration with the GoR team and an increasing sympathy with the RPF. The participants who made these comments skirt around the language, but it appears that the dynamic was essentially a result of the perceived incompetence of the GoR delegation, contrasted with the discipline of the RPF team. That shift in sympathy may account for the fact that Tanzania, which had to this point played an honest broker role, supported the RPF's bid for a 50-50 split. This support for the RPF, combined with the RPF's on-the-ground victories, left the GoR delegation—and the Habyarimana regime—in no position to oppose the RPF's negotiating tactic. The government's capitulation on this issue would prove to be a hollow victory for the RPF team. In the short run, however, it was the final element of the peace package: the Arusha Accords were signed by both sides and all observers on 4 August 1993.[46]

Adjacent Processes

The Arusha process was not the only forum in which third parties contributed to the peace process. Simultaneous with Arusha were second-track processes and neutral military interventions, by both the OAU and the United Nations, that affected negotiations.

Chapter 3 details the formation, composition, and repeated realignment of the OAU's Military Observer Group. This mission was substantially modified in June 1992, when the Arusha talks got under way. Its successor, the NMOG, had a composition that was reworked to draw in more remote participants.[47] This mission did deploy, reporting to the JPMC.[48] There is some evidence that the NMOG had a limited role in confidence-building between the two parties. Some reports of cease-fire violations and the like were raised at the JPMC by NMOG during the negotiation process, and although they were never substantiated by evidence, discussion of these incidents at JPMC did serve to lessen tensions. Yet some diplomats reported that NMOG was ineffective, its performance hampered by its reliance on support from the FAR, which was able to control its movements and keep it clear of sensitive areas. On balance, it seems as if the JPMC made a more substantial contribution to confidence-building than did NMOG.

As mentioned earlier, following the events of February 1993 the RPF agreed to turn over the territory gained during its advance to the UN-sponsored DMZ. As part of the same negotiations, a UN military observer group was deployed to the Uganda-Rwanda border. This mission, UNOMUR, was to play a similar role to NMOG and, indeed, cooperated with it—the first ever UN-OAU military collaboration on the ground. Although taken more seriously than NMOG by many of the players in Rwanda, the UNOMUR was confined to a border that had long since outlived its strategic significance and had only a small force—roughly 80 men—to patrol even that border (along one hundred mountainous kilometers). In practice, UNOMUR proved as ineffectual as its regional predecessors, with one exception. Its reports were taken more seriously at Arusha than were those of NMOG; thus, one could say that UNOMUR was providing good information, except that its mandate was so limited, its observational scope so constrained, that this information was of tertiary importance to the conflict resolution process.

More significant was the role played by second-track conflict resolution processes, as well as multitrack efforts. In the second-track realm, a very important role was played by the Vatican/Rwandan church team that had helped get the Arusha negotiations under way.

Of particular importance was an effort by Bishop Nsengiyumva, once again supported by the Vatican's Bertollo, to create the Groupe de Contact within the Rwandan church, which met regularly throughout 1993 and lobbied the Habyarimana regime on the peace process. When, during the Arusha talks, the Habyarimana delegation was proving particularly intractable, the Groupe de Contact would deploy its moral and political clout to push the government toward more moderate positions. Most important was the group's role in convincing the Habyarimana regime to accept a moderate position on the question of powersharing.[49]

The backing of the Vatican was critical to the success of the Groupe de Contact.[50] Following the start of the Arusha process, Bertollo had begun to convene an informal grouping known as the

Five Musketeers, comprising France, Belgium, the United States, Germany, and the papal nunciature. Meeting in an unofficial capacity, the five representatives shared information and strategized—notwithstanding the different policies supported by their respective governments. At important junctures, this informal grouping was used to defend Nsengiyumva's efforts. For example, when the Groupe de Contact was pressuring the Habyarimana regime on the issue of powersharing and came under attack from the government for doing so, the Five Musketeers managed to convince the French ambassador to call on Habyarimana and chastise him for his attack—this despite the fact that the Groupe was supporting a position at odds with that of the French government. Bertollo's argument to the French ambassador, and his to Habyarimana's, was that whatever the substance of the disagreement, the church had to be allowed to express a view without coming under attack from the government.[51]

Another process that should be considered is that of the JPMC. It seems not unreasonable to argue that the JPMC, albeit technically part of the first-track Arusha process, nevertheless provided a forum that in some ways resembled a second-track process. Participants at Arusha uniformly referred to the JPMC as a forum in which problems could be aired, reviewed, and solved, steam could be let off, and information, options, and solutions could be shared, usually by second-level members of delegations rather than delegation heads, all without interrupting or disrupting the main Arusha talks. A good example of the function of the JPMC was provided by the question of the integration of the armed forces. At one stage, discussions broke down over a technical question, namely, how ranks in the two armies would correspond for purposes of integration into one joint armed forces structure. The issue was kicked to the JPMC, where the military advisers of the main delegations played with different ideas. In the end, the solution came from the U.S. military adviser, Lieutenant-Colonel Marley, with help from the French military attachés. Marley used a simple chart detailing ages, years of experience, education, function, and nature of command to determine how the two armies' command structures related to one another. Once technical agreement was reached, then the talks moved back into the main Arusha forum, where they were integrated into the armed forces protocol. Although this example suggests that the JPMC was more of a technical clearinghouse than anything else, there were other instances when it put forward ideas—at the time seemingly unacceptable in Arusha—in a forum where they could be discussed as just that—ideas—without having the status of proposals or positions that would have restricted participants from bringing them forward.

Also of some note was a community-based mediation effort launched by OXFAM.[52] OXFAM Rwanda, the in-country arm of the international nongovernmental aid organization, launched a program to tackle public attitudes to the violence and conflict in Rwandan society. OXFAM was, according to diplomatic sources, one of the few development agencies in Rwanda with power in Kigali. Its influence came not through its high-level connections among official circles but through its important role as a major funding agency for so-called civil society groups. OXFAM used its position to attempt to diminish the recourse to violence in Rwanda society. Most visible among its efforts was a program called Education for Non-Violence and Democracy (ENVD), run under the umbrella of a Catholic Church program called Justice et Paix (Justice and Peace).[53] The experience illustrates many of the challenges that face community-based mediation.

The ENVD program was advertised through local parishes and brought people together and sought to raise their awareness of issues such as ethnic relations, democratic process, and human rights. Its strength was that the issues addressed were those raised by participants. The program had some success, at least in that OXFAM received calls from participants for more opportunities to engage in this type of dialogue. However, the program was limited in scope—never, for example, attempted in Kigali, the absolute power center of Rwandan society. In 1993, as the crisis in Rwanda began to deepen, the ENVD was in hiatus, in a period of adjustment as the lessons of the early round were absorbed.

The program suffered from major weaknesses, recognized by OXFAM staff who participated in the program, either in Kigali or from Oxford. Most important is the question of having run the program through the Catholic Church. Anne Mackintosh, the country director responsible for the program, later argued that OXFAM might have done well to have involved Protestant churches. OXFAM did attempt to involve Rwandan human rights organizations, but without success. The Catholic Church itself was grappling with the thorny issue of ethnicity in its own ranks.[54]

Notwithstanding the limitations of the ENVD program, hindsight gives reason for regret that it was not conducted more widely and sustained further, in particular that it was never run in Kigali. As a result, the program was never able to forge important linkages between grassroots discussions and the middle-range leadership of the parties, army, and government in Kigali. The absence of such connections would prove important, for as the peace process moved from mediation to implementation, community fears and perceptions about security and threats, from both the war and the Arusha settlement, were of critical importance. Leading members of the Habyarimana regime increasingly used such fears to lay the groundwork for their opposition to the implementation of Arusha; there was no third-party process to counter their message.

The question of opposition to Arusha raises the issue of the nature of the final settlement; it is to an analysis of that issue that we now turn.

Analysis of Arusha

Arusha was at the heart of the third-party process in Rwanda. Almost everything that came before fed into the Arusha talks, and the peace accords conditioned everything that came after.

Two competing accounts of Arusha warrant critical analysis. The first, which we can term the "diplomatic perspective," suggests that Arusha was almost perfect preventive diplomacy. Western negotiators and diplomats have argued that the Arusha peace deal was the best such agreement in Africa since Lancaster House and, moreover, was the best agreement that could possibly have been reached.[55] From this perspective, the collapse of the accords is attributable exclusively to manipulation by Hutu extremists who were outside the control of the Arusha process. The *content* of the Arusha deal is strongly defended.

The second perspective, which has been forcibly presented by René Lemarchand, a noted scholar of the region, takes issue with the diplomatic perspective:

> The transition bargain in Rwanda emerges retrospectively as a recipe for disaster: not only were the negotiations conducted under *tremendous external pressures,* but, partly for this reason, the concessions made were seen by Hutu hard-liners as a sell-out *imposed by outsiders.* For the Tutsi "rebels" to end up claiming as many cabinet posts in the transitional government as the ruling MRND (including Interior and Communal Development), as well as half of

the field-grade officers and above, was immediately viewed by extremists in the so-called *mouvance presidentielle* (presidential movement) as a surrender to blackmail. Many indeed wondered whether the Arusha Accords would have been signed in the absence of repeated nudging from the OAU, Tanzania, France, the United States, and Belgium. If there were any doubts about the intense disagreements within the MRND concerning the wisdom of making these concessions to the RPF, these were quickly dissipated by the outbreaks of Hutu-instigated violence that both preceded and followed the accords.[56] [Emphasis added]

Although Lemarchand makes several points that will be dealt with in turn, his concern is not only with the outcomes; he argues a flawed *process* generated the outcome. Considering some aspects of both process and content helps determine the validity of these competing perspectives.

The Process

From a theoretical perspective, the Arusha *process* had much to commend it. The process was, first of all, inclusive: All the parties to the conflict were represented in Arusha; and although three of them were in effect lumped together in one delegation, that did not stop any one from presenting opinions or positions or communicating with other delegates. The process was not the kind of sustained all-nighter that produces agreement through exhaustion, the kind of process represented, for example, by the Dayton Accords, and presumed to produce agreements that will not last without external enforcement. Rather, the lengthy, sustained process of meetings outside Kigali, where discussions were off the record and seemingly quite open, roughly conformed to the outlines of the kind of facilitative process that should, in theoretical terms, more likely lead to sustainable resolution. And indeed, at least on paper the Arusha Accords were a richly detailed blueprint for the resolution of the underlying causes of the Rwandan conflict, not merely for a short- or medium-term cease-fire.

Furthermore, far from being the kind of standard international mediation process, the Arusha process contained many of the elements of a facilitative, communicative process. The primary facilitator of Arusha, Ambassador Mpungwe, deliberately designed a process wherein the parties would have sufficient contact and communication to overcome the kinds of totalistic perceptions of others that tend to derail peace talks. Moreover, several of the third parties engaged in practices designed to facilitate communication between the primary parties and to solve problems. The JPMC was used to allow the parties to channel frustrations and blockages into a formal discussion that nevertheless would not undermine the spirit of Arusha. Notwithstanding the pathologies of the CDR, some success in this realm can be seen in the breadth and depth of the transition package.

The process of Arusha thus seems relatively strong, and not just for these reasons. Yet Lemarchand's comments do not fully capture the nature of the relationship between international and Rwandan actors. Although it was true that the extent of pressure on the Habyarimana regime was certainly considerable, this was not a key aspect of the negotiation process.[57] The external pressure on the regime *within* the Arusha process cannot be seen as overwhelming because of the presence of supportive regimes like France and Zaire. What's more, at several points the external delegations, or observers, actually tried to limit the concessions made in Arusha, the most important example being the U.S. delegation's attempt to convince the Arusha participants that the deal on the armed forces had moved past what was acceptable in Kigali. True, the observers would at times nudge the parties in one direction or another, but it is also the case that various observers at times backed up the delegations and used their influence to restrain concessions, especially by the GoR delegation. It was not repeated nudging from the observers and facilitators that produced the positions taken on the contentious elements; especially in the case of the exclusion of the CDR, this key decision was taken precisely *contrary* to the strong positions taken by observers. Accordingly, to argue that the content of the Arusha deal resulted from a flawed process, in which the Habyarimana regime was elbowed into making concessions by outsiders, misses important dimensions of the real dynamics.

On the issue of moderates, several provisions were essentially negotiated deals between moderates within the regime and the RPF. This was certainly true of the early protocols, a critical aspect of the negotiations. Here the issue of party cohesiveness raises its head again: although the Arusha process was designed to facilitate communication between the parties, little had been done to deal with the fact that one of the parties was deeply riven. This resulted in some situations where, according to Western observers, the only way in which deals were reached was when Ngulinzira and the prime minister decided to take draft deals and "ram them down Kigali's throat."[58]

The issue is more complex that this, however. Even though the GoR delegation was led by opposition-party moderates, two other delegation members fulfilled other functions. Colonel Bagasora was present for the entire process and provided a direct link to the Hutu extremist groups in Kigali. Ambassador Kanyarushoki, seen by Western delegates as the eyes and ears of Habyarimana, was also present. The fact that these two political communities—the Hutu extremists, and Habyarimana and his closest supporters, respectively (these are, by 1993, not precisely the same groups)—were represented in Arusha is demonstrated on occasions when the process was suspended in order to refer proposed agreements to Kigali, where they were then rejected by Habyarimana. When provisions were rejected in Kigali, they came back to the Arusha process, as occurred repeatedly on questions pertaining to the BBTG and the integration of the armed forces. Ngulinzira thus had to take hard-line opinion very much into account while negotiating with the RPF or risk having his agreements repudiated in Kigali.

It is thus too simple to blame the failings of Arusha on a moderate-RPF compact or on the nudgings of foreigners. Yet when we turn to content, we see that the Arusha deal had several key problems.

The Content

Again, from a theoretical perspective there is much to commend the content of the Arusha deal. The deal laid out, in rich and complete detail, the basis for a new political order in Rwanda, one based on the rule of law, on democratic processes, and on the rights of refugees and returnees. Moreover, these were not mere abstract principles taken from the Western diplomatic bag of tricks; they responded in strong terms to the issues that can be seen as the underlying causes of the war itself: the exclusive nature of Rwandan politics, captured by the oligarchy; the arbitrary nature of the execution of their power; and the long-standing issue of the refugees who had fled political violence in the late 1950s. These issues, as previously argued, formed the underlying structure of conflict in Rwanda; the Arusha peace deal responded on each of these fronts.

Furthermore, the agreement fulfilled several conditions often viewed as critical to success. First, the agreement, at least on paper, was detailed enough to leave little room for maneuver and collapse during the implementation phase; no key issues were left aside for "later discussion." The agreement also clearly spelled out the roles to be played by parties, in particular the international community, during the transition toward the new order. The provision of the NIF for the transition phase recognized the potential for security fears and sought to neutralize them.

Yet the accords went well beyond the realm of a mutually acceptable agreement. Two sets of issues proved especially unacceptable in Kigali.

The first was the distribution of seats in the Cabinet and parliament. Much noise was generated over the exclusion of the CDR, but this was not the major point. Rather, it was that the distribution agreed to in the final days of Arusha left the MRND in a 33 percent minority position. In power terms this was critical, because it meant that even with the one CDR seat in parliament, added at the last minute, and various allies within splinter factions of the opposition parties, the MRND would have a very difficult time attempting to command a majority in parliament. In contrast, by containing only a small degree of splinter, the RPF could join forces with the opposition and gain a clear majority. The MRND had gone from an oligarchic party in control of the state to a minority party that wouldn't be able to win a vote.

The second unacceptable element was the distribution of the armed forces. The RPF was given a powerful share in what was to become an integrated national army, composed of RPF and FAR troops in a 40-60 split but commanded by a 50–50 split of RPF and FAR officers.[59] Also, both sides were to decommission troops down to a joint force of 20,000 soldiers; with the larger army, the FAR would feel the impact of demobilization more heavily. Moreover, during the transitional phase the RPF was to install a force of 600 men inside Kigali to protect its members in the transitional government.

From the perspective of the ruling elites in Kigali, then, the loss of control over the armed forces, combined with relegation to a minority position in the government they had so far dominated and the physical reminder of these losses in the form of an RPF battalion in Kigali, left a bitter taste. For the *akazu*, the deal represented a major loss of power, from oligarchic control over the state to a position of weak minority in the power structure of Rwanda, thereby losing the capacity to ensure their position through the military. The settlement was met with outrage and hostility by extremist forces in Kigali. The weak position of the MRND was put to good effect by its opponents, who represented the bargain as a sellout and a Trojan horse, through which the RPF would gain entry to Kigali, only to oust the weakened MRND.

Thus, at a minimum, the Arusha *process*, notwithstanding its strengths, fell short of achieving the kind of mutually acceptable agreement upon which truly sustainable outcomes can be built. How, then, can we account for the gap between the good process of Arusha and its flawed outcome?

Process Versus Content: The Role of the Parties

The critical explanatory variable—which is missing from both the preventive-diplomacy and Lemarchand accounts—has to do with the nature and positions of the parties themselves. One aspect of this has already been alluded to: the superior position of the RPF, both on the ground and in the negotiating room. Among the several reasons for RPF superiority, however, the most important was the RPF's field position, illustrated by the tremendous success of the February 1993 offensive. It not only moved the RPF close to Kigali; it also displaced over a half-million people from Ruhengiri and Byumba, two of Rwanda's breadbasket regions, thus intensifying the economic pressures on the Habyarimana regime.

The key point is that the provisions of the Arusha Accords that generated such hostility in Kigali—the distribution of seats and the formulas for the integration of the armies—were both finalized *after* the February offensive. It seems reasonable to conclude that the RPF's success on the battlefield was what turned the tables in Rwanda and, arguably, transformed the Arusha Peace Agreement from a resolution package into a victory deal. It was thus RPF bargaining strength, as well as what to many observers seemed like intransigence over the question of CDR inclusion and the percentages in the armed forces, that made the final agreement read like a victor's deal rather than a meeting of the minds fostered by the aid of third parties.

On this last point, it is not reasonable to hold the RPF solely to account on the question of the CDR. For the CDR repeatedly made use of not merely totalistic but downright apocalyptic rhetoric during negotiations. Colonel Bagasora became infamous in East African diplomatic circles for having taken the floor in Arusha and stating that should the Arusha Accords be signed, there would be "an apocalypse in Rwanda." More substantively, it is certainly understandable that the RPF would wish to have no part of powersharing with a group whose explicit purpose was the radical defense of *akazu* power and who made no bones about threatening all kinds of violent repudiation to any form of negotiated settlement with the RPF.

However, on both the power-sharing and military-split issues, RPF intransigence was a salient factor. Negotiating "victories" in these two realms would prove hollow, as they were unpalatable to important constituencies in Kigali. Patrick Mazimpaka, chief negotiator for the RPF, would later recognize this, admitting: "You can't ask a dictator to become a democrat overnight. We did this, and it was a grave tactical error."[60]

Thus, the preventive-diplomacy argument and the Lemarchand critique each contain an aspect of truth but conflate a critical distinction between *content* and *process*. As preventive diplomacy *process*, Arusha got several things right. There was, arguably, the right mix of relevant regional players, committed international players, and neutral elements around the table; the use of the JPMC to negotiate military elements while having peace negotiations continue was innovative and effective; the GoR delegation represented the major power groupings in Kigali; the agreement itself, in many dimensions, addressed and resolved fundamental causes of conflict (such as the question of refugees) as opposed to merely containing the fighting; and the need for a neutral international force to secure the transition was foreseen and called for.

However, the final *result* proved to be a recipe for disaster because it pushed well beyond what was acceptable in key sectors in Kigali on distribution of command posts and the distribution of seats in the BBTG. Thus, the exemplary preventive-diplomacy analysis, although correct in terms of process, must be rejected in terms of the content of the final deal.

What becomes clear is that the responsibility for the outcomes rests with the parties themselves: with the CDR for its virulent, hateful rhetoric and general hostile disposition to the Arusha process; and with the RPF, in part, for seeking a deal beyond what was acceptable, despite urgings to the contrary even from trusted allies such as Uganda. These factors, not the "nudgings" of outsiders, produced the somewhat lopsided deal that was taken back to Kigali on 4 August.

Assessing the Outcome:
Spoilers, Losers, and the Arusha Deal

Although we can emphasize that Arusha did not produce a mutually acceptable agreement as prescribed by facilitative conflict resolution theory and the convenors, it is debatable whether Arusha was the appropriate outcome in Rwanda. Given the totalistic attitudes of the CDR and its allies, and what would prove to be a predatory nature, was it appropriate that they were all but excluded from transitional arrangements? Was Arusha, as diplomats argued, the best deal available?

The content of the Arusha Accords violated key tenets of conflict resolution within the context of protracted social conflicts. First, by excluding the CDR from power (one seat in the TNA does not constitute power), Arusha diverged from the tenet that those forces who comprise the problem must be made part of the solution. Second, Arusha failed to properly balance the profound security concerns of the combatants. The twin negotiating victories won by the RPF—on the CDR and the structure of the integrated forces—created a situation in which a powerful political force in Kigali was deprived not only of direct *military* control over security forces in Rwanda but also the opportunity to exercise any *political* control over those forces. This created uncertainty and fear, particularly among uncommitted members of the MRND, as well as an important opportunity for the CDR and the hard-line wing of the MRND.

In retrospect, however, there is an argument that excluding the CDR from Arusha was the only appropriate solution; they were spoilers determined to violate any peace deal that was put forward.[61] Excluding from a negotiated settlement the groups that refuse to negotiate seems sensible; although it clearly shifts the burden of peacemaking to the implementation phase, where much must be done to contain the threat posed by such spoilers, it is arguably the only credible option. Was such the case in Rwanda?

This issue is critical. However, to fully develop it in detail, we must first discuss the implementation phase of the agreement. The political battles waged in Kigali following the signing of the Arusha Accords; the battle to implement or undermine Arusha; the battle for control of the moderates—all these processes shed light on the question of outcomes. Moreover, given that there were spoilers in Rwanda, there was bound to be some form of reaction against Arusha, irrespective of its content. In assessing the overall outcome, therefore, it is necessary to consider the types of interventions deployed during the implementation phase. What was done to contain extremist reaction? What role did the Neutral International Force play? What was done to bolster Arusha, to defend against the extremists? How was the totalistic rhetoric of the CDR countered? And what role did third parties play in the political battle for control over the implementation process? It is impossible to make a final assessment of the appropriateness, or even the nature of the outcome, of Arusha without addressing these issues.

* * *

As with the prenegotiation phase, the mediation phase of peacemaking in Rwanda illustrates the complexity of third-party efforts and the obstacles they can pose.

The mediation phase conclusively demonstrates the importance of the cohesiveness, or noncohesiveness, of parties to peace negotiations. The notion that parties to conflict are in fact shifting coalitions of interest that change through time characterizes the fluid nature of what would very inaccurately be called the "government" side. Obviously, the GoR delegation to Arusha contained at least three parties to the conflict: representatives of the ruling MRND, representatives of the CDR, and members of opposition parties. The shifting nexus of interest among these three groups was a critical aspect of the mediation process, a fact even more strongly revealed during the next phase. Still, it is worth noting that by all accounts the RPF was a remarkably disciplined, unitary actor within the Arusha process, not to mention the battlefield. Here we find no significant fractures or factions, no shifting dissent or need for consensus. These differing degrees of cohesiveness among the two sides were a salient factor in shaping the course of the mediation process.

Also as in the prenegotiation phase, a variety of interconnected roles was evident during the mediation phase. In Arusha, the OAU was both convenor and legitimator; Tanzania, aided to a certain degree by Senegal, facilitated discussions; the United States played the role of enskiller, through its training of the delegations in negotiating techniques; the OAU and the UN both had monitoring roles; Uganda and France acted to ensure and reassure the parties to the negotiations; and a number of observers at Arusha, especially the United States and France, sought to envision solutions to the stickiest problems.

These roles were interconnected with third-party roles prior to Arusha or outside its framework. For example, the regional summitry process early on laid the groundwork for Arusha, as seen in the use of documents such as the Dar-es-Salaam Declaration as the building-blocks for the Arusha Protocols (in this example, on refugees). There were also negative interconnections regarding third-party roles, that is, areas where the outcomes of one intervention are limited by the *absence* of another. First, there was no one in Arusha able to play the role of "unifier," someone to deal with the tendency to splits and factions within deep-rooted social conflict. The fractiousness of the government delegation was a considerable barrier to achieving good outcomes, and the absence of a unifier role was keenly felt in that context. Second, the weakness of community-based processes for tackling the totalistic perceptions and rhetoric arguably weakened the overall mediation process. In particular, the fact that the ENVD program never managed to make connections to midlevel leadership in Kigali was most unfortunate. Absent any meaningful effort to counter their rhetoric and propaganda, the extremists were allowed to continue to ratchet up that rhetoric, to demonize the RPF without a strong contradictory message being generated from other spheres. This would have ramifications within the implementation process.

On this last point, the mediation phase also underscores the importance of subjective aspects of conflict, as well as the deep challenge posed by totalistic perceptions and rhetoric. This became evident in the difficulties of negotiating around the apocalyptic rhetoric of the CDR. The barriers to successful resolution posed by these factors would only increase with the shift to an implementation phase. In similar fashion, the issue of security fears was significant for the negotiations, complicating issues surrounding military integration. Of course, there were efforts to address both totalistic perceptions and security fears, the first through such processes as ENVD, the latter through agreement on the international force. But both of these elements would prove wholly insufficient. During the implementation phase, the combination of totalistic perceptions and real security fears would prove an explosive mix—and a potent obstacle to efforts to implement the Arusha deal.

Notes

1. Cohen, Snyder, and Mpungwe, author interviews; Quai d'Orsay officials, confidential author interviews.

2. In early 1993, the Africa Bureau of the State Department received a visit from James Gasana, the minister of defense, and a senior intelligence official (both senior members of the government and close associates of Habyarimana) while on their way to visit Nicaragua. The two also took U.S. advice to investigate the Lancaster House provisions from Zimbabwe. Lieutenant-Colonel Marley, U.S. Department of State, author interview, Washington, DC, December 1994.

3. Author interviews, Dar-es-Salaam, December 1993; author interviews, Africa Bureau, State Department, Washington, DC, June 1993.

4. This according to Ambassador Mpungwe; this account was confirmed by French and U.S. representatives in the talks.

5. The following account draws on confidential interviews conducted in Dar-es-Salaam, December 1993–January 1994; Ottawa, March 1994, Washington, DC, December 1994; and on confidential documents relating to the Arusha process to which I was given access in Dar-es-Salaam by officials who were participating as observers to the talks.

6. One Western diplomat described Bagasora, the CDR delegate to Arusha, as a "loyal thug." Bagasora has since been deeply implicated in the planning and implementation of the genocide.

7. This quotation was given in two separate author interviews; Lieutenant-Colonel Marley and Ambassador Mpungwe.

8. Filip Reyntjens, *L'Afrique des Grands Lacs en Crise: Rwanda et Burundi, 1990–1994* (Paris: Khartala, 1994), 248–256.

9. Patrick Mazimpaka, Minister for Social Rehabilitation, RPF, author interview, Kigali, June 1996.

10. Marley, author interview.

11. This case is made strongly by Canadian High Commission documents, Dar-es-Salaam, August 1992.

12. On Salim's perceptions, see Adotey Bing, "Salim A. Salim on the OAU and the African Agenda," *Review of African Political Economy* 50 (1991): 60–69.

13. UNOMUR was created by Security Council Resolution 846 (1993) on 22 June 1993 and subsumed NMOG under its command.

14. Author interview, Africa Bureau, State Department, Washington, DC, June 1995.

15. On U.S. policy in post–Cold War Africa, see esp. Chester A. Crocker, "Afterword: Strengthening African Peacemaking and Peacekeeping," Smock (ed.), *Making War,* 263–270.

16. For example, a French official commented that the Americans refused to cooperate with them in supporting GoR positions on the composition of the gendarmerie.

17. Prunier, *The Rwanda Crisis.*

18. Author interviews, officials of the embassy of France to the United States, Washington, DC, December, 1995. For one full week, the author was given repeated access to officials in the embassy who had previously been involved in the Arusha process, on condition of not naming the officials or directly citing material provided by them.

19. The eventual victory of the RPF over government forces in July 1994, and the subsequent negative relations between France and Rwanda, lend further credence to the analysis of the French foreign ministry.

20. U.S. and Canadian diplomats, confidential author interviews, Dar-es-Salaam, Tanzania, December 1993.

21. Fuller, author interview; Mpungwe, author interview.

22. René Lemarchand, "Managing Transition Anarchies: Rwanda, Burundi, and South Africa in Comparative Perspective," *Journal of Modern African Studies* 32, 4 (December 1994): 581–640.

23. It has been suggested that the Tanzanian government supported the RPF, and although this may well be true in the sense of sympathy, it does not appear to have been true in the sense of taking sides.

24. Zaire had supported the Habyarimana government; the Tutsi-dominated government of Burundi was seen as allied to or at least sympathetic with the RPF; Uganda evidently supported the RPF; and Kenya's President Daniel Arap Moi had a long-standing animosity to Uganda's President Yoweri Museveni. See K. Matthews, S. S. Mushi, and J. K. Nyerere, *Foreign Policy of Tanzania, 1961–1981: A Reader* (Dar-es-Salaam: Tanzania Publishing House, 1981); Timothy Shaw and Olajide Aluko, *The Political Economy of African Foreign Policy: A Comparative Analysis* (Aldershot, Harts, UK: Gower, 1984); P. Godfrey Okoth, "The OAU and the Uganda-Tanzania War: 1978–1979," *Journal of African Studies* 4, 3 (Fall 1987): 152–162.

25. Author notes, Paul Kagame, Panel Discussion, Royal Institute for International Affairs, December 1995; author notes, Theogene Rudasingwa, "Open Forum on Rwanda," International Alert, March 1996.

26. This section was developed using cables from the U.S. and Canadian embassies in Dar-es-Salaam that reported on progress in Arusha; interviews with Arusha delegates and observers, already cited; an unofficial timeline and analysis compiled by a UN observer (unsigned); the multiple texts of the Arusha protocols, statements, interim agreements, and declarations; and secondary literature, primarily that of Reyntjens.

27. Because the observer teams to the Arusha negotiations and the JPMC overlapped, the JPMC often met in Arusha instead of Addis Ababa.

28. *N'Sele Ceasefire Agreement Between the Government of the Rwandese Republic and the Rwandese Patriotic Front, Amended* (Gbadolite, 16 September 1991; and Arusha, 12 July 1992), art. 4, 7 (hereafter the Arusha ceasefire). The Arusha ceasefire had restructured the NMOG (from that point on referred to as NMOG II), such that it was composed of ten officers from each of Nigeria, Senegal, Zimbabwe, and an African country selected by the chair of the OAU in collaboration with the president of Tanzania; and five officers each from the GOR and RPF.

29. OAU document JPMC/RWD/OAU/1 (I) Rev. 2, "Rules of Procedure for the Joint Political-Military Commission (JPMC)"; JPMC/RWD/OAU/2 (I), "Terms of Reference of the Neutral Military Observer Group."

30. Marley, author interview.

31. "Joint Communiqué Issued at the End of the First Part of the Second Round of Political Negotiations between the Government of the Republic of Rwanda and the Rwandese Patriotic Front, Held in Arusha, from 7th to 18th September 1992." Arusha, Tanzania, 18 September 1992.

32. Reyntjens, *L'Afrique des Grands Lacs*, provides an excellent analysis of this protocol, on which I have drawn.

33. "Protocol of Agreement on Power-Sharing Within the Framework of a Broad-Based Transitional Government Between the Government of the Republic of Rwanda and the Rwandese Patriotic Front," Arusha, Tanzania, 30 October 1992.

34. It should be noted that although the Arusha talks formally adjourned between these periods, discussions and negotiations continued in Kigali, Kampala, Addis Ababa, and Dar-es-Salaam throughout these intervals, both under the aegis of the JPMC and in informal meetings at various embassies and high commissions in the region.

35. Official of the French embassy to the United States, confidential author interview, June 1995.

36. Author interview, Africa Bureau, State Department, Washington, DC, June 1995.

37. State Department official, confidential author interview, Washington, DC, June 1995.

38. "Joint Communiqué Issued at the End of the Third Round of the Political Negotiations on Power-Sharing Between the Government of the Republic of Rwanda and the Rwandese Patriotic Front Held in Arusha from 24 November 1992 to 9 January 1992." Arusha, Tanzania, 9 January 1993.

39. It should be recalled that Walter highlights this issue as the key stumbling block in internal negotiations; see Barbara F. Walter, "Why Negotiations Fail," Diss., University of Chicago, 1996.

40. *Africa Research Bulletin* (1–28 February 1993): 10902.

41. Confidential U.S. document, Dar-es-Salaam, December 1993.

42. "Joint Communiqué Issued at the End of Negotiations Between the Government of the Republic of Rwanda and the Rwandese Patriotic Front on the Repatriation of Rwandese Refugee Problem and the Resettlement of Displaced Persons Held in Arusha, United Republic of Tanzania, from 2–6 June 1993." Arusha, Tanzania, 9 June 1993.

43. For details, see Amare Tekle, "The OAU," in Adelman and Suhrke (eds.), *The Path of a Genocide,* 111–130.

44. Author interview, Anthony Marley, U.S. Department of State, Washington, DC, June 1995.

45. Confidential U.S. government document, U.S. Embassy in Dar-es-Salaam; Lieutenant-Colonel Marley, author interview, confirmed this perception, although not the existence of the document.

46. "Peace Agreement Between the Government of the Republic of Rwanda and the Rwandese Patriotic Front." Arusha, Tanzania, 4 August 1993.

47. NMOG was composed of ten Nigerian, ten Senegalese, ten Zimbabwean, and ten other African officers, plus five representatives each of the RPF and the government of Rwanda.

48. The Arusha ceasefire; also, "Terms of Reference of the Neutral Military Observer Group," JPMC/RWD/OAU/2(1).

49. Confidential author interview.

50. Monsignor Bertollo, interview by the author, and Astri Suhrke, Rome, April 1995; also, Patrick Mazimpaka, former lead negotiator, RPF, author interview, Kigali, July 1996.

51. Bertollo, interview by the author, and Astri Suhrke.

52. Anne Mackintosh, Oxfam Rwanda Country Director, 1990–1993, author interview, Oxford, UK, April 1995.

53. Jean-Pierre Goding, former animator, ENVD program, author interview, Nairobi, Kenya, December 1996. Other OXFAM activities included channeling information to Amnesty International and other human rights agencies.

54. The papal nuncio in Kigali at the time had been sent out specifically to help the local church come to grips with the divisive ethnic relations within its own ranks. He had begun to register what appeared to be some small successes when the genocide was launched—with the connivance and participation of most of the church's leading figures, including Monsignor Nsengiyumva.

55. This argument was made by a number of the architects of Arusha, including Tanzanian, French, and U.S. diplomats interviewed in Tanzania in December 1993; more interesting is the fact that this argument was also made by U.S. diplomats interviewed in 1995 and 1996 in Washington, DC.

56. Lemarchand, "Managing Transition Anarchies."

57. A number of the pressures on Habyarimana have been elucidated by Peter Uvin, *Development, Aid, and Conflict: Reflections from the Case of Rwanda* (Helsinki: UNU/Wider, 1996). Western pressure for democratic reforms had pushed Habyarimana to accept, in principle, multiparty democracy in 1989; falling world coffee prices had sharpened economic decline in the country; the war with the RPF had exposed Rwanda to Western human rights monitors, who were working with Rwandan groups to expose extrajudicial executions, disappearances, and other violations by the regime; and Habyarimana was certainly pushed into negotiations by his Western allies (Belgium and France) and pulled into them by his regional counterparts.

58. Confidential cable, U.S. Embassy in Dar-es-Salaam, May 1993.

59. Prunier, *The Rwanda Crisis*.

60. Mazimpaka, author interview.

61. Stedman, "The Spoiler Problem."

5
UN Peacekeeping and the Collapse of Arusha: Implementation Efforts

The signing of the Arusha Peace Accords in August 1993 launched a new stage of international response in Rwanda, one characterized by efforts to solidify and implement the Arusha agreement, as well as by the deployment of a UN peacekeeping mission to secure its implementation. However, key international actors, especially the United Nations, too readily assumed that the signing of the Arusha Accords meant that they were ready for implementation. In Rwanda itself, the period from August 1993 until the start of the genocide was characterized by ferocious negotiations that grew in bitterness and violence as the Arusha peace deal came closer to being realized. Indeed, seen from within Kigali, the signing of Arusha stands not as the first step to peace but as the critical spur to radical polarization of politics in Kigali, to greater demonization of the RPF and its allies, and to mobilization for the massively violent repudiation of Arusha that was the Rwandan genocide. The collapse of Arusha and the launch of the genocide in April 1994 left international third parties, and especially the United Nations, facing the challenge of responding to the swiftly unfolding crisis. In both the diplomatic and military realms, third-party responses were anemic. The result was disastrous: a wholesale failure to halt or contain the genocide that swept through Rwanda with brutal efficiency.

"Securing" the Implementation Phase: The Deployment of UNAMIR

The term *implementation* conveys the idea that agreement had been reached and had merely to be put in motion. Although this was true on paper, in fact the so-called implementation phase constituted two key tasks that were resisted by anti-Arusha forces: the establishment of a transitional government; and the overseeing of that transition process by the Neutral International Force.

The Neutral International Force

The Arusha negotiations had reviewed the need to provide a neutral international force to secure the implementation of the Broad-Based Transitional Government, which would govern Rwanda until national elections could be held twenty-two months later. The agreement specified that the neutral force should be deployed within thirty-seven days of the signing of the agreement and should provide security and protection to the members of the BBTG as well as continuing the task, to that point performed by NMOG, of monitoring the DMZ.

Discussions about the force started with a proposal that the OAU should provide the neutral force, building on its experience in managing NMOG. This proposal met resistance from three quarters. First, the government of Rwanda had reservations about an OAU force, seeing the OAU as predisposed to the RPF position and not reliable. Second, several international observers at Arusha, on the basis of the poor performance of NMOG, argued that the OAU was not capable of mounting an effective security force. Third, the proposal was resisted by the United Nations.

The nature of UN resistance was an unwillingness to provide the kinds of backup and support that the OAU would need were it to take the lead with the NIF.[1] Put simply, the OAU would require financial as well as logistical support from the United Nations to mount an operation. Such support was not forthcoming from the UN leadership, and the UN response amounted to a poison pill: if the United Nations were to support the force, then it would have to run the command-and-control functions—which means, in effect, that it would be a UN force. This was unworkable. Faced with opposition from the United Nations, the OAU looked to its own resources and quickly concluded that it was unable to mount an effective operation.[2]

The discussions around the NIF thus turned to proposals to have a UN-led force. In fact, the GoR, with backing from the French, had been lobbying for a UN force from the outset of discussions. The RPF initially resisted that proposal, fearing that France's position on the Security Council would allow it to control the UN force in a way that would threaten RPF security. In the end, however, the RPF had to give way when its preferred option (an OAU-led force) fell through. An agreement was reached that the United Nations would provide the NIF in the form of a Chapter 6 peacekeeping operation. The transfer of responsibility from the OAU to the United Nations, as the process moved from mediation to implementation, would prove to be disastrous.

Planning and Deploying UNAMIR

On 15 August 1993, UN Secretary-General Boutros Boutros-Ghali decided to send a reconnaissance mission to Rwanda, which departed on 19 August under the leadership of Brigadier-General Romeo Dallaire (who would subsequently be named force commander of the UN operation).[3] In meetings in Kigali, Rwandan officials stressed the urgency of the mission and the fact that it had been asked, by the Arusha Peace Accords (which the United Nations had signed), to guarantee security throughout the country.[4] They also stressed that the deployment of the mission was central to the whole peace process, especially to the establishment of the BBTG. RPF officials warned that late deployment of a neutral force would give an opportunity to hard-line opponents of the peace deal, who would use the interim to thwart the accords.

The mission reported serious risks for any peacekeeping operation in Rwanda and, on the basis of this assessment, argued (in an initial, informal report) that an optimal mission would comprise 8,000 troops, with 4,500–5,000 men as the responsible minimum.[5] Nevertheless, the conclusion from the reconnaissance mission was that UNAMIR was achievable, despite the risks. Diplomats in the region who were consulted by Brigadier-General Dallaire recall his optimism: "We can do this thing," Dallaire reported to the Canadian mission in Dar-es-Salaam.[6]

Back in New York, it quickly became clear that support for a large mission was nonexistent. The larger figure was never put to the UN Security Council: advance messages from the U.S. delegation in particular made it clear that there would be no support for a large mission in Rwanda.[7] The UN Department of Peacekeeping Operations (DPKO) thus had to recommend a mission designed mindful of "what the traffic would bear" (i.e., bearing political considerations in mind).

The Security Council agreed to send a force, deployed in four phases, to Rwanda after a compromise agreement was brokered by

France. In Phase I, starting immediately, 1,428 troops were to be sent to Rwanda to establish a presence in the DMZ and await the departure of French forces from Kigali—a condition of deployment established by the Arusha negotiations. Phase I was estimated to have a duration of ninety days. Phase II was to commence after the establishment of the transitional government and would focus on preparations for disarmament and demobilization of the armed forces. During this phase, UNAMIR would also provide security in Kigali and in a weapons-free zone surrounding the city. Troop strength would rise during this period to 2,217. These reinforcements would, during Phase III, oversee the demobilization, disengagement, and integration processes. The force would gradually be thinned out during Phase IV, which would maintain a security presence during the transition to elections.

UNAMIR's mandate was strictly Chapter VI (i.e., it was a classic peacekeeping operation based on the consent of the parties). Specifically, it was mandated to perform the following tasks:

> to contribute to the security of the city of Kigali, *inter alia,* within a weapons-secure area established by the parties in and around the city;
>
> to monitor the observance of the cease-fire agreement, which calls for the establishment of cantonment and assembly zones and the demarcation of the new demilitarized zones and other demilitarization procedures;
>
> to monitor the security situation during the final period of the transitional Government's mandate, leading up to the elections;
>
> to assist with mine clearance, primarily through training programmes;
>
> to investigate, at the request of the parties, or on its own initiative, instances of alleged non-compliance with the provisions of the Protocol of Agreement on the Integration of the Armed Forces of the Two Parties, and to pursue any such instances with the parties responsible and report thereon as appropriate to the Secretary-General;
>
> to monitor the process of repatriation of Rwandan refugees and resettlement of displaced persons to verify that it is carried out in a safe and orderly manner;
>
> to assist in the co-ordination of humanitarian assistance activities in conjunction with relief operations; and
>
> to investigate and report on incidents regarding the activities of the *gendarmerie* and police.[8]

The mandate given to UNAMIR by the Security Council conformed with some of the tasks foreseen for it in the Arusha Accords but altered key provisions. Missing from the Security Council resolution was any reference to the primary tasks ascribed to the NIF by Arusha, namely, ensuring overall security in the country, providing security for civilians, tracking arms flows, and neutralizing armed gangs.[9] The rules of engagement established by UNAMIR reflected this restricted mandate. The force commander's directive establishing the rules stated that "the use of weapons is normally authorized for self-defence only. The use of force for deterrence or retaliation is forbidden."[10] This reflected his philosophy that "the whole *raison d'être* of peacekeeping is that peace should be achieved without the use of military force."[11]

UNAMIR was thus established as a small mission with a limited mandate, further weakened by the extraordinarily tortuous budget procedure that accompanies UN missions.[12] The initial budget for UNAMIR went to the UN Fifth Committee on 3 January 1994; the Advisory Committee on Activities and Budgetary Questions (ACABQ) began consideration of the budget on 17 March. ACABQ issued its recommendations to the Fifth Committee on 30 March; they were endorsed on 4 April.[13] On 18 April, requests were issued to contributors for $61 million, the first installments of which were received on 26 August. In short, UNAMIR's budget was approved two days before the start of the genocide, and the first funds were received one month after its completion. During this period, UNAMIR was put in the position of operating hand-to-mouth, at one stage borrowing from UNICEF simply to remain operational. At the time, UNAMIR was described as "financially and logistically very weak."[14]

Quite apart from bureaucratic obstacles in New York, on the ground UNAMIR was challenged from the outset. The force commander and an advance party of twenty-one troops arrived in Kigali between 21 and 27 October 1993, several weeks after the Arusha-scheduled arrival. On the day the force commander arrived, the Tutsi-dominated army of Burundi assassinated the newly elected president, Melchior Ndadaye, a Hutu, an act that sparked widespread killing, resulting in the deaths of a *reported* 150,000 Burundians. The assassination and killings were rich material for the extremists in Rwanda, who used the events to bolster their claim that the Tutsis of the RPF were returning to Rwanda to reestablish their historic dominance over the Hutu. The contrast could not have been more stark between the violence in Burundi and the late, partial arrival of the NIF, whose ostensible task—at least in Rwandan eyes and in the language of Arusha—was to "secure" the implementation phase. UNAMIR's role as guarantor of the peace agreement was already in jeopardy. The Burundi killings had a second adverse impact on UNAMIR, namely, a large refugee influx into Rwanda. Immediately upon arrival, some of UNAMIR's troops had to be deployed to the Rwanda-Burundi border to monitor potential instability stemming from the refugee movement.

Starting on 1 November, the first contingent of troops assigned to UNAMIR deployed in five sectors: in the DMZ; in Kigali; in RPF-held territory; in GoR territory; and along the Uganda-Rwanda border, incorporating the eighty-one observers of the UN Observer Mission to Uganda-Rwanda. In Kigali, UNAMIR was deployed in several small detachments, rather than as a concentrated force. UNAMIR slowly built up its presence. By 27 December 1993, UNAMIR had 1,260 troops on the ground from Belgian, Bangladeshi, Tunisian, Ghanaian, and Canadian contingents.[15] Despite the fact that the transitional government had not been established, the UN Secretary-General's December report recommended that a battalion be sent early to Rwanda, and on 6 January additional troops for UNAMIR were approved by the Security Council, bringing UNAMIR's total strength to 2,548.

Strikingly, UNAMIR was never provided with two things that would have proved useful: a strong intelligence capacity; and defensive equipment, such as armored personnel carriers (APCs).[16] No member state contributed an armed unit, so DPKO found spare equipment from the UN operation in Mozambique, and commercial contractors were contacted. In the end, the APCs that arrived from Mozambique were largely nonfunctional. What intelligence capacity UNAMIR had was provided informally by the Belgian contingent (the 1st Paratroop Battalion). On these two issues, a staff officer serving Force Commander Dallaire would later comment that the experience of Rwanda established, first, that "the UN must drop its aversion to intelligence operations," and second, that "the continued deployment of contingents without the requisite equipment . . . placed a large, immobile and largely ineffective force in the middle of an increasingly hostile environment."[17]

The Management of UNAMIR: Politics in New York

Ironically, given the UN's earlier resistance to an OAU force, when discussions finally moved from Rwanda to New York the idea of a

UN peacekeeping mission for Rwanda ran into serious resistance.[18] The period was mid-1993, when U.S. hostility to the United Nations had reached a peak and U.S. views toward UN peacekeeping had been soured by the cost and ineffectiveness of the UN operations in Somalia and Bosnia, to which the United States was contributing a 33 percent share of funds.[19] The United Nations also had ongoing, expensive missions in Cambodia, Haiti, and elsewhere. At the Security Council, the United States and Russia initially objected to yet another peacekeeping operation, this time for a small country with a small civil war that was barely on the radar screen.

Moreover, among the actors involved in Security Council deliberations, only France had interests in Rwanda. As J. Matthew Vaccaro establishes, the political will to engage seriously in Rwanda was generally absent among those actors with sufficient capacity to do so.[20] However, France took the lead in backing the mission. The director for Africa at the Quai d'Orsay was considered by his colleagues to be a strong internationalist and a strong backer of the United Nations, and his support for a UN mission was critical.[21] Eventually, the French delegation in New York at the Security Council brokered a compromise. At the same time that Rwanda was being discussed, Russia was seeking Security Council support for a mission in Georgia, and the United States was seeking support for a mission in Haiti. France let it be known that its support for those missions would be contingent on U.S. and Russian support for the Rwandan operation. A deal was brokered wherein the United States, Russia, and France would all agree to support each other's desired missions. The UN Assistance Mission in Rwanda was voted into effect on 5 October 1993 (SC/RES/872).

The "risky but achievable" assessment reached by DPKO's reconnaissance mission was toned down for Security Council consumption. Indeed, by the time proposals were being floated to the Permanent Five, Rwanda was increasingly being depicted as a winnable mission, a potential success story that could restore the tarnished image of UN peacekeeping. Adding to this perception was the fact that the United Nations received a joint request for peacekeeping assistance from the GoR and the RPF. Moreover, at no point during deliberations in the Security Council was the Tanzanian mediation team invited to share its perspectives on the potential challenges the mission might face. Thereby failing to coordinate even in the most basic way with those engaged in mediation, the United Nations opened up a critical disjuncture between the negotiation and implementation elements of the peacemaking process.

Accordingly, the assessment of the mission in New York was part confusion (as to the degree of support for Arusha among the parties, as well as little awareness of the lack of cohesion within the government), and part misrepresentation (the Security Council was not likely to authorize a risky mission, given the trauma of the UN operations in Somalia and Bosnia). However, the perception that Rwanda was achievable meant that the mission was approved with minimal political backing, reflected in its limited strength; this would prove disastrous.

The political reluctance that attended the birth of UNAMIR shaped its destiny. At key moments, the lack of political support within New York would place serious limitations on UNAMIR's ability to interpret its mandate broadly, communicate effectively with its political masters, respond to events and information on the ground, and in other ways help shape the implementation phase in Rwanda.

Seen in retrospect, the decision to send a small, weak mission to Rwanda seems absurd; seen in perspective of the organizational and political constraints on the Department of Peacekeeping Operations, it was hardly surprising. DPKO was simultaneously managing the ill-fated mission in Somalia, the troubled mission in Yugoslavia, as well as the longer-running and (at that point) more successful missions in Cambodia and Haiti.[22] Whatever the explanation or reason, the fact is that the United Nations sent a small, poorly equipped, reactive mission possibly capable of monitoring a generally accepted peace to a country in which the peace deal was a source of aggravated disagreement. Critically, the local force most adamantly opposed to the Arusha deal controlled key elements of the FAR. This fact alone should have been cause for concern and sufficient justification for contingency planning for serious opposition. Moreover, this fact was established by the DPKO reconnaissance mission to Rwanda, yet this was never reflected in the strength, composition, mandate, or rules of engagement assigned to UNAMIR.

Writing about UNAMIR, Vaccaro argues that "within the constraints imposed by the Security Council, UNAMIR was a well-planned operation, reflecting newly developed competencies within the UN Secretariat."[23] This characterization seems questionable and is certainly at odds with the reflections of many senior UNAMIR officials. Yet even if we assume that the early design, deployment, and financing were in fact well-planned, there was at the very least a major failure of strategic planning. Part of this, of course, as is implicit in

Vaccaro's statement, was a function of Security Council decisions: sending a mission into Rwanda based on the concept that "peace should be achieved without the use of military force" ensured that UNAMIR would never be able to fulfill the real task ascribed to the NIF by the architects of Arusha. Lack of contingency planning for fierce opposition to UNAMIR meant that the mission was comprised, financed, equipped, and deployed on the basis of dangerously false planning assumptions.

End-Game:
The Collapse of Arusha and Withdrawal of UNAMIR

As UNAMIR was deployed and during the months that followed, elements of the Rwandan political system and the United Nations struggled to implement Arusha, especially with respect to the establishment of the transitional institutions, principally the BBTG. As the forces of peace struggled to get the implementation phase off the ground, extremist forces methodically and efficiently undermined their efforts.

The Extremist Response:
Demonization, Mobilization, and Polarization

Efforts to establish the BBTG began with the appointment of the MDR's Faustin Twagiramungu to the prime ministership, as agreed in the final days of Arusha. Simultaneously, the opposition parties in Kigali began to splinter. Twagiramungu's party itself splintered into factions, and intense squabbles broke out among the Parti Libéral and the Parti Socialiste Démocratique.

The splintering of the opposition parties was far from accidental; rather, it was part of the three-pronged strategy being put into effect by extremist forces—leading figures within the *akazu,* including the CDR, members of the MRND, and elements of the FAR and Presidential Guard. This strategy, as outlined in Chapter 2, entailed, first, *demonization*: a substantial increase in the volume of hate and fear propaganda against the RPF. Extremists flooded the country with pamphlets, radio broadcasts, and newspapers that depicted the RPF as a threat to Rwanda and emphasized the threat to all Hutus if the RPF were allowed to enter government. Arusha was depicted as a sellout, those who supported it, traitors.[24] The second part of the strategy was *mobilization:* the CDR and elements of the MRND began the process of mobilizing armed opposition to the RPF, especially through the creation of the *interahamwe* and *impuzamugambi* militias. Logistical planning for opposition also was stepped into high gear. The third, and critical, element of the strategy was *polarization:* the committed opponents of Arusha fought hard in the political war for control of the center—the moderates in the regime and the opposition parties that formed a third corner of power between the RPF and Arusha's enemies.

The political war for the center was a process that led to massive polarization in Kigali. The major development during this phase was the emergence of the so-called power factions within some of the opposition parties.[25] The power factions represented hard-line opinion within otherwise more moderate parties and political groupings. Their emergence was directed by the CDR and elements within the MRND. The major tactic was a classic combination of sticks and carrots. The central message was that the regime was going to emerge victorious either from the current process or from later elections and would remember its friends; direct and indirect threats against party members reinforced this message. Joining forces now with the regime was the key to survival. Successful use of these tactics so effectively divided the opposition parties that even when Faustin Twagiramungu (of the MDR) was appointed prime minister as the first step toward establishing the BBTG as per Arusha, his appointment was criticized by members of his own party.

The fracturing of the opposition parties delayed the establishment of the transitional government. The emergence of factions played havoc with the math used in the distribution of seats in Arusha and tied up the parties in internal fights. The so-called power factions were seen within their respective parties as fronts for the MRND and CDR; this caused massive dissension within the parties. For example, attempts to convene the BBTG failed on 8 January 1994 because of deadlock within the Mouvement Démocratique Républicain and the Parti Libéral. By 10 February the deadlock within the Parti Libéral was so intense that the other opposition parties, and the MRND, agreed to go ahead and establish the BBTG without Parti Libéral participation.

Before this could occur, Felicien Gatabazi, the secretary general of the Parti Socialiste Démocratique, was assassinated in Kigali; the next day Martin Bucyana, a key figure within the CDR, was killed. On 23 February the opposition parties all boycotted an MRND attempt to hold the installation ceremonies for the BBTG. On 24 February UNHCR's Michel Moussali issued his prescient warning of "a bloodbath of unparalleled proportions." The bloodbath was already in preparation.

Early Warning, Weak Action

UNAMIR, its resources stretched by the general deterioration in Kigali, provided little security against the growing sense of chaos and impending catastrophe that increasingly pervaded Rwanda. Its ability to contain the disintegrating situation was minimal, a weakness matched by the diplomatic efforts to control the situation: in both the military and diplomatic realms, international responses to the extremists' strategies of polarization, demonization, and mobilization were anemic.

From the late Arusha period onward, it had been clear that there was fierce opposition to the Arusha process, especially to the final deal. Moreover, the groups that opposed the deal, especially the CDR, used totalistic rhetoric and even apocalyptic references to signal their opposition. The risk to Arusha and to general stability was widely noted by diplomats in the region.[26]

Awareness of the growing threat to Arusha has been interpreted ex post facto as an early warning. At the time, however, such was not the case in most Western capitals, and certainly not in New York. Yet the fact that important forces might attempt to undo Arusha, and that such efforts would destabilize the situation, became increasingly clear. But the potential magnitude of mass genocide was less clearly understood. The apocalyptic rhetoric of the CDR was seen as posturing, and some of it was farcical: the papal nuncio, for instance, was repeatedly accused of plotting to overthrow the government and of being an RPF conspirator. Such accusations diminished the seriousness with which the hate rhetoric was received by the international diplomatic community.[27]

By early January, however, there was new evidence that the rhetoric reflected a plan for violent opposition. In what has become the most infamous moment of pregenocide Rwanda, an informant reached UNAMIR and revealed the existence of a plan of opposition to Arusha.[28] The informant revealed the existence of arms caches, of plans to attack members of the transitional government as well as UN-AMIR in order to force its withdrawal, and of plans to disrupt efforts to implement the BBTG. The informant also revealed that the architects of this plan had compiled lists of Tutsi throughout the country and had the capacity to kill 1,000 Tutsi every twenty minutes. As we have already seen, this conformed precisely to the genocide plan as it was implemented, although the rate was exaggerated somewhat. This information was cabled to New York on 11 January 1994.

Again, this has subsequently been interpreted as a signal for genocide, a warning of what was to come. This is problematic. First, the informant was deeply involved in the political process in Kigali, a senior figure in the government being accused of hatching the plan; given the heated politics of Kigali, an insider was scarcely to be trusted. Second, the threat of killing 1,000 Tutsis every twenty minutes could signal a genocide on the extraordinary scale that occurred, or a very bloody few hours. The RPF, listening to CDR rhetoric about an apocalypse, and on the basis of its own intelligence, calculated that it would risk losing 10,000 Tutsis in Kigali if events unfolded as the CDR foretold.[29] Although dire, this assessment was still enormously at variance with what actually occurred. Third, the information contradicted many other signals from political actors in Kigali. Notably, UN Special Representative Roger Booh-Booh was sending more positive reports to New York.[30] In the context, there was no a priori reason to trust either the message or the messenger.

However, even if it does not stand as a clear warning about a future event, the 11 January cable certainly underscored a growing risk to the peace deal as well as to UNAMIR. The Tanzanians in particular were very worried. Their intelligence on the CDR was better than that of the United Nations, and it was telling them that the threat to Arusha was serious.

Additional warnings were received in New York, especially from Belgium. On 11 February the Belgian foreign minister warned the UN Secretary-General that the situation was deadlocked and could result in new violence. Evidently, Belgium was increasingly aware of what was brewing. On 25 February the Belgian foreign ministry wrote to its ambassador in New York warning that "public opinion would never tolerate having Belgian peacekeepers remain passive witnesses to genocide and having the UN do nothing."[31] The Belgian ambassador discussed Brussels's warnings with the UN Secretariat; whether he used the word *genocide* is unclear.

Nevertheless, warnings and signals coming out of Rwanda were falling on mostly deaf ears in New York. Warning signs, although they were arriving amid signals that seemed to indicate only a general threat to Arusha and not a specific threat of genocide, were processed by the UN Secretariat but not highlighted or brought to the attention of the Security Council. Given the presumption of an easy mission, the rapid deterioration in Rwanda was overlooked in the Security Council despite the fact that national intelligence units were beginning to foresee the possibility of wider violence. Notably, the CIA conducted a desk study of possible scenarios, one of which suggested a worst-case scenario of 500,000 dead. This report was never shared beyond the CIA, and certainly not with the United Nations, a decision justified retrospectively by an unwillingness to reveal sources.[32] The consequences of this omission were tragic indeed.

Five years after the event, a UN-commissioned independent report on Rwanda criticized several UN officials for mishandling the 11 January cable.[33] The report is compelling in its critique of senior UN peacekeeping officials for their nonreaction to the cable. However, the report reinforces a popular misconception, namely, that the United Nations knew about the genocide before its start.

The argument that receipt of the cable constituted foreknowledge of the genocide cannot be sustained. Although the cable was mishandled in that its warnings were not adequately investigated, it seems equally clear that no one with a decisionmaking role in the United Nations truly understood the seriousness of the threat of genocide. Rather, what was understood in New York was a growing threat of a repudiation of Arusha and new violence—not genocidal violence. This seems evident from expressed perceptions of Western diplomats in the region in late 1993 and early 1994;[34] from the fact that the majority of other information being received in New York did not corroborate the informant's picture of the evolving situation; and from recollections by Western diplomats after the fact.[35] This is corroborated by the RPF's own intelligence assessment, which did not suggest an event anywhere close to the scale of what occurred. Tellingly, the United Nations actually *downgraded* the security rating of Rwanda in March 1994 (it had been raised following the Bucyana assassination).[36]

The purpose of this argument is not to exonerate any party. The possibility of reaction against Arusha, even on a smaller scale than what occurred, was sufficient reason to prepare contingency plans and to energetically move to reinforce UNAMIR.

Importantly, the evidence suggests that although the international actors in Rwanda probably had sufficient pieces of the puzzle, they did not possess a cultural or political analysis of Rwanda that would allow them to put those pieces together. The fact that the CIA generated a worst-case scenario of 500,000 dead indicates that it was possible to reach the right conclusion; and a few international actors, such as Moussali, had more prescience. But in general terms, international actors missed the specific threat of genocide in their general concern for the viability of Arusha. This has been referred to as "the shadow of Arusha," that is, a kind of quasideliberate blindness to opposition resulting from a strong commitment to the success of Arusha. The shadow of Arusha combined with a limited range of cultural references to blinker the United Nations and most other Western implementers. Among the key Western governments involved, only the Belgians seemed to have had a clear idea about the nature of the threat.

Notwithstanding these limits on international perceptions, UNAMIR was being managed in a way that minimized its relevance and its ability to influence the course of events. As the force commander reported a worsening situation and sought approval to interpret his mandate widely in order to respond, he was consistently denied. The critical juncture came in response to the 11 January cable, with its reports of arms caches. The force commander requested approval to conduct a search for weapons. DPKO's response was that the matter should be raised with the Rwandan government as well as local ambassadors, and that no weapons searches should be undertaken. The DPKO noted that the mandate referred to a weapons-free zone established "by the parties."

The unwillingness of New York to take an expansive view of the mandate was in part a consequence of the weak political support for UNAMIR. The timing was not auspicious: the Security Council was still reeling from the news of the disastrous results from a similar hunt-and-destroy mission in Mogadishu that resulted in a UN death toll. A clear "Mogadishu line" had been set, and it was not to be crossed. This mood, coupled with the basic lack of support for UNAMIR, limited the mission's capacity to investigate the growing signals of opposition to Arusha. The combination of political indifference, poor intelligence, and lack of cultural awareness meant that the direction of the political war, and signals of impending violence, went unheeded in New York.[37] Even as the signals grew louder, and civil violence in Kigali and throughout the country increased with each step toward implementation, New York failed to respond. No proactive measures to block Arusha opponents were taken; no contingency planning occurred. UNAMIR was thus denied the tools that might have helped generate better options when the violence of the political war overtook the peace process in the military war.

At the diplomatic level, efforts to rescue the situation were not quite as hapless, but they were equally ineffective. The bloody episode in Burundi had made it more and more clear that the potential for disaster was real. Some Western diplomats warned of a possible return to violence—meaning a return to civil war—that could come from the army's rejection of the Arusha Accords. In general terms, however, the diplomatic response was mismatched with the evolving realities on the ground. The diplomatic community's main channels of communication were to the regime itself, and it was the regime that was the problem.

Moreover, Habyarimana and the Cabinet showed considerable diplomatic prowess in fending off international pressure. For example, a joint diplomatic démarche raised the issue of hate radio and asked Habyarimana to take RTLMC off the air. Habyarimana responded that since the West had pressured him to move toward democratic government, he no longer had the power to control the airwaves; democracies guaranteed free speech, did they not?[38] The reality, of course, was that Habyarimana would not control RTLMC not because of free speech laws but because he did not have sufficient power, or sufficient will, to control the CDR and its extremists allies. The extremists were now moving beyond planning and into deliberate escalation toward genocide.

As events spiraled out of control in Kigali, diplomatic efforts to contain the hostilities continued. A Special Representative of the Secretary-General (SRSG), Roger Booh-Booh of Cameroon, who was sent to Rwanda to oversee UNAMIR and to support the diplomatic process, met with the RPF on 1 March to put the peace process back on track.[39] Booh-Booh's efforts met with little success. Tanzania also kept up efforts to persuade the sides to implement the agreement. Ultimately, Tanzania persuaded Habyarimana to attend a meeting in Dar-es-Salaam on the crisis in Burundi, with the intention of pressuring him to reaffirm his commitment to the BBTG. Habyarimana attended the meeting and did issue a statement reaffirming the Arusha deal; returning from this conference on 6 April, the plane carrying Habyarimana and President Cyprien Ntaryamira of Burundi was shot down, killing all aboard.

Within hours, roadblocks were thrown up around Kigali by the Presidential Guard and elements of the FAR, and the same armed units began a carefully planned program of assassination. The first victims of the genocide, as noted in Chapter 2, were the moderate members of the opposition parties, that is, elements within the regime that might pose an alternative to the radical effort that was under way. These politicians were hunted down and brutalized. The new constellation of forces that would become known as *les génocidaires* was composed of members of the CDR, hard-liners from the MRND, members of the Presidential Guard, and some leaders of the FAR. Committed to the program of genocide, they moved to clear the ground of opposition before launching the main, murderous thrust of their plan.

Last-Gasp Diplomacy and the Withdrawal of UNAMIR

Tanzanian authorities tried desperately to renew the Arusha process and thereby restore order in Rwanda. On 7 April, Tanzania ordered gasoline shipments to Rwanda to be held at the border in order to put pressure on what remained of the government to negotiate with UNAMIR and the RPF. On 19 April, President Ali Hassan Mwinyi called for a return to Arusha on 23 April. On 22 April, the RPF agreed to attend and to talk, not to the putative government but to the Rwandan army. Also on 23 April, an RPF delegation turned up in Arusha ready to announce a unilateral cease-fire; no government delegation presented itself at Arusha.[40]

As it turned out, Zaire's Mobutu Sese Seko had disastrously chosen this moment to reassert his authority as formal mediator of the Arusha process. He had called the government of Rwanda to parallel talks in Zaire on 23 April. The effective government had gone to Zaire, ready to announce a unilateral cease-fire. The Tanzanian government's outrage was expressed diplomatically when it "regretted" Mobutu's interference, saying simply that "two unilaterally decided cease-fires do not add up to one that is effective."[41] Although it is not clear that the two cease-fires would have been mutually acceptable or could have returned order to Rwanda, it is certainly evidence that Mobutu's interference denied the Arusha process a last chance (however slim) to stop the killings in Rwanda.

Undeterred, Tanzania called both sides to another Arusha round on 3 May; both the RPF and the GoR, such as it was by this point, attended. The provisional government was represented by Minister of Transportation and Communications André Ntagerura; Brigadier-General Marcel Gatsinzi; Agnes Ntambyauro, who held the justice portfolio; and Ambassador Munyaneza, Rwanda's envoy to Zaire.[42] The RPF sent a senior delegation composed of Colonel Alexis Kanyarengwe and General Secretary Rudasingwa. The two teams stayed in Arusha for 3 and 4 May but refused at any point to meet with each other. The RPF rejected attempts by SRSG Booh-Booh to act as a mediator. By 5 May it was clear that these talks would achieve nothing, and they were abandoned.

The fifth day of May 1994 thus marks the end of the Arusha process. Tanzania would twice more attempt to launch new peace initiatives for Rwanda, both times without success. The 3–4 May summit was the last point when the Arusha partners would attempt to bring the RPF together with Rwandan government officials to negotiate a restoration of order. The jaws of genocide had already closed around Rwanda.

As the grip tightened, the United Nations was in no position to respond. When the genocide plan was put in motion on 6 April 1994, UNAMIR was among the early, successful targets. The targeting of UNAMIR had actually been revealed to the United Nations in the 11 January cable; the plan included killing peacekeepers to cause the withdrawal of the UN force. Ten Belgian peacekeepers were detained by the FAR after an unsuccessful effort to provide protection to the prime minister.[43] The peacekeepers radioed in for instructions; the head of the Belgian contingent, Colonel Luc Marchal, told them they should make their own decision, as they were the ones who were best placed to assess the situation. Later, as the situation deteriorated, a Belgian commander suggested it would be best to cooperate with the FAR and lay down their arms. The peacekeepers were taken to an FAR encampment. A lengthy interval ensued, possibly because the FAR was waiting for UNAMIR's response. After several hours, ten Belgian peacekeepers were attacked and killed.

As Astri Suhrke makes clear in her detailed account of this episode, the fact that the Belgians did not respond more robustly to this attack on their men was influenced by three factors.[44] First, the scattered deployment of UNAMIR around Kigali meant that neither UNAMIR nor the Belgian battalion was well positioned to respond with force. Second, the rules of engagement for the Belgian battalion reflected the mandate and the general UN conception regarding UNAMIR's limited, pacific role. Finally, it is unclear that UNAMIR had adequate strength to respond to such a situation—a damning indictment of its overall capacity and relevance.

It seems clear that the attack on the Belgian peacekeepers was a test for UNAMIR, consistent with the plans revealed to the United Nations in January. If so, UNAMIR utterly failed. Discussing the attack, a Rwandan official familiar with the planning of the genocide talked about the inspiration for the attack as having come from watching the UN's experience in Somalia: "We watch CNN, too, you know."[45] The extremists believed—correctly—that the Western nations supplying the core of the force would not be able to stomach any casualties. The attack on UNAMIR was designed to ensure its withdrawal; the plan unfolded as foreseen and produced the intended result. Within five days, Belgium announced the imminent withdrawal of its UNAMIR contingent.[46]

It is difficult to know what would have happened had UNAMIR been in a position to respond more robustly to this attack. Had it had adequate capacity to respond, and had it done so, the impact *might* have been meaningful. The fact that UNAMIR was among the first targets for attack suggests that the *génocidaires* were relying on UNAMIR's evacuation; thus, had UNAMIR been able to respond forcefully to the attack, it would have weakened the *génocidaires'* position. In a best-case scenario, the *génocidaires'* plan could have been frustrated by their failure to achieve what the 11 January cable spells out as a first-step goal, namely, the removal of the UN force. Given that they would then have had to assume that the United Nations would respond to further attacks, the implementation of the genocide would have been more difficult. It is not inconceivable that the genocide plan could have imploded at this stage under the combined opposition of moderates within the regime and the United Nations. Far more likely, however, is a scenario whereby resistance by the United Nations would at best have slowed the *génocidaires'* progress, forcing them to spend more time consolidating their position in Kigali and dealing with the UN force. This would have delayed implementation of the genocide in the countryside and probably speeded the RPF's military progress. The net result would have been a lower death toll from the genocide, although how much lower is impossible to assess.

More significant, this episode demonstrates that had UNAMIR been mandated as an enforcement operation—with a robust mandate and the muscle to respond to attacks—its capacity to respond at this initial stage to the implementation of the genocide, and thereby to frustrate the extremists' plans, would have increased. The course of the genocide might then have been very different indeed.

Ten days later, the United Nations decided to draw down its force to symbolic levels (UN Security Council Resolution 912).[47] The decision to draw down UNAMIR followed heated debate in the corridors of the Security Council. Notable in this debate was the effort of Nigeria, then seated on the Security Council, to generate a substantive response. The UN Secretariat provided options for reinforcement, maintenance of the status quo, and evacuation of the force.[48] However, the withdrawal of the Belgian contingent had already crippled the mission. In addition, Belgium's defense minister, Willy Claes, actively sought to persuade other nations to join Belgium in withdrawing their troops from UNAMIR.[49]

It is evident that UN Secretary-General Boutros Boutros-Ghali failed to provide leadership within the UN Secretariat and Security Council at this critical juncture.[50] Although the responsible parts of the UN Secretariat were enormously overworked (as Vaccaro points out, two weeks earlier U.S. troops had withdrawn from Somalia, leaving the United Nations in the lurch; at the same time, the United Nations was facing the Serb attack on Goradze in Bosnia), its failure to respond with vigor drastically undermined its moral credibility and thus its ability to prompt action from the Security Council. Moreover, the sense of responsibility of some actors within the Secretariat lagged from the outset. One senior peacekeeping official admitted later that it was only after the outbreak of the genocide that he learned of the Genocide Convention and of the UN's legal capacity and moral obligation to respond to genocide.[51]

The net result was that on 21 April the bulk of UNAMIR's troops withdrew from the Kigali airport. Belgian peacekeepers cut up their blue berets in disgust, forced as they were to abandon a mission that had already claimed the lives of ten Belgian soldiers. Apart from the small contingent left behind, the United Nations effectively left Rwanda's genocide planners a clear field to put their killing machine into motion.

The Nonresponse to Genocide

The withdrawal of the bulk of UNAMIR's troops from Rwanda left the population unprotected from the *génocidiares*. Two subsequent military interventions were putatively geared toward protecting Rwandans from the genocide: France's Operation Turquoise, and UNAMIR II. The former was a substantive military force, but its real purposes were largely other than stated; the latter clearly had real humanitarian purposes but was utterly ineffective.

By the end of April 1994, some 470 UNAMIR troops remained in Kigali, and these vulnerable forces in fact managed to protect tens of thousands of civilian Rwandans.[52] By May, reports of genocide in Rwanda and the gut-wrenching images, particularly of bloated victims floating downriver into Lake Victoria, combined with the destabilizing fact of hundreds of thousands of refugees pouring into Tanzania, generated sufficient political pressure to force the Security Council to reconsider its decision and move to reinforce UNAMIR.

UN Peacekeeping Revisited: UNAMIR II

The story of the decisionmaking surrounding UNAMIR II has been recounted in detail elsewhere.[53] The basic facts are simple to recount. On 29 April, according to statistics from UNHCR, just more than 250,000 Rwandans crossed into neighboring Tanzania. Such a massive outflux focused attention on the scale of events inside Rwanda. At the same juncture, the United Nations issued an estimate that more than 200,000 people had been killed inside Rwanda. These facts managed to jolt the Security Council into action, if we can call it that: on 6 May it reopened the debate on Rwanda and asked the UN Secretariat for contingency plans. This resulted, by 17 May, in Resolution 918, under which the Security Council sought to reinforce UNAMIR to a total strength of 5,500. However, requests to contributing nations produced no readily available troops. A Nigerian proposal to send Nigerian and other African troops to Rwanda with U.S. and other Western governments' equipment quickly bogged down in discussions of insurance and cost issues, and in the end no Nigerian troops were ever deployed. Indeed, no new troops were deployed to UNAMIR II, as the force became known, until the middle of August, by which point the genocide and the civil war were well over.

Writing about this period, Michael Barnett has critiqued what he calls the "politics of indifference."[54] This was indeed a significant factor. After the 20 April vote to draw down UNAMIR, the UN Secretariat recovered from its earlier paralysis and "assumed the role of a model executive branch: it asserted the moral and political need for action, assessed the problem, formulated an innovative and bold response, and actively sought to mobilize resources for its realization."[55] Yet interviews with U.S. officials about their reasons for not responding positively to Nigerian proposals to use U.S. equipment to protect African peacekeepers revealed attitudes of callousness and indifference.[56] Even the official view—there was too high a cost associated with not being able to recover APCs and other equipment that might have been lent to Nigeria or other potential troop-providers—is staggering in its callousness when contrasted to the human reality.

Indeed, U.S. President Bill Clinton later apologized to the Rwandan people for the inexcusably slow U.S. response to the genocide. However, the United States did more than respond slowly; it actively sought to downplay the genocide in Rwanda, thereby diminishing the likelihood of response. In particular, the U.S. government issued instructions that U.S. diplomats should avoid using the word *genocide* in respect of Rwanda and, instead, refer to "acts of genocide."[57] The government was afraid that if the killings in Rwanda were acknowledged to be a genocide, then public pressure to respond would be overwhelming and the United States would be dragged into a military engagement it did not seek and did not want.

Operation Turquoise

While the genocide was under way, France sent a unilateral, but UN-mandated, intervention force to southwestern Rwanda: Operation Turquoise.[58] Its publicly stated purpose was to halt the genocide and facilitate humanitarian access to victims of genocide and displacement. In fact, Operation Turquoise established a presence only in a part of Rwanda where the genocide had already been largely completed; elsewhere, it did little to halt the genocide. Although it is arguable that perhaps 10,000 lives were saved by the operation, it is difficult to interpret Operation Turquoise as a serious response.

As with UNAMIR II, the decisionmaking and events surrounding the deployment of Operation Turquoise have been well documented elsewhere.[59] Turquoise was approved by the Security Council under Chapter VII of the UN Charter on 22 June 1994. In the official UN account of this period, the operation appears as one proposed by France, subject to Security Council authorization.[60] In point of fact, it is quite clear that France intended to intervene in Rwanda irrespective of whether the Security Council endorsed its action. Indeed, the issue was brought to the Security Council only on 20 June; by 21 June France had already begun moving troops from its African bases in the Central African Republic and Chad toward Goma, which would be the rear base of operations for Turquoise (indeed the advance force had landed in Goma before the vote occurred).[61]

The first question surrounding Turquoise is that of its purposes. The French government had provided both military and political backing to the Habyarimana regime. Several governments and humanitarian organizations feared that France would use Turquoise to support the FAR, notwithstanding the stated humanitarian purposes of the intervention. As noted by Vaccaro, these doubts were strong enough to persuade Nigeria and New Zealand—governments that had actively sought a peacekeeping response to the genocide—to abstain from the vote on Turquoise.[62]

The question of Turquoise's purpose remains a difficult one. Prunier, who was closely involved in French decisionmaking surrounding Turquoise, suggests that its genesis was a complex mix of domestic political competition; shame that French allies were engaged in horrific acts of civilian slaughter; the importance of distancing France from the genocide in the eyes of the international community; and loyalty to the forces that the French army had cooperated with only a year earlier.[63] Many were convinced of the humanitarian purposes of the French when they established the Safe Humanitarian Zone in western Rwanda and worked closely with NGOs and UN humanitarian agencies there (see Chapter 7).[64] Others remain convinced that France had diabolical motives from the outset.[65]

To judge by the actions rather than intentions, the record of Turquoise as a humanitarian intervention is decidedly mixed. Turquoise had several specific consequences. First, it protected and evacuated roughly 10,000 people from western Rwanda in the first days of its presence. Yet even Prunier has argued that Turquoise, by entering western Rwanda first in small foot patrols and, in the process, reassuring several Tutsis who were in hiding, actually exposed *more* civilians to the *génocidiares,* who rounded up Tutsi during the period between Turquoise's first foot patrols and their return (roughly 36 hours later) with sufficient trucks to evacuate survivors.[66]

Second, Turquoise did establish the Safe Humanitarian Zone in western Rwanda and, in that zone, worked diligently to support the humanitarian efforts of the United Nations and NGOs. Later, Turquoise also supported humanitarian activities in Goma when that city was flooded with refugees from western Rwanda (see Chapter 7). There is no doubt that the French operation provided critical support to those operations, saving thousands of lives imperiled by dysentery and other diseases.[67]

Third, with one minor exception, Turquoise did not clash with the RPF, as some had feared. When it was announced that Turquoise would respond to any military aggression against or within the territory it occupied, the RPF chose not to test the point. According to Prunier, who handled the negotiations, RPF members quickly came to realize that Turquoise did not intend to attack them and that they could avoid a high-cost battle simply by staying out of Turquoise-occupied territory.[68] RPF sources largely confirm that account, adding that their own military assessment showed that they could defeat the French only at substantial cost in time, troops, and equipment.[69]

The most important aspect of Operation Turquoise was its impact within Zone Turquoise and Goma on the course of subsequent events. By declaring a safe zone and threatening to respond to any incursion into it, Turquoise effectively created a sanctuary for retreating leaders of the genocide, as well as some retreating FAR units.[70] This allowed a portion of the genocide movement to leave Rwanda intact, allowing them to establish a presence inside Zaire (near Bukavu) under less military pressure than they would otherwise have faced. Second, the presence of the French in Goma was a deterrent to the RPF, which briefly entered Goma in chase of the retreating FAR but returned to Rwanda. Again, this contributed to the ability of the genocide regime to establish itself in Zaire under less pressure than there would otherwise have been. The presence in eastern Zaire of the remnants of the deposed Rwandan regime hugely destabilized that specific region and, later, the wider subregion; remnants of this force continue to bedevil peace efforts in central Africa to this day.[71]

Finally, Turquoise by all accounts did nothing at all to halt the FAR's genocidal attacks on civilians. By the time Turquoise established itself in western Rwanda, the genocide in that territory was virtually complete. In effect, Turquoise occupied the only section of Rwanda in which there was both no RPF presence and no ongoing killings. These facts led Prunier to conclude that Operation Turquoise was primarily an effort by the French government to "wash its hands in public," that is, it was a public-relations exercise by which it distanced itself from the FAR without actually having to fight against it or to engage the RPF.[72]

French intervention, then, did nothing to aid the process of war termination or conflict resolution; rather, it had some positive humanitarian outcomes. But even those positives were outweighed by the negative outcome: recycling the war when it might otherwise have been concluded through a decisive RPF victory.

Between the two operations, Turquoise and UNAMIR II, there is little to choose. UNAMIR II was mandated to protect civilians in a more direct manner than was Turquoise, but it did not materialize until after the killing was completed. Turquoise did materialize—just in the wrong place and with the wrong effects. Put simply, there was no international intervention of any seriousness designed and deployed to halt the Rwandan genocide.

Parenthetically, the RPF's assessment sheds light on an important but debated point, namely, whether UNAMIR II would have been able to affect the course of war had it been provided with troops in May. The argument made by Vaccaro and others is that UNAMIR II would have faced opposition by the FAR and would have been unable to impede the progress of genocide.[73] Against a presumed rebuttal—that Turquoise controlled one-third of Rwanda with only 2,600 troops—Vaccaro counterargues that the experience of Turquoise is not relevant because it was operating in what amounted to friendly territory. Although this is true, the fact remains that the larger, better-equipped, and more disciplined of the two Rwandan armies—the RPF—assessed the 2,600 French troops as an opponent capable of imposing costs and delays in its offensive. If this force, which soundly defeated the opposing FAR, saw 2,600 French troops as an impediment, it suggests that 5,500 well-armed, well-trained, and properly mandated UN troops may well have been able to be an obstacle to the smaller, less well trained, less well motivated, and less well equipped FAR. A rapid-reaction force of the kind sent to East Timor in 1999 would probably have been sufficient; it is even instructive to note the stabilizing impact that roughly 500 British paratroopers, rapidly deployed, had on the conflict in Sierra Leone in May 2000 when the Revolutionary United Front launched an attack on government forces several months after signing the Lomé peace accords.

The stronger argument, of course, is that UNAMIR would have been able to impede the genocide had sufficient troops been present in Rwanda *from the outset*. As Alan Kuperman has pointed out, the time involved in deploying reinforcements to Rwanda would have been substantial, and they would have arrived when the genocide forces were spread throughout the countryside, thus making the containment challenge more difficult. Had 5,500 well-equipped, well-trained, properly mandated troops been deployed to Rwanda from the outset, their impact could well have been definitive. This was the conclusion of a panel of military experts convened by the Carnegie Commission on Preventing Deadly Conflict.[74]

For all of the debate around UNAMIR and UNAMIR II, for all of the noise that accompanied Operation Turquoise, for all of the last-ditch diplomacy, nothing of substance was done to mute the demonization of the RPF and the Kigali moderates, counter the polarization of the politics of implementation, block the mobilization of force against Arusha, or halt the genocidal escalation. Three and a half years of peacemaking efforts came to naught as Rwanda was consumed by the extremists' deadly plan.

Themes: Complexities of Peacemaking

When genocide commenced, the United Nations withdrew its peacekeeping force, abandoning the Rwandan peace and Rwandan civilians to their fate. The reasons for the withdrawal had largely to do with the lack of great power interests in Rwanda, as well as the resultant unwillingness of capable powers to risk troop casualties in protecting the Rwandan peace. It was also a cultural, conceptual, and planning failure.

Had the United Nations more fully understood the dynamics of the conflict, had it more fully understood the cultural legacy of Rwandan history, the need to engage in contingency planning for encounters with a forceful opposition would have been apparent. However good the peacemaking process might have been, the Arusha peace deal would ultimately have been attacked in some fashion by the extremist forces. Some military role in support of implementation was indispensable in the process of generating the least violent of possible outcomes in Rwanda. The ideal intervention during the early stages of genocide would have been a robust peace enforcement mission from the United Nations, one capable of halting the military actions of the extremists. The main purpose of such a force would have been the protection of civilians. The idea that peace should be obtained without the use of force—as Dallaire's force directives stipulated—was never more than fantasy.

The larger failure, however, was a moral failure on the part of member states of the United Nations to respond to genocide, given the international legal right, clear moral responsibility, and ample military capacity to do so. Whatever the failings of Arusha, however much earlier third-party processes had complicated the task, the fact remains that in the face of the genocide an international obligation to respond was utterly repudiated; Rwanda was abandoned to its bloody fate. The tragedy of the UN withdrawal is that a stronger UN presence would have done much to impede the genocide.

The deepest irony is that a primary reason for the Security Council's unwillingness to respond in April or May was that it had learned the lesson of Somalia; it was not going to cross the Mogadishu line between impartial peacekeeping and peace enforcement. But Rwanda was not Somalia. The Rwandan genocide was not a case of a widespread and diffuse conflict between a fractious set of warlords, or a situation where the population was unsympathetic to containment efforts. The Rwandan genocide was tightly controlled by its leadership and waged war against an unarmed population. Rwanda's extremists, not the UN Security Council, had learned the *real* lesson of Mogadishu: UN peacekeeping was a bluff, mere diplomatic sleight-of-hand.[75] In this case the extremists called the UN's bluff, to the terrible detriment of the Rwandan population and international peacemaking capacity at large.

Indeed, what is striking in retrospect is the overall negative impact of the complex organizational dynamics of the United Nations on the peacemaking process. The complexity of political decisionmaking in New York and the bureaucratic obstacles faced there are not typically considered in analyses of peacemaking initiatives, but in this case they undercut an already faltering Rwandan peace process. The challenge of comprehending the nature of the conflict, and what type of intervention is required when, is one thing; a whole other task is involved in managing the intervenors themselves. This complexity is simply a feature of any system for international conflict resolution. Because organizations involved in such a system will likely be involved in multiple actions and initiatives at any given time, there will always be issues surrounding deployment of resources, political will, management of information, and other issues pertaining to the nature and degree of involvement in any one operation. Moreover, these issues are pertinent not only for major international organizations such as the United Nations but also for diplomatic bodies and NGOs. Also striking is the importance of coordination between organizations, particularly in terms of the disjunctures that arose from a shift between OAU-led mediation and UN-led peacekeeping. This coordination gap, which was part of the politics that led to an inadequate force being sent to implement Arusha, emerges as a critical flaw in the overall international effort.

These two issues—the weakness of international institutions, and the paucity of coordination between them—emerge as major themes in the overall dynamic of peacemaking in Rwanda.

Notes

1. *Report of Meeting Between H.E. Dr. Salim Ahmed Salim, Secretary-General, and Mr. James Jonah, Under-Secretary-General for Political Affairs,* OAU Headquarters, Addis Ababa, 25 May 1993.

2. Mpungwe, author interview.

3. Much of the data presented in this section is contained in chapters 3 and 4 of Adelman and Suhrke with Jones, *Study II of the Joint Evaluation.* Research on UNAMIR during the Joint Evaluation was undertaken by the author, Astri Suhrke, Howard Adelman, and Turid Lægreid. During this process, the author either conducted or coconducted author interviews with Kofi Annan, Under-Secretary-General for Peacekeeping Operations; General Maurice Baril, Chief Military Adviser to the Secretary-General, DPKO; Hedi Annabi, Director, Africa Division, DPKO; Elizabeth Lindermeyer, Principal Officer, Africa Division, DPKO; Margaret Carey, Peacekeeping Affairs Officer, Africa Division, DPKO (hereafter, DPKO interviews); and with members of the UK, U.S., Canadian, and Belgian missions to the United Nations. The section on Operation Turquoise also draws on documents supplied to the Joint Evaluation by the French government, as well as primary and secondary sources referenced in the text.

4. UN Department of Political Affairs, "Report of the Reconnaissance Mission" (New York: United Nations, March 1993): 4–6.

5. DPKO interviews.

6. U.S. Embassy and Canadian High Commission, confidential author interviews, Dar-es-Salaam, December 1993.

7. DPKO interviews.

8. Security Council resolution establishing UNAMIR for a six-month period and approving the integration of UNOMUR into UNAMIR. UN Doc. S/Res/872, 5 October 1993.

9. See *The United Nations and Rwanda, 1993–1996, with an Introduction by Boutros Boutros-Ghali* (New York: Department of Public Information, United Nations), 1996, 23; see also Des Forges, *Leave None to Tell the Story,* 132.

10. UNAMIR, "Force Commander's Directive No. 01: Rules of Engagement" (October 1993): 1.

11. UNAMIR, "Force Commander's Directive," 1.

12. Confidential author interviews: Diplomatic mission, Permanent Member of the Security Council, official in charge of UN budgetary issues, New York, June 1995.

13. UN Doc., A/RES/48/248, 5 April 1994.

14. UN Doc. UNAMIR/IC/08, 14 December 1993.

15. *The United Nations and Rwanda, 1993–1996,* 28.

16. For details about the process by which UNAMIR was supplied and equipped, see Adelman and Suhrke with Jones, *Study II of the Joint Evaluation.* See also Turid Lægrid, "U.N. Peacekeeping in Rwanda," in Adelman and Suhrke, *The Path of a Genocide,* 231–252.

17. Confidential document, given to the Joint Evaluation team by a senior officer in UNAMIR, New York, June 1995.

18. This section based in part on unofficial author interviews with the following: Laurie Shesteck, First Secretary, U.S. Permanent Mission to the UN, New York, 27 June 1995; Patricia Holland, First Secretary, UK Permanent Mission to the UN, 27 June 1995; and Eli Jensvik, First Secretary, Norwegian Permanent Mission to the UN, 21 June 1995; officials of the Belgian Permanent Mission to the UN, and the French embassy to the United States; as well as the DPKO interviews referenced above.

19. For an interesting account of U.S. views about UN peacekeeping operations, in particular with respect to Rwanda, see Michael Barnett, "The Politics of Indifference: The Professionalization of Peacekeeping and the Toleration of Genocide," unpublished paper, December 1995.

20. J. Matthew Vaccaro, "The Politics of Genocide: Peacekeeping and Disaster Relief in Rwanda," in William S. Durch (ed.), *UN Peacekeeping, American Politics, and the Uncivil Wars of the 1990s.* 1st ed. (New York: St. Martin's Press, 1996), 374.

21. French Embassy Official, confidential author interview, Washington, DC, June 1995.

22. For details on the workload of DPKO at the time, see Adelman and Suhrke with Jones, *Study II of the Joint Evaluation,* 42.

23. Vaccaro, "The Politics of Genocide," 379.

24. See Kakwenzire and Kamukama, "Development and Consolidation."

25. See Prunier, *The Rwanda Crisis;* and Bihozigara et al., "Analyses de la situation rwandaise," in Guichaoua (ed.), *Les crises politiques.*

26. For example, on 29 November 1993 Canadian diplomats sent the following message to Ottawa: "Country is tense as political actors maneuver to keep or gain advantage among three shifting corners of power: President and his MRND party, RPF, and opposition parties (several of whose members are cabinet ministers). Within each corner, there are divisions and intrigue which contribute to general sense of unease over likelihood that Arusha Accords can be fully implemented and peace maintained." Canadian High Commission, Dar-es-Salaam, Cable, 29 November 1993.

27. Vatican official, author interview, Rome, April 1995.

28. Philip Gourevitch, "The Genocide Fax," *The New Yorker* 74, 11 (5 November 1998): 42.

29. Mazimpaka, author interview.

30. Des Forges, *Leave None to Tell the Story*, 173.

31. Quoted in ibid., 165.

32. U.S. Department of State, confidential author interview, Washington, DC, December 1995. This was confirmed in separate interviews by Astri Suhrke and Howard Adelman at the U.S. Central Intelligence Agency.

33. Ingvar Carrlson et al., *Report of the Independent Inquiry.*

34. Author interviews, Dar-es-Salaam, with U.S., Canadian, and French diplomats involved in Arusha, December 1993.

35. See Adelman and Suhrke with Jones, *Study II of the Joint Evaluation.*

36. UN cable from the UN Security Coordinator to the Designated Security Official, March 1993; the cable cites the stabilizing situation and downgrades the security conditions to the second-lowest possible level.

37. Jones and Suhrke, "Failure to Act."

38. Confidential author interview, U.S. Department of State, June 1995.

39. *The United Nations and Rwanda, 1993–1996,* 24.

40. This chronology compiled from reporting by the U.S. and Canadian missions in Dar-es-Salaam; confidential documents supplied to the author, December 1995.

41. Canadian High Commission Cable, Dar-es-Salaam, 23 April 1994.

42. For details on the provisional government, see Prunier, *The Rwanda Crisis,* 232–233.

43. For details on this episode, see esp. Astri Suhrke, "Facing Genocide: The Record of the Belgian Battalion in Rwanda," *Security Dialogue* 29, 1 (1998): 37–47. On the circumstances of the prime minister's murder, U.S. Department of State officials, confidential author interview with Astri Suhrke, Washington, DC, June 1995.

44. Suhrke, "Facing Genocide."

45. Confidential author interview, Kigali, June 1996.

46. Letter from the Belgian Permanent Representative to the United Nations to the UN Secretary-General, New York, 13 April 1994.

47. The decision to draw down was never fully implemented. Only 270 officials were supposed to remain in Rwanda; in fact, more than 450 stayed. Adelman and Suhrke with Jones, *Study II of the Joint Evaluation,* chap. 5.

48. Ibid.

49. Official of the Belgian Permanent Mission to the United Nations, confidential author interview, New York, June 1995.

50. Adelman and Suhrke with Jones, *Study II of the Joint Evaluation,* chap. 5; see also Barnett, "The Politics of Indifference." This point is also made by the *Independent Report on Rwanda.*

51. Confidential author interview, United Nations, New York, June 1995.

52. Humanitarian officials stationed in Kigali during the genocide stated that UNAMIR forces on a number of occasions engaged FAR snipers and

other troops, in contravention of orders. Quite apart from such attacks, the physical protection of such sites as the Hotel Milles Colines, Amohoro Stadium, and others saved the lives of the thousands of Kigali citizens who took refuge there. Confidential author interviews, Kigali, July 1996.

53. See esp. Adelman and Suhrke with Jones, *Study II of the Joint Evaluation,* chaps. 5 and 6; Vaccaro, "The Politics of Genocide"; Prunier, *The Rwanda Crisis.*

54. Barnett, "The Politics of Indifference."

55. Adelman and Suhrke with Jones, *Study II of the Joint Evaluation,* 49.

56. U.S. Department of State, confidential author interviews, June 1995; also, notes, U.S. Department of State, Astri Suhrke interviews, Washington, DC, June and July 1995. One U.S. Department of Defense official put it bluntly: "We weren't going to put any damn niggers in our APCs."

57. Adelman and Suhrke with Jones, *Study II of the Joint Evaluation,* chap. 5.

58. Government of France, *Terms of Reference, Opération Turquoise* (Paris, 1994).

59. Again, see Vaccaro, "The Politics of Genocide," Prunier, *The Rwanda Crisis,* and Adelman and Suhrke with Jones, *Study II of the Joint Evaluation,* chaps. 5 and 6.

60. *The United Nations and Rwanda, 1993–1996,* 53.

61. Vaccaro is particularly clear on this point; see "The Politics of Genocide," 385.

62. Ibid.

63. Prunier, *The Rwanda Crisis,* chap. 8; also, discussions with the author; and Gérard Prunier, U.S. Committee for Refugees, presentation for the Workshop for Study II of the Joint Evaluation, Washington, DC, December 1995.

64. For details on the reaction by humanitarian agencies to Operation Turquoise, see Jones, *NGOs in Complex Emergencies: The Case of Rwanda.*

65. See esp. Xavier Verschave, *Complicité de génocide? La politique de la France au Rwanda* (Paris: La Découverte, 1994).

66. Discussions with the author; also, Prunier, U.S. Committee for Refugees.

67. For details, see John Borton, Alistair Hallam, and Emery Brusset, "Humanitarian Aid and Effects," *Study III of the Joint Evaluation International Response to Conflict and Genocide: Lessons from the Rwanda Experience* (Copenhagen: DANIDA, 1996).

68. Prunier, *The Rwanda Crisis,* chap. 8; also, Prunier, U.S. Committee for Refugees.

69. Interviews with RPF officials, Kigali, June 1996.

70. Vaccaro, "The Politics of Genocide," 388.

71. As this book was being completed in April 2001, fighting was continuing in what was by then known as the Democratic Republic of Congo (formerly Zaire), notwithstanding a peace agreement between external parties to the conflict and the decision to deploy a UN force to observe its implementation.

72. Discussions with the author; Prunier, U.S. Committee for Refugees.

73. For a debate on the prospects for reinforcing UNAMIR, see Alan J. Kuperman, "Rwanda in Retrospect," *Foreign Affairs* 79, 1 (January/February 2000): 94–118. Also the response: Alison L. des Forges, "Shame: Rationalizing Western Apathy on Rwanda," *Foreign Affairs* 79, 3 (May/June 2000): 141–144.

74. Carnegie Commission on Preventing Deadly Conflict, *Preventing Deadly Conflict: Final Report* (Washington, DC: Carnegie Commission on Preventing Deadly Conflict, 1997).

75. DPKO officials actually commented to this effect, i.e., most peacekeeping operations were in fact little more than a bluff, given that few of them had any capacity to respond to serious breaches of peace agreements. DPKO interviews.

6
Genocide, Crisis, and the Renewal of War: The Consequences of Failure

Against the determination of the CDR to resist a negotiated settlement, the failures of coordinated strategy between mediation and implementation, and the absence of political will on the part of Western powers, the peace process in Rwanda was no match for the massive violence of the *génocidaires.* The failure to prevent or halt the escalation of violence in Rwanda could not have been more complete.

The scale and intensity of human suffering in Rwanda during the three bloody months of genocide are shocking. The Introduction to this book gave some Western reference points to illustrate the enormity of the death toll, and it is impossible to overstate the scale of the killing. But simple comparisons, bald figures, convey only part of the horror. Stalin's famous aphorism—that one death is a tragedy and a million deaths a statistic—does not hold in the case of Rwanda.

What is most striking in listening to survivors' accounts is the sense of totality. As one survivor expressed: "You cannot imagine the whole of the killing. You look up after a terror, and not just one person is killed, not just one brother or one parent; everybody is killed. There is nothing there. Everything is killed."[1] In this context, the concept of survival becomes suspect. To say that one "survived" the genocide is to say only that one was not physically slaughtered. Most who escaped with their lives lost entire families; often they had endured the torture of hiding out on rooftops or in sealed rooms while gangs of militia members tortured and killed their family members. Others were forced to maim and kill their own brothers, sisters, and children before being attacked by machete and left for dead. It is difficult to imagine what it means to "survive" such an encounter.

When "everything is killed," peace and harmony are distant prospects at best. Modern Cambodia, fully twenty years after its own genocide, continues to be plagued by the long shadow of the murderous Khmer Rouge.[2] There is every reason to expect that the shadow of the CDR will darken Rwanda for at least a generation.

Clearly, the human suffering of the genocide was the overwhelming consequence of the failure to contain the escalation of the Rwandan war, overshadowing all other consequences. Yet other consequences were significant. First among them, in chronological terms, was the humanitarian crisis produced by the genocide, wherein more than half of the Rwandan population was displaced from their homes. This crisis generated an overwhelming response from the international relief system and the wider international community. Literally hundreds of relief organizations flooded into Rwanda to respond to some portion of the misery. No fewer than eight nations sent military contingents to assist the relief process. The United Nations provided the reinforcements to UNAMIR that had not been forthcoming during the genocide itself. In the first five months of the response, the international community spent more than $1.2 billion dollars responding to the humanitarian aftermath of the genocide. The fact that the response to the aftermath dwarfed in scale and commitment the response to the actual genocide was an irony not lost on Rwandans.

Second, as quickly became clear, the humanitarian aftermath of the 1994 genocide contained within it the seeds of renewed conflict. The enormous international energy that characterized response to the humanitarian crisis was not matched by similar energy with respect to preventive efforts to halt the renewal of conflict. Instead, the international community engaged in what Susan Woodward has called "humanitarian containment."[3] The result was continued instability and insecurity in Rwanda. This insecurity was in turn the direct cause of yet another round of violent conflict: the civil and regional war for control of Zaire and the subregion starting in 1996.

Humanitarian Crisis and Response

Even those who were not killed during the genocide suffered.[4] Fully half of all surviving Rwandans were displaced from their homes by the war and genocide, many of them repeatedly. At the end of the war, rough figures suggested 2.2 million refugees in Tanzania, Burundi, and Zaire, with an additional 1.7 million internally displaced persons scattered throughout southern and southwestern Rwanda.[5] The international aid response to the crisis has been denigrated ever since it was mounted. In fact, however, the humanitarian effort was wide-ranging, compassionate, in parts sophisticated, in moments courageous, yet deeply flawed and ultimately part of the problem (primarily because of the continued failings of political response by the Security Council).

The humanitarian response preceded the launch of the genocide. International and local aid agencies, present in Rwanda for development purposes, began to respond to humanitarian needs during the later part of the civil war. The war produced thousands of internally displaced persons in its early days, especially in the north where RPF attacks on Rwandan territory disrupted economic and civic activity, especially in 1992. By early 1993, this number had grown to 400,000, significant for a country of less than 8 million people.[6]

The February 1993 offensive caused the number of internally displaced persons to swell, reaching 900,000 by the end of the offensive.[7] Although many returned to their homes following the implementation of the Kinihira cease-fire in March 1993, emergency relief continued in large quantities. The October coup in Burundi sent roughly 150,000 refugees into southwestern Rwanda, adding to the relief problem. However, these numbers were dwarfed by the humanitarian crisis that followed.

When the genocide broke out, a handful of international NGO staff remained in Rwanda despite extraordinary risks. The International Committee of the Red Cross (ICRC), supported by a few Médecins sans Frontières staff doctors, continued to provide emergency medical treatment in three locations in downtown Kigali; a senior ICRC official estimated that 1,000 Rwandans were saved by their presence.[8] Furthermore, the United Nations, having withdrawn all its staff in the first days of genocide, sent a handful of consultants back into Kigali to distribute aid that was being flown into Kigali airport by the Canadian armed forces. This UN Advance Humanitarian Assistance Team (UNAHAT) distributed several planeloads of food to the population of Kigali, sometimes with UNAMIR protection, sometimes relying on their negotiation skills to navigate the dozens of roadblocks now established around Kigali, and always at considerable personal risk.[9] The courage of the NGO and UN staff who remained in Kigali during this period has gone largely unmentioned but was unparalleled in the entire international response to Rwanda.

As the war advanced, large-scale humanitarian operations began in the RPF-occupied northwest. These operations were mounted from southern Uganda and involved at least thirty different international NGOs and UN aid agencies.[10] As the RPF swept south and west, what seemed at the time like a massive wave of people fled the fighting. On 29 April, 170,000 crossed into Tanzania in a single day.[11] UNHCR called it the largest-ever movement of refugees; it was shortly to be dwarfed. In the meantime, the international aid community began mounting a second major response in western Tanzania. Apart from the sheer scale of the need, the logistical problems of getting adequate relief supplies across Tanzania's execrable roads proved challenging.

In June, the launch of Operation Turquoise into southwestern Rwanda meant that yet another territory opened up for humanitarian access. Aid agencies launched a third major humanitarian operation, this time from Burundi, to respond to the needs of hundreds of thousands of Rwandans in the southwest who had been displaced by the fighting. The establishment of the so-called Humanitarian Safe Zone, known as Zone Turquoise, allowed aid agencies to move about more or less freely.

By June the humanitarian response was already multifaceted and operating on an enormous scale. But when the RPF defeated the FAR in Ruhengiri, on Rwanda's western border with Zaire, the humanitarian floodgates were opened. On 14–15 July, 1.2 million refugees poured across the border into the Goma region of Zaire in just under twenty-four hours. Humanitarian agencies were left scrambling to respond when the refugees arrived.[12]

There is some evidence to suggest that the movement of refugees into Zaire was only partially a spontaneous response to flee the fighting.[13] An additional factor was that the *génocidaires* deliberately moved displaced populations along with them as they retreated westward toward the Zaire border. The purpose of this tactic was to create a human shield between their forces and those of the advancing RPF. When the refugees crossed into Zaire, the tactic paid off: the mass of people crowding Goma impeded an initial cross-border raid by the RPF designed to capture the remaining forces of the *génocidaires*.

The response to the Goma outflux was the largest, most complex humanitarian operation ever mounted. At its peak, it would involve fifteen UN agencies, more than 250 international NGOs, and several national missions from major aid-giving countries. It also involved military missions from no less than seven countries: the United States, Canada, Ireland, Japan, Germany, Britain, and Israel. These missions were sent to Goma not for security or military purposes, however, but to assist in the enormous logistical effort of mounting a humanitarian response to more than 1.5 million people.

As estimated by a multidonor evaluation of the emergency effort, fast response in Goma saved as many as 50,000 lives when a cholera epidemic struck the refugees camps around Goma.[14] However, the same evaluation discovered that lapses in coordination also cost lives and wasted resources, as duplication of effort, inappropriate responses, and other forms of inefficiency weakened the overall effort. The United Nations had a de facto lead agency in Goma, the UNHCR, but its authority extended primarily to those NGOs that relied on the United Nations for funding or that routinely worked with the United Nations in crisis situations. Dozens of NGOs operated in Goma on the basis of private funding and were not responsive to UN concerns or direction.

The cost of mounting this operation would reach $1.2 billion by December 1994. This figure does not include the costs of what was called, with no trace of irony, Operation Support Hope, a large-scale U.S. military-humanitarian operation that airlifted large quantities of heavy equipment, personnel, and troops to support the relief effort in Goma. Over the following two years, maintaining this massive presence would cost the aid community a total of $2.5 billion.[15]

Indeed, looking at the cost figures drives home the point that the relief response to the humanitarian crisis was by far and away the largest element of the overall international presence in Rwanda. The cost of the relief effort can be compared to those of prior international roles: roughly $3 million for the Arusha process,[16] and $25 million for UNAMIR prior to the genocide. In other words, money spent on responding to the humanitarian consequences of the genocide exceeded by ninety times money spent on efforts to resolve the Rwandan civil war.

The sum of money spent can be looked at from another angle, which highlights its relative scale: the cost of relief in the eight months from April to December ($1.2 billion) exceeded by 20 percent the prewar annual gross national product of Rwanda, spent on roughly one-quarter of the prewar population.[17] It is hard to imagine that a set of outside actors could deploy such resources without having a profound impact on the target society. And, indeed, humanitarian relief did affect an important Rwandan dynamic, one that should have been addressed by political and security actors: the ability of the genocide forces to recuperate and resuscitate, inside Zaire, and thereby to pose a continuing threat to Rwanda.

Political Response

Chapter 5 has already made the point that the most important form of potential international response to the genocide—that is, a strong intervention to halt the killings—was not forthcoming. The unwillingness to send a significant military mission to Rwanda to thwart the *génocidiares* continued to weaken the international response.

When the refugees crossed into Goma, a good portion of the FAR crossed with them. Indeed, as the RPF had pursued the FAR across Rwanda in its five-pronged attack, the FAR surrounded themselves with an ever-growing human shield; this human shield was pushed across the border when the FAR abandoned Ruhengiri. It should be recalled that they were crossing into territory controlled by a government, Mobutu's Zaire, that had supported them both politically and militarily. The FAR was allowed to cross into Zaire unchallenged, in many cases with weapons and vehicles intact. The military leadership of the FAR, as well as senior members of the regime, created their own camp in Lac Vert, just south of Goma; thousands of soldiers encamped nearby. Some soldiers, however, and thousands of militia members, as well as much of the political and community leadership of Rwanda, mixed in with the wider refugee population.

Additional elements of the FAR were still at large—and armed, although inactive—in Zone Turquoise. When Operation Turquoise was withdrawn at the end of August, coinciding with the arrival of UNAMIR II, the rest of the FAR, the Presidential Guard, and the ancien régime crossed into Bukavu, Zaire, roughly 100 kilometers south of Goma, along with a further outflux of refugees. It was, of course, impossible for anyone to distinguish noncombatant refugees from militia members, and even soldiers could easily blend into the refugee population simply by shedding their uniforms. Thus, by the fall of 1994 the international community was facing the growing realization that the regime responsible for the genocide had not been truly defeated, merely chased out of the country—some of them thanks to Operation Turquoise—and were now encamped on Rwanda's immediate border in a country run by a political ally.[18]

Concern over the situation eventually led to consideration in the Security Council of the innovative idea of sending a peacekeeping operation to the refugee camps. As early as mid-August, the UNHCR had suggested to the UN Secretary-General and to DPKO that the situation was beyond their scope as well as their mandate. DPKO began considering various alternatives. UNHCR, however, considered them to be somewhat unrealistic and therefore began on its own initiative to negotiate with the government of Zaire for internationally directed, Zairian-provided security for the camps. At the end of September, UNHCR took this proposal, which had been successfully negotiated, to the Secretary-General for his support.[19] The UNHCR was told by the Secretary-General to put the program on hold while DPKO explored more robust options.[20]

An 18 November DPKO report made clear that the ideal goal was the separation of soldiers from refugees but that this was a difficult goal to achieve.[21] DPKO laid out a series of options to the Security Council, the most ambitious of which was designed to reach the ideal goal.[22]

Option A was to send a relatively large number of troops under Chapter VII to separate the soldiers from the refugees and, in so doing, disarm them. The proposal was designed to meet the ideal goal; significantly, its purpose was to enhance the physical protection of refugees by removing the sources of the threat. The report estimated that 7,000 well-armed troops would be required to fulfill the mission, with 4,000 devoted to the North Kivu region (Goma) and 3,000 for South Kivu (Bukavu). According to DPKO sources, the department knew full well that this option was a nonstarter, that the Security Council would never consider a Chapter VII humanitarian operation so soon after the disasters in Somalia. They were right: Option A was dismissed in the Security Council as a "fantasy."[23]

Option B was considerably more moderate, involving 3,000–5,000 troops under Chapter VI in what came to be dubbed the "salami approach." The idea was to have a smaller number of troops secure a small slice of the camps and "clean" it, that is, disarm the soldiers and leave behind a protection structure to ensure the safety of refugees after the departure of the troops. It was argued that the cleaning process would require 3,000 troops for North Kivu only,

5,000 for both North and South Kivu. This option was the preferred option of the UN Secretary-General. It was based on the perception that a Chapter VI operation was easier to handle (i.e., make it past the Security Council) than a Chapter VII option and that the solution it invoked required only the formal agreement of Zaire, not its operational involvement. It was this option that received further exploration, although it was eventually rejected.

DPKO also floated Option C, a truly innovative alternative: use a private-sector security company to provide protection. DPKO received an informal proposal from an experienced British company in which the firm offered to provide training and logistical support to Zairian troops. The perceived attraction was that Option C would avoid the political difficulty that had scuppered the UNAMIR option: countries unwilling to face the political repercussions of body bags returning from an operation in Zaire that their populations little understood. The proposal did receive some support in the Security Council, including one member of the Permanent Five, as a practical solution to a difficult situation.[24] Other states, however, rejected it because of high costs and on the basis of principle. Some states argued that using a private security company to fulfill an international public responsibility was tantamount to shirking that responsibility. Those who supported Option C responded that principle was all well and good if one were willing to act upon it; given that opponents were unwilling to provide troops to a UN force, it did seem reasonable to pursue such practical solutions.[25] Nevertheless, the nay-sayers won the day.

On 30 November, the UN Security Council asked DPKO to continue its investigation of options. Discussions in the Security Council and in the corridors clearly favored Option B among the three being offered. The United States, in discussions with DPKO, expressed its support in principle for Option B and noted that on the basis of its own assessment the force should have as its backbone one strong, well-equipped battalion. When DPKO asked if the United States was offering to supply such a battalion, it received a curt "no" in response, as well as a list of countries that the United States felt were capable and might be willing to supply the battalion.[26] However, at the same time, the Security Council requested that DPKO look further into the question of supporting Zaire's troops in providing protection. Clearly, the Security Council was sensing the difficulties of actually establishing a peacekeeping force for the camps—and wanted to keep its options open.[27]

A joint DPKO/UNHCR mission was sent to Rwanda to assess the appropriateness of the various suggestions to date, in particular Option B, the "salami approach." The mission found that the task was in fact more difficult than anticipated and would require more troops (between 5,000 and 7,000 rather than the 3,000–5,000 initially suggested). Simultaneously, DPKO began the process of approaching states for troop contributions. Of the sixty states approached to contribute troops, only one gave a positive response, and it did not translate into a "strong" battalion. Option B was dead before it started.

The unwillingness of potential troop-contributing nations to go into Zaire was a function of several factors, some similar to those that had constrained the deployment of UNAMIR. First, Zaire was perceived as a quagmire into which entry would be difficult and exit both expensive and potentially bloody. Second, nobody's interests were at play, with the possible exception of France, which had already been engaged through Operation Turquoise and was not about to reenter the region. Finally, there was no major power backing the operation. The conventional wisdom in New York is that to get a peacekeeping force approved one needs a major power—essentially, one of the Permanent Five—to back the plan; this ingredient was absent. Although the Security Council in its deliberations had determined the presence of former army and militia members in the camps as a threat to international peace and security, members were unwilling to act to neutralize the threat these people posed both to the refugees and aid workers in Goma and, more important, to the long-term security and stability of the region.

With no peacekeeping option in the offing, the DPKO followed up on the second part of the Security Council's request: explore the option of providing support to the Zairian army in protecting the camps. DPKO proposed an International Police/Military Observer Group, which would marry Zairian troops with an international military/police supervisory, training, and observation function. However, this option quickly ran into opposition from Zaire itself on the grounds of sovereignty. Although Zaire was willing to allow the Security Council to send peacekeeping troops into Zaire, it was unwilling to have its own troops serve under other nations' military authority.

Finally, in January 1995 the UN Secretary-General acknowledged that the efforts to find a suitable option had failed and asked the UNHCR to revive the proposal it first explored in September 1994. This proposal—which became the Zairian Camp Security Operation

(ZCSO)—was ultimately deployed in February 1995, a full six months after originally being proposed by the UNHCR. The ZCSO comprised the Zairian Camp Security Contingent (ZCSC) staffed by a unit of the Zairian Presidential Guard, flown into the region from Kinshasa at UN expense and reporting to the Civilian Liaison Unit (largely staffed by Dutch police officers on loan). The operation was civilian in structure despite the presence of Zairian soldiers in the ZCSC.[28]

Notwithstanding the fact that protection was being provided by soldiers under the direct command of the ancien régime's closest ally, many in the humanitarian community reported improvement in what was a rapidly deteriorating situation.[29] Later reports question the role of the ZCSC. In any event, the role of the ZCSC was not to tackle the underlying security threat posed by the presence of the ancien régime on the Rwandan border.[30] The ZCSC was an exercise in camp control, not conflict management.[31]

Indeed, despite this massive international response to the humanitarian crisis, there was no serious effort at conflict management. The immediate consequence was a renewal of hostilities on the Rwanda-Zaire border, as well as enormously heightened instability in a fractured region. Already by early 1995, it was clear that if the situation were left unresolved, it would lead to renewed warfare in eastern Zaire and Rwanda.[32]

Renewing the Cycle of Conflict: Toward Zaire

Another ominous sign was equally clear.[33] The presence of a massive humanitarian aid effort in the absence of a security response would contribute to the process of recycling the Rwandan conflict.[34] Indeed, from the outset the ancien régime had used the aid flows into Goma to its political advantage, and to the detriment of refugees, and had begun reestablishing its fight to reclaim power in Rwanda.

Both the FAR (along with the associated militias) and the deposed regime had crossed into Zaire essentially intact, albeit in disarray. The unwillingness of the UN Security Council and member states to field a peacekeeping operation to the camps allowed enough space to regroup and reassert political control over the refugee population. The mechanisms they used included taking political control of the relief process in the camps, continuing the campaign of rhetoric and intimidation to stop the population from returning to Rwanda (despite various exhortations to do so), and forging alliances with local actors who could assist them politically and militarily.[35]

The purpose of controlling the refugee population was threefold: (1) the refugees were a form of political base for the deposed regime; (2) the refugees attracted massive aid flows, from which taxes could be extracted; and (3) the mounting of a major aid operation in eastern Zaire, which had to operate with the consent of Zairian authorities, created a new alliance of interest between the ancien régime and its Zairian hosts, at both the local and national levels.

The ability of the deposed regime to control the relief process in eastern Zaire, and through it to assert political control and extract taxes, was in part the function of aid agencies' efforts to follow "best practices" and "lessons learned" from prior emergencies. One of the most important lessons learned, especially in dealing with the Somali refugee population in Kenya, was that aid was most efficiently (and least disruptively) distributed when it was channeled through existing local political structures.[36] Rather than attempt to establish their own structures of authority in a camp, and thereby displace local authority and potentially undermine longer-term social and political processes of rehabilitation and development, aid agencies learned to rely on local leadership. When 1.2 million refugees crossed into Goma in a single day, working through existing leadership structures seemed the logical choice. Moreover, those leadership structures rapidly asserted their authority among the refugee population. Thus, partially out of sheer need, partly on the basis of best practices, aid agencies in Goma and the surrounding regions used local and regional governance structures of Rwanda, now displaced into Zaire, as the channel for distribution and designation of relief supplies in the camps.[37] The local and regional structures of Rwanda, however, had been largely controlled by the deposed regime, comprising *akazu* members and appointees, and were instrumental in the implementation of the genocide. Thus, inadvertently, aid flows into eastern Zaire helped reconstitute the deposed regime by giving it political credit and partial control over aid flows, which, it will be recalled, were on the order of Rwanda's gross national product.

As the cholera crisis passed and the situation in eastern Zaire stabilized somewhat, several aid agencies began to pay more attention to the underlying political situation of the camps. Some tried to assert their own control over the aid process. When they did so, they were attacked by the FAR and militias. CARE, in attempting to wrest control away from the ancien régime, was forced out of the Katale camps almost at gunpoint; thirty-five local CARE employees were murdered.[38] Reacting to the perversion of humanitarian relief, several agencies—including CARE, OXFAM, and thirteen others—withdrew from the Katale camp. However, other NGOs immediately replaced them. Moreover, those agencies that had withdrawn continued to support the relief pipeline.[39]

Aid agencies thus faced a dilemma. If the UN Security Council and member states were unwilling to deploy a peacekeeping operation to eastern Zaire, then the ancien régime would continue to pervert the aid process and intimidate and harass refugees who would challenge their rule in the camps. Thus, humanitarian assistance was the handmaiden to the resuscitation of the genocide movement. Yet full withdrawal of the aid presence would mean that tens of thousands of legitimate refugees would perish. By late fall 1994 and certainly by 1995, the aid agencies were aware that they were feeding *génocidaires* and refueling a genocide movement, but there was little choice other than to remain in place.[40]

The aid agencies have been roundly criticized for this position. However, if one looks at the structure of the situation, is seems clear that there was no real choice, as there never is in a true dilemma. The source of the dilemma, of course, was primarily the willingness of the ancien régime to use the refugee population as buffer, resource base, and pawn. Secondarily, the dilemma stemmed from the unwillingness of the UN Security Council and member states to act on the real security threat posed by the ancien régime.

By mid-1995 the FAR had regrouped, primarily in the Mugunga camp south of Goma, and began a series of small, provocative attacks in western Rwanda. These created tension and instability in western and southwestern Rwanda, which impeded the new regime's efforts to establish control and legitimacy inside the ravaged country. The new regime, dominated and controlled by the RPF (although containing some non-RPF members), faced the compound challenges of rebuilding the Rwandan state, reconstructing the Rwandan economy, and trying to establish a degree of legitimate authority over the population at large. The FAR continued its attacks on Rwanda throughout 1995 and into 1996, further destabilizing eastern Zaire as well as western Rwanda.

Reports from humanitarian agencies on the situation in eastern Zaire reached the UN Secretariat but received minimal response. One report called for a UN political presence to mitigate and contain the conflict before it spread, but this also was put aside in New York.[41] Once again, in the absence of a serious political or military response at the international level, and despite the ongoing need for massive humanitarian response, conflict was allowed to escalate.

Accordingly, the increasing frustration with the situation in eastern Zaire, mounting insecurity in western Rwanda, and continuing unwillingness of international actors to respond led to a growing belief in the military option. Colonel Frank Mugambage, cabinet director in the president's office and a key RPF figure in government, argued in June 1996 that the RPF saw the solution in eastern Zaire as the relatively simple task of "taking the war to Goma."[42] The purpose of such a war was purportedly to break the ancien régime's control over the refugee population and, ideally, to disperse that population away from the Rwandan border. As Mugambage put it at the time, if the leadership were "decapitated," then the refugees could be pushed west into Zaire and dispersed to the extent that they would no longer pose a threat to Rwanda.

In the two years since the FAR had fled into Zaire, the regional political situation had changed in a way that increased the RPF's capacity to wage war in eastern Zaire. Developments in the fractious and dangerous politics of neighboring Burundi brought to power a regime that also faced rebel opponents supported from eastern Zaire.[43] And in the fall of 1996, a nebulous group called the Alliance of Democratic Forces for the Liberation of Congo-Zaire (ADFL) emerged as the constellation of rebel forces involved in the fighting in eastern Zaire, under the leadership of Laurent Kabila, a longtime Zairian revolutionary with dubious credentials.[44]

An alliance of interest led in the early fall of 1996 to a Rwandan incursion into eastern Zaire, with passage through northwestern Burundi. By September and October 1996, two fronts had opened up in eastern Zaire. In North Kivu, the local Mai-Mai forces—temporarily allied with the RPF against their Zairian opponents—attacked refugee camps and Hutu populations. Regional engagement in the war widened. First, the RPF opened a new front near Goma. Officially, the GoR denied having troops inside Zaire. It was, however, an open secret that "our troops" were winning victories inside Zaire. The fact that the RPF was behind this offensive was subsequently acknowledged by Paul Kagame, Rwanda's minister of defense.[45] At the same time, it is widely believed that Ugandan troops crossed into Zaire, not so much to open another front as to close off an escape route for the erstwhile FAR.[46]

By January 1997, what once seemed like a war for control of the Rwanda-Zaire border area had become a war for the Kivu region and then a war for the whole of Zaire.[47] On 15 March, after some days of heavy fighting, the most important city in central Zaire, Kisangani, fell to the ADFL/RPF. At this stage, the Angolan government began to provide support, including air transport, to the rebels. This support allowed the ADFL to rapidly cross the western half of Zaire. Incredibly, a mere nine weeks after the fall of Kisangani, the ADFL entered Kinshasa after a brief battle around the nearby airport. On 18 May, the ADFL took control of Kinshasa, Mobutu having fled Zaire two days earlier.

Quite apart from direct fighting between military combatants, this war had enormous civilian costs. As the former FAR retreated from the RPF/ADFL attack, refugees and local populations were used as human shields. At key points in the war, especially at Kisangani, refugees placed between warring parties were killed by the thousands. Moreover, although it has never been fully documented, it is evident that the RPF, along with the ADFL, conducted large-scale massacres of civilians in eastern Zaire, probably killing tens of thousands of civilians. One Rwandan official blatantly defended the killings, arguing that "we had to kill those criminals [the *génocidiares*], and if there were women and children in the way, we can't be naive; this is war."[48] Estimates of those killed during the fighting range from 50,000 to triple that number.[49] These killings were repeatedly denounced by human rights organizations but were met with silence from the international community.

International Response

As the fighting in Zaire spread during the fall of 1996, the United Nations and Western powers began a search for response options. In late October, UN officials began discussions with the government of Canada about the deployment of a Multinational Force (MNF) to eastern Zaire. On 9 November, the UN Security Council passed Resolution 1078, calling for governments to begin working toward an MNF, and on the same day the Canadian government agreed to lead it. On 13 November, the U.S. government expressed its commitment in principle to providing up to 5,000 troops to the MNF. In total, with contributions from France, Spain, and others, the proposed force was to comprise 10,000–15,000 troops.[50]

Notwithstanding some initial lack of clarity about the point, the Canadian government made clear to the United Nations that the military force was not being provided for the purpose of separating armed elements from refugees, as some had hoped. Rather, the MNF would seek to secure humanitarian operations, perhaps by providing secure corridors for the return of refugees to Rwanda.[51] Concerns about how such an operation would work on the ground caused the U.S. Department of Defense to scale back its proposed involvement. The purpose and mission of the MNF became entangled in debate: among those who wanted the MNF to undertake military action, those who wanted it only to secure humanitarian space, and those who argued that it could not secure humanitarian space without undertaking military action and was thus ill-advised.[52]

Any momentum behind the MNF stalled when, on 14 November, RPF-led forces attacked the eastern Zaire refugee camps, where the mass of refugees and the former FAR had congregated. This attack triggered a massive forced repatriation of refugees, with more than 500,000 crossing back into Rwanda during the next few days. On 19 November, the U.S. government further scaled back its proposed involvement, in what was taken by many to be the death knell for the mission. Some Rwanda analysts have argued that the potential deployment of the MNF had actually spurred Kigali into advancing the timetable of the attack on the Mugunga refugee camps in order to rob the MNF of a coherent agenda.[53] Evidence for such an interpretation is sketchy, however.

With the MNF's intended role now obviated by events on the ground, the governments that had contributed to it debated the options. War continued unchecked, and the humanitarian consequences continued to mount. In November and December, the RPF/ADFL's concentrated on consolidating its gains in Goma, even as fighting continued north of Goma. At this time, there were initial reports about RPF/ADFL massacres of refugees and other civilians; later international estimates (including by this author) would suggest that the RPF/ADFL had possibly killed as many as 80,000 refugees in eastern Zaire. Also at this time, aid workers began to express grave concern about the fate of the refugees from the South Kivu camps, arguing that as many as 200,000 refugees were unaccounted.[54] Humanitarian actors prevailed on the advance military contingents of the MNF to use their capacities to track the missing refugees. However, such options were rejected by the MNF commander, Brigadier-General

Maurice Baril of Canada (ironically, the same individual who had received General Dallaire's infamous 11 January cable from Rwanda).

Having failed to identify an appropriate role, the MNF advance force was withdrawn in early 1998; no MNF forces had been deployed on Zairian soil. The international community's largest military response to the Rwandan and regional conflict amounted to naught. The irony of having authorized the deployment of 15,000 soldiers, and then not being able to use them, two years (and $2.5 billion) after having failed to send 7,000 soldiers to do the job, was not lost on the sponsoring nations.[55] More horrific—while the MNF stood idle—refugees were suffering under appalling conditions while civilians were being slaughtered by the tens of thousands.

Conclusion

Tragically, humanitarian assistance in the *postgenocide* period was in fact one of the most significant dimensions of international engagement in the conflict. It doubtless saved tens of thousands of lives, and it was well intentioned. Still, its effects were not all salutary. In the political vacuum created by nonresponses to the underlying security situation, humanitarian assistance in fact transformed the structure of the conflict at a critical juncture. The delivery of international aid provided means and method to Rwanda's extremist political structure to reinforce its strength and reengage its opponents.

The idea that aid can have a conflict-transformation dimension has gained increasing currency in recent years.[56] The process of providing relief in conflict, it has been argued, produces a series of unintended consequences, of inescapable dilemmas from which no clean outcomes are available.[57] This has raised political and ethical questions about the viability and desirability of providing relief in conflict situations. Rwanda supports the unintended-consequences thesis; simultaneously, it shows that consequences arise because of failures in the political response. Specifically, Rwanda shows that the actual cause of unintended consequences is the security vacuum created by the unwillingness of the international community to tackle the political and security elements of the wider crisis in which humanitarian aid is given. It is also clear that the political and security responses to the postgenocide crisis in Rwanda were wholly insufficient in the face of events on the ground.

The human consequences of the postgenocide crisis did not rise to the level of suffering experienced during the genocide yet are extraordinary by any other standard. As many as 80,000 civilians were killed; hundreds of thousands of refugees were forced back into a country where their security was far from guaranteed; Africa's second-largest country was embroiled in war; and eastern Zaire became a battleground of regional competition. A small civil war became a genocide, and a genocide in a small country became a war in a huge region. The failures of peacemaking in Rwanda and the subregion could not have been more complete.

Notes

1. Survivor, name withheld, author interview, Butare, July 1996.

2. See, e.g., Philip Gourevitch, "Letter from Cambodia: Pol Pot's Children," *The New Yorker* 74, 23, (10 August 1998): 40.

3. Susan Woodward, *Balkan Tragedy: Chaos and Dissolution after the Cold War* (Washington, DC: Brookings Institution, 1995).

4. Many of the chronological facts presented below are taken from UN and CARE Rwanda reports (see below), and from author interviews with UN and NGO officials, some of them conducted during the course of a study commissioned by the Department of Humanitarian Affairs, which I cowrote with Sue Lautze and with inputs from Mark Duffield: *Strategic Humanitarian Coordination in the Great Lakes Region, 1996–1997: An Independent Study for the Inter-Agency Standing Committee* (New York: Office for the Coordination of Humanitarian Affairs, March 1998): inter alia from UN Department of Humanitarian Affairs (Yasushi Akashi, Martin Griffiths, Charles Petrie, David Shearer, Randolph Kent), UNHCR (Sergio Vieira de Mello, Pierce Gerety, Dennis McNamara, Jiddo Van Drunen, Imran Riza, Paul Stromberg, Fillipo Grande), UNDP (Omar Bakhet, Mizra Khan, Michel Kassa), UNICEF (Peter O'Brien, Peter McDermott), World Food Programme (David Bulman, Rigobert Oura, Jean Luc Siblot UN High Commissioner for Human Rights (Mary Robinson, Ian Martin), OXFAM (Nick Stockton, Anne Macintosh, Alexandre Guy Banville), SCF UK (Robert Ffolkes, Anne Martin), CONCERN (Nick Guttman, Clea O'Reilly), CARE (John Watson, Nancy Gordon, Jude Rand, Shawn Lowry, Ralph Hazelton, Rowland Roome), ICRC (Geoff Loane), and officials from Médecins-sans-frontières (MSF), the International Rescue Committee (IRC), the UN Food and Agriculture Organization (FAO), the World Health Organization (WHO), Christian Aid, and the European Community Humanitarian Office (ECHO).

5. See esp. Borton et al., "Humanitarian Aid and Effects," 35–46.

6. CARE Rwanda, *Internal Reports, 1992–1993*, Kigali, 1992–1993, and CARE Rwanda, *Internal Reports, 1992–1994*, Ottawa, 1992–1994. UN Rwanda Emergency Office (Goma) and UN Rwanda Emergency Office (Nairobi), Daily Reports, April-August 1994. From late 1995 until mid-1997, the author worked as a policy consultant for CARE Canada on its Great Lakes program, including researching and drafting *NGOs in Complex Emergencies: The Case of Rwanda*. In this capacity, the author was given complete access to CARE Canada's internal files for the 1990–1994 period. Because CARE Canada was the parent organization of CARE Rwanda, this included all internal reporting from CARE Rwanda during the civil war period. CARE Rwanda was the principal NGO contracted by UNHCR to manage refugee camps in eastern Zaire. During this consultancy, the author was also given access to the archived files of the UN Rwanda Emergency Office, housed in the offices of the UN Integrated Regional Information Network (IRIN) in Nairobi.

7. CARE Rwanda, Monthly Report, February 1993.

8. ICRC Regional Office for the Great Lakes, confidential author interview, Nairobi, August 1996.

9. Jerry McCarthy, formerly with UN Advance Humanitarian Assistance Team (UNAHAT), author interview, Nairobi, June 1996; and Gregory Alexander, also formerly with UNAHAT, author interview, Kigali, November 1997.

10. CARE Rwanda weekly reports; also, from May 1994 onwards, UN Integrated Regional Information Network (IRIN), Daily Reports, Nairobi/Goma.

11. Borton et al., "Humanitarian Aid and Effects," 31.

12. For details on the preplanning for refugee movements, and on the first days of response, see ibid., chap. 2, and Jones, *NGOs in Complex Emergencies: The Case of Rwanda*, sec. 4; also author interviews, CARE and UNHCR officials.

13. CARE Rwanda, Internal Reports, July 1994.

14. Borton et al., "Humanitarian Aid and Effects," 74.

15. Ibid., 111–118; see also Alistair Hallam, "ODA to Rwanda," *Background Note/Joint Evaluation* (London: Overseas Development Institute, 1995).

16. Author calculation based on a review of cables from the U.S. Department of State and the French foreign ministry, Washington, DC, May 1995.

17. For details on the gross national product of Rwanda before the civil war, see C. Newbury, "Rwanda."

18. Officials of the UN Department of Humanitarian Affairs, author interviews, New York, June 1995.

19. Soren Jessen-Petersen, Director, UNHCR Liaison Office, author interview, New York, June 1995.

20. Jessen-Petersen, author interview; notes from interviews by Kate Halvorsen, with UNHCR officials, Geneva, 1995; see also, *The United Nations and Rwanda, 1993–1996.*

21. United Nations DPKO, *Internal Report* (New York: United Nations, 18 November 1994).

22. The following based primarily on DPKO interviews (see Chapter 6). See also Romeo A. Dallaire, "The Changing Role of UN Peacekeeping Forces: The Relationship Between UN Peacekeepers and NGOs in Rwanda," in Jim Whitman and David Pocock (eds.), *After Rwanda: The Coordination of United Nations Humanitarian Assistance* (London: MacMillan Press, 1996), 205–218.

23. Confidential author interview, New York, June 1995.

24. Confidential author interview, New York, June 1995.

25. The "principled" view was given by a Scandinavian diplomat, the riposte by a UN Secretariat official. DPKO and Security Council missions to the UN, author interviews, New York, June 1995.

26. DPKO and Security Council missions to the UN, author interviews, New York, June 1995.

27. On decisionmaking during this period, see esp. Vaccaro, "The Politics of Genocide."

28. Government of Holland. "Report of the Zairian Camp Security Contingent." Dutch Police Contingent. Unofficial document. Goman, Zaire, March 1995.

29. CARE Canada, *Internal Reports,* January-June 1995. Also, UNHCR officials, confidential author interviews.

30. Norah Niland, Department of Humanitarian Affairs, author interview, New York, June 1995; Charles Petrie, former Deputy Head of the UN Rwanda Emergency Office (UNREO), author interview, New York, June 1995; Randolph Kent, former Head of UNREO, author interview, London, October 1996.

31. For further details, see Bruce Jones, "Refugee Camps in Zaire," *Background Report for Study II of the Joint Evaluation*; and Kate Halvorsen, "Refugee Camps in Zaire: Humanitarian Issues," *Report Prepared for Study II of the Joint Evaluation of Emergency Assistance in Rwanda* (Bergen: November 1995).

32. For an early version of this argument, see Bruce D. Jones, "'Intervention Without Borders': Humanitarian Intervention in Rwanda, 1990–1994," *Millennium: Journal of International Studies* 24, 2 (Summer 1995): 225–249.

33. Material for this chapter was published in Lautze and Jones with Duffield, *Strategic Humanitarian Coordination in the Great Lakes Region.* Additional material was published in Bruce D. Jones, "NGOs in Complex Emergencies: The Case of Rwanda," CARE Canada, Ottawa, October 1996.

34. For an early version of this argument, see Jones, "'Intervention Without Borders.'"

35. CARE Rwanda, camp officials, author interviews, Kigali and Nairobi, June 1996.

36. A 1993 UNHCR internal review of best practices was shared with the author. The document impressively traced the articulation of lessons from past operations, their translation into doctrine, their application in new operations, and again the new lessons learned. The document had been written during the Somali refugee crisis and articulated lessons about the importance of working through existing local structures in order to maximize communication with the local population. Also, author interviews, CARE officials, Ottawa, May 1996, and Nairobi, June 1996.

37. For more details, see Jones, "NGOs in Complex Emergencies."

38. CARE Canada officials, author interviews, Ottawa, December 1995; CARE Rwanda officials, author interviews, Kigali, June 1996; also internal CARE reports.

39. CARE International, *Internal Reports, Zaire*, August-November 1994. For more details, see Jones "NGOs in Complex Emergencies."

40. Officials from UN Department of Humanitarian Affairs, the UN High Commissioner for Refugees, CARE, Médecins sans Frontières, and OXFAM, author interviews.

41. United Nations, *Department of Humanitarian Affairs Mission Report* (Masisi, Zaire: United Nations, May 1996). See Lautze and Jones with Duffield, *Strategic Humanitarian Coordination in the Great Lakes Region.*

42. Colonel Frank Mugambage, Office of the Prime Minister, author interview, Kigali, July 1996.

43. See Johann Pottier, "The 'Self' in Self-Repatriation." As Pottier makes clear, there were long-standing links between the Tutsi population in eastern Zaire and the RPF.

44. In July 1996, the author received from local contacts a copy of a document being circulated in Nairobi and Kigali: Executive Committee of the Rwandaphone Zaireans Association, "Memorandum on the Tragedy of the Rwandaphone Zaireans with some Proposals and Recommendations" (Nairobi: June 1996). The document outlined the history of the "Banyamulenge" population (primarily Tutsis in eastern Zaire), i.e., the argument that the Kivu regions had historically been part of Rwanda and the need for the regions' governments to act to defend the Rwandaphone Zaireans.

45. During most of the Zairian offensive, the Rwandan government denied its active role in eastern Zaire while making clear its political support for the Banyamulenge. More recently, Vice President Paul Kagame has acknowledged the active military presence of the Rwandan army in the eastern Zaire campaign. See John Pomfret, "Rwandans Led Revolt in Congo," *Washington Post,* 9 July 1997: A01. Also see Mahmood Mamdani, "Why Rwanda Trumpeted Its Zaire Role," *Mail and Guardian,* 8 August 1997.

46. As early as June 1996, the Belgian newspaper *Le Soir* reported Ugandan People's Defence Forces (UPDF) activity in the North Kivu region. Cited in Pottier, "The 'Self' in Self Repatriation."

47. The time line that follows is drawn from the UN's IRIN daily reports, as well as from Refugees International, "The Lost Refugees: Herded and Hunted in Eastern Zaire" (Washington, DC: Refugees International, September 1997).

48. Dr. Ephraim Kabayija, adviser to the president, author interview with Sue Lautze, Kigali, 24 October 1997.

49. For a variety of estimates and surrounding debates, see Refugees International, "The Lost Refugees."

50. Department of Political Affairs, author interviews with Sue Lautze, New York, October 1997.

51. Officials of the Canadian Permanent Mission to the UN, author interview with Sue Lautze, New York, October 1997.

52. For example, proposals to establish secure humanitarian corridors for the safe return of refugees did not provide clear answers to the question of how refugees would enter the corridors without a potentially large-scale firefight between the MNF and the former FAR.

53. UN official, confidential author interview, Kinshasa, November 1997.

54. For an account of what became known as the "numbers game"—accusations and counteraccusations between the military contingents and humanitarian agencies about the number of missing refugees—see Nicholas Stockton, "Rwanda: Rights and Racism," unpublished paper, Oxford University, 1998, and Refugees International, "The Lost Refugees."

55. See Raymond Hnatyshyn, "Lessons Learned from the Multi-National Force" (Ottawa: Government of Canada, 1998).

56. Among the earliest works on this topic is Robert Miller (ed.), *Aid as Peacemaker: Canada's Development Assistance and Third World Conflict* (Ottawa: Carleton University Press, 1992).

57. Michael Bryans, Bruce Jones, and Janice Stein, *Mean Times: Humanitarian Action in Complex Political Emergencies—Stark Choices, Cruel Dilemmas* (Toronto: Programme on Conflict Management and Negotiation, University of Toronto, January 1999).

7

The Dynamics of Peacemaking in Rwanda: Conclusions and Implications

The wide-ranging peacemaking process for the Rwandan civil war did not forestall escalation into massive genocide. Four main factors are responsible. First, inside the Rwandan regime a core group of extremists, the so-called spoilers, complicated the peace effort throughout. Second, the third-party strategies for containing the threat posed by the extremists were inconsistent and incoherent. Third, the RPF's negotiating strategy became intransigent following its battlefield victories in the late stages of the war. And fourth, international interest in Rwanda was limited, which caused less attention to be paid and fewer resources to be devoted to conflict management than the situation demanded.

Obstacles to Peaceful Resolution

That there were significant obstacles to conflict resolution in Rwanda is clear. Key features of the conflict itself, including security fears and mistrust, posed barriers to effective peacemaking. This was true of the difficulties of reaching agreement during the mediation process, even of reaching the mediation stage itself. Most particularly, it was true of the implementation phase, which was frustrated and ultimately undermined by polarization and demonization efforts. Furthermore, totalistic perceptions and rhetoric, especially as wielded by the CDR, posed a challenge to third parties during Arusha as well as after. Indeed, the months prior to the genocide were characterized far more by security fears, mistrust, and totalistic rhetoric than by any positive efforts to implement the Arusha peace deal.

As for security fears and rhetoric, they were *deliberately* amplified by the opponents of Arusha. Whereas security fears are often treated as a natural outcome of the dynamics of conflict, Rwanda demonstrates that fear and distrust can also be used to exacerbate a conflict. In this regard, it is useful to distinguish between the fears and rhetoric of leaders and those of other groups. At its core, opposition to Arusha arose primarily from the vested interests of the oligarchic *akazu*. The opposition may well have been amplified by security fears. But more important, the security fears and concerns of *other* elements of the leadership were deliberately preyed upon by the extremists to aid their mobilization efforts. Totalistic rhetoric was also used to generate and amplify security fears in the population as a whole, a first step toward creating the necessary political space for genocide. In the hands of Rwanda's extremists, then, security fears were *tools* of conflict, not just outcomes of it.

The totalistic rhetoric of Rwanda's extremists reflected the actual, totalistic nature of their program and objectives. They were, indubitably, *spoilers* who were implacably opposed to any compromise peace deal. Their very presence complicated the search for peace in Rwanda. Yet the presence of spoilers is not, in and of itself, sufficient to explain the failure of the peace process. Rather, the evidence suggests that the opposition of spoilers could have been overcome by a peace process that differed within reasonable parameters from that which occurred. This is so because the spoilers had to expend considerable energies to win the support of less committed groups within the regime prior to launching the genocide campaign. Their targets were political leaders who appeared to have lost out in the Arusha bargain. As *losers* from Arusha, they were susceptible to the powerful combination of threats and inducements used by the *génocidaires* to widen their base of support. A peace process that resulted in a better deal for moderates within the regime would have augmented the prospects of implementation.

Failures of the Peacemaking Process

If the presence of hard-line and extremist opponents of peace was a central feature of the conflict, this reality was not reflected in third-party peacemaking initiatives. There were some efforts to contain the threat, but they were limited, inconsistent, and incoherent. The peacemaking process was never informed by an overall strategy for tackling extremism or extremists. Prenegotiation efforts focused on diffusing the influence of hard-liners by widening the range of interlocutors, specifically by bringing opposition groups into government. In the mediation phase, the strategy of international actors was based on inclusion, that is, buying off extremists by bringing them into the fold. The strategy failed, first because the room for maneuver had already been restricted by strategies employed during the prenegotiation phase, and then because the RPF at a decisive moment in Arusha proved intransigent on the question of including the CDR. The RPF's position stemmed from battlefield victories and the extremists' rhetoric. That fact that the resulting deal failed to include extremists was complicating but possibly manageable; the fact that it marginalized more moderate forces in the Habyarimana regime proved disastrous.

The Arusha deal was met in Kigali with outrage and hostility. Why? If those who would ultimately repudiate the peace accords were a priori committed to repudiate *any* deal, why should they react harshly or loudly to the particulars of Arusha? If one rejects a process in its entirety, why fight over details? Because the reaction of the CDR and other anti-Arusha forces was deliberate, its purpose was to capture the political support of MRND members not already part of the extremist core, politicians from within the regime who had kept their options open through the Arusha process. These moderate forces now found themselves saddled with a deal that looked like a sellout, their regime reduced to minority-party status. The CDR worked energetically to bring the losers on board with their strategy of opposition, and they found the provisions of Arusha to be a powerful tool. The level of rhetorical and substantive planning for the genocide began to grow.[1]

On their own, the inner core of the CDR had insufficient weight to repudiate the entire Arusha process. But increasingly they were supported by a wider spectrum of political actors. With no incentives to cooperate, no guarantees of security, and caught in a process of deliberate polarization, many of the losers joined forces with the extremists. This combination of spoilers and losers created a constellation of opposition to peace that nurtured the growing genocide movement.

After Arusha was completed, the main strategy pursued by the implementers and ostensible guarantors of Arusha, especially the

United Nations, was tantamount to ignoring the threat posed by the extremists. Even though early reports showed the potential for opposition to Arusha, UNAMIR was composed as if it were being sent to oversee a mutually agreed-upon peace. When evidence of growing opposition to Arusha reached the United Nations, little was done. The responsibility lies at the doorstep of the Security Council for adopting a minimalist approach to Rwanda. Its failure to act was compounded by UNAMIR and especially the UN Secretariat's inadequate reading of the dynamics of the Rwandan conflict, which resulted in their doing too little to inform the Security Council of the potential for opposition. In the event, the extremists forces launched an attack on UNAMIR and Arusha, and nothing was done to counter it. The unwillingness of the major powers to act decisively to reinforce UNAMIR in April and May 1994 stands as the most important failure. But the compounding failure of the United Nations was in not reacting earlier to forestall or at least prepare for this growing threat. And the greatest flaw in the overall peace process, arguably, was marginalizing moderate forces through incoherent approaches and thereby leaving the extremists an open field.

The evidence suggests that the outcome of the conflict resolution process is not ascribable to any single third-party effort. Rather, it was the weakness of the collective effort that hamstrung the peace efforts. Two major disjunctures occurred: the first was between prenegotiation efforts and the mediation process, the second between the OAU-sponsored Arusha process and the UN peacekeeping effort. Thus, a lack of coordination between the three principal elements of the peace process created gaps that allowed the genocide to be implemented. Once the genocide was under way, lack of will on the part of major powers sealed Rwanda's fate.

What Might Have Been Done? An Alternative History

In theory, could it have been possible to overcome the extremist threat? Perhaps. But even if the third parties had developed a consistent strategy for containing extremism and forging an alliance with moderate forces, it is likely that the opposition would have mounted some form of attack on Arusha. Yet such an attack would have been less virulent and more amenable to response. The peace process had multiple fault lines, and it is not difficult to imagine an alternative process that would have resulted in better outcomes.

If no concerted pressure had been placed on the single-party Habyarimana regime to open itself to multiparty politics, then outcomes might have been better. The regime might eventually have agreed to the Arusha process notwithstanding the absence of opposition parties. (After all, it had earlier agreed to the regional porocess, as many other oppressive regimes have agreed to negotiate in the past—perhaps with the bilateral donors exercising their influence in this direction.)

If no meaningful opposition was present at Arusha, then a more equitable bargain might have resulted. Rather than assigning the patchwork of seats in the transitional institutions across several opposition parties, Arusha might have reflected a 50–50 or 60–40 power-sharing scheme.

Assuming that talks did not break down completely, let us also assume that second-track and community-based efforts (e.g., by groups like OXFAM as well as the Vatican) were more vigorous. This might have countered the demonization strategy of the CDR throughout 1991–1993, thereby weakening the effects of their propaganda on the Rwandan population.

How would this scenario have affected the politics of Kigali? Would a 50-50 (or close to it) power-sharing arrangement have pacified the CDR? Not likely. However, if Arusha had not relegated the MRND to minority status, the moderates within the MRND may have been able to support the deal. Regardless, the CDR probably would have attempted to polarize politics in Kigali and obstruct the peace process. But it is also likely that a degree of MRND support for Arusha would have at least impeded the CDR's genocidal plans. Stronger efforts by second-track and community-based groups would have given voice to moderate forces in Kigali, which may have been able to live with a more balanced power-sharing deal.

Finally, let us assume that the UN Security Council authorized a peacekeeping mission of some 5,000 troops with sufficient defensive equipment. Such a mission could have been authorized to enforce the peace or at least defend itself under certain circumstances as well as to conduct contingency planning for an attack on the peace process by known hard-line and extremist forces.

With these assumptions in mind, it is possible to envision a scenario in which extremist forces attempted but failed to implement a program of radical opposition to Arusha. Their strategy of demonization would have been undermined by education and facilitation efforts at the second-track and community-based levels. Their support in Kigali would have been narrowed, as moderate voices within the MRND and elsewhere would have had the political space to operate, and mediators might have had a better chance to convince uncommitted actors within the MRND. The *génocidaires* attacks probably would have been less vicious, in turn making it easier for the strengthened UNAMIR to contain or delay the plan. A weaker attack might have been met with a more rapid response in the Security Council, perhaps including reinforcements for UNAMIR in April 1994, when something could have been done to stop the killing.

All of these assumptions are reasonable; indeed, some are conservative. And the evidence suggests that if events had unfolded as outlined just above, the death toll might have been much lower. Facing moderate opposition within its own ranks and from the MRND, the *génocidaires* would have had to fight *government* forces in order to launch their genocide campaign. During the first days following the assassination of President Habyarimana, the *génocidaires'* first order of business was to assassinate political rivals *within* government ranks. Had there been opposition from some political and military leaders within the regime (i.e., those who stood to gain from the Arusha transitional structures), the *génocidaires'* efforts to clear the ground for an all-out attack on the Tutsis would have been more complicated. In fact, pro-Arusha forces might have been able to call on FAR and Presidential Guard elements to support them.

This suggests two alternative outcomes: First, the genocide machine would have collapsed in the face of internal opposition; second, the *génocidaires* would have had to concentrate their forces and efforts in the battle for political control of Kigali for a much longer period. Even if they were victorious, they would have been weakened before the RPF counterattack. Even this second scenario would have resulted in a far quicker RPF victory, which in turn translates into tens and possibly hundreds of thousands of lives saved.

Thus, a more consistent strategy for bringing moderates on board and containing extremists, including more robust peacekeeping action, might have resulted in a lower death toll. At best, it might have collapsed the genocidal structure before it fully mobilized.

In reality, however, the peacemaking process in Rwanda was no match for the more focused, more brutal strategy of its opponents. A core of brutal individuals handily overcame sustained and wide-ranging international peace efforts, a damning indictment of our current international systems for conflict management.

Implications for Research and Policy

Some important lessons from Rwanda have already been learned by UN officials, diplomats, and aid workers. Within the humanitarian and development communities, Rwanda illustrates the need to infuse aid strategies with greater political sensitivity and awareness of the connections between aid and conflict resolution.[2] In political and peacekeeping circles, the failure to provide an adequate peacekeeping presence to respond to the genocide stands as a lingering indictment.[3] An echo of Rwanda surely could be heard in the British government's decision to bolster UN peacekeeping forces in Sierra Leone, when events in May 2000 could otherwise have forced the United Nations to abandon that country to a bloody fate.

Yet one of the principal lessons of Rwanda has been mislearned. Whereas Rwanda is viewed as a failure of early warning and conflict prevention, the events instead reflect a failure of concerted conflict management efforts: not a failure to take action, but a failure of actions taken. When the focus is shifted from the weak international response toward the more concerted international actions during the civil war, Rwanda is more correctly seen as a cautionary tale about the limits of peacemaking as it is currently practiced.

Returning to I. William Zartman's notion, cited in the Introduction, of a gap between sophisticated methods and brutal outcomes, Rwanda suggests that perhaps our current methods are not so sophisticated after all. However sophisticated the *individual* methods for conflict resolution, the means by which these combine into an overall *process* are problematic indeed. The international community has many tools at its disposal, but when they are used separately by different actors on various targets, is it any wonder that they collectively miss the mark?

The utter irony is that Rwanda saw a huge range of conflict resolution initiatives and methods: UN peacekeepers, official mediators, church-based facilitators—all playing to their own tune. Each initiative had its strengths and weaknesses, and there were positive and negative connections among these initiatives. Within those interconnections we can see the dynamics of failed peacemaking in Rwanda. We review each element in turn below.

Premature Democratization

To begin with the prenegotiation phase, the use of democratization as a conflict resolution tool was problematic. The pressure placed on the Habyarimana regime to open itself to multiparty democracy occasioned important changes in the structure and texture of interparty negotiations. From this limited perspective, the democratization efforts can be seen as successful. But the victory was hollow, as the resultant fracturing of political power in Kigali complicated the mediation and peace implementation processes. The push for democratization had unforeseen and ultimately negative effects, and it was a key tactical error. Two years after the genocide, former RPF chief negotiator Patrick Mazimpaka's ruefully concluded: "One does not turn dictators into democrats overnight."[4]

* * *

In general, why would the international community pursue democratization within the fractious context of civil war? If an oligarchy or dictatorship is in power, democratization by definition weakens the existing regime. If that regime is already under attack, additional pressures can collapse all political authority or lead to an aggressive defense by the entrenched powers.

Charles Tilly, perhaps the foremost historian on this topic, has argued that the process of democratization and state-building in Europe reveals a pattern whereby excessive democratization in weak states leads to challenges. These come from internal actors, who use the weakness of the state to mount successful coups, often steering the state toward more oppressive policies; or from external actors, who take advantage of weakness to mount a campaign to overtake internal authorities.[5] The tension between opening the state to civic and democratic participation, on the one hand, and retaining a degree of state authority, on the other, requires a fine balance. There are echoes of this tension even in modern liberal states: most modern democracies retain clauses in their constitutions allowing them to suspend civil liberties in times of national emergency. The general concept is that, during periods of threat, state cohesion takes precedence over democratic liberties.

In this light, the experience of Rwanda lends credence to those who have challenged one of the orthodoxies of the 1990s: that democratization is necessarily a positive tool for the peaceful resolution of conflict.[6] Of course, Rwanda is only one case, but it suggests caution in the use of democratization as a strategy for conflict resolution.

Mediation and Facilitation

The Arusha process constituted an interesting blend of the facilitation and mediation models for conflict resolution. Whereas political negotiations by official government delegations typically follow traditional mediation processes, Arusha reflects unofficial second-track facilitation. The facilitator of Arusha deliberately designed a process wherein the parties would have sufficient contact and communication to overcome obstacles arising from perceptions and mistrust. The use of a lengthy, sustained process of meetings outside Kigali, where discussions were often open, reinforced the prospects for real communication. This process was distinct from the high-pressure, short-duration talks that often characterize official mediation processes. The latter tend to produce quasiagreements through exhaustion. By contrast, several of the third parties in Arusha facilitated communication between the parties to solve problems through mutual agreement. (Elements of the process were similar to those used in the Oslo process, another example of mixed facilitation and mediation methods, one that produced historic breakthroughs in an entrenched conflict.[7])

Accordingly, the Arusha process generated important outcomes, at least on paper. The Arusha Accords were a detailed blueprint to resolve the underlying themes of the Rwandan conflict. They went far beyond merely short- or medium-term cessation of hostilities; they laid out a clear process for implementation of a new political order.

But the spoilers on the GoR negotiating team, and the intransigent bargaining position of the RPF, thwarted these goals in the later stages of the talks. Two lessons can be learned: First, the use of a creative mix of mediation and facilitation techniques, at the level of the top political leadership, can generate an important degree of communication and problem-solving between parties, resulting in far-reaching agreements; and second, even a sophisticated process of this type may not be sufficient to overcome totalistic rhetoric and the presence of spoilers. In theorizing and managing conflict resolution processes, it is critical to recall that it is ultimately the parties themselves that will, or will not, make peace.

Community-Based Mediation

Related to these issues is the second mediation-phase issue: the impact of limited community-based mediation and intergroup reconciliation. Community-based efforts, such as those by the ENVD program run by OXFAM and the Catholic Church, had minimal effects. More robust attempts to counter the CDR's demonization and polarization could have changed the landscape, as they might have developed or protected political space wherein moderate voices could be heard. Rwanda was sorely lacking such political space, especially during the implementation phase of Arusha. The limits of peacebuilding efforts during the conflict were a major weakness of the overall third-party process in Rwanda.

In the years since the Rwandan genocide, more attention has been paid to such processes. The rapid growth of the nongovernmental conflict resolution sector has been a salient factor in generating more community-based mediation and peacebuilding efforts, both during and after conflicts.[8] However, as some practitioners have made clear, there is ample room for further research and further work on how to ensure that such efforts have a positive impact on related efforts at the level of the political leadership.[9]

Planning for Opposition

In the implementation phase of peacekeeping operations, the most important issue is planning for the prospect of violent opposition. Failure to do so in Rwanda meant that the UN "security guarantee" of Arusha was meaningless. This failure had multiple dimensions: the late transfer of responsibility from the OAU to the United Nations; lack of sensitivity, within the United Nations, to Rwandan history and political culture; limited interest in peacekeeping in Rwanda among the major powers; and an organizational culture in the United Nations that limits contingency planning for worst-case scenarios.

But the issue of transferring responsibility from the OAU to the United Nations is only one aspect of a larger problem of failures of interconnection. Limited local knowledge, inadequate contingency planning, and limited interest in Rwanda reinforced one another in damaging ways.

There is little doubt that UNAMIR and the UN Secretariat did too little to sensitize themselves to the dynamics of the Rwandan conflict. Lack of awareness is a recurrent problem in international organizations.[10] In institutions such as the United Nations, a small core of staff members typically manages simultaneous operations in diverse contexts. It is all but impossible to ensure that sufficient regional expertise exists among these staff (such expertise is, of course, available outside the core staff). At the United Nations, poor administrative systems thwart the ability to take advantage of outside expertise.[11] There is also a tendency to only partially draw on the expertise of local or regional actors. In Rwanda, the United Nations essentially shoved aside the OAU and the Tanzanians, notwithstanding their greater involvement to date and their far better intelligence and political analyses of Rwanda and Arusha. Finally, there is the tricky question of how international actors identify appropriate local expertise and sources. When foreign intervenors arrive in a local context and seek knowledge, local expertise, and contacts, they risk being captured by a single politicized view and having their policies distorted as a result.[12] This remains an ongoing problem for the United Nations and other international organizations.

With little understanding of the local context, the United Nations had a limited capacity to interpret the sounds of growing opposition to peace. But the more general question was one of planning for the *contingency* of hostile opposition. One need not determine with certainty the future scenarios, but failure to plan for worst-case contingencies is a recurrent problem in UN operations, whether peacekeeping missions or humanitarian operations. For example, a major review of UNHCR's operations in Kosovo found significant failures to plan for worst-case scenarios, notwithstanding a general assessment that such scenarios were possible.[13] The result was delays in UNHCR's response when large-scale refugee outflows accompanied the NATO bombing campaign. Similar problems beset the UN's operation in East Timor. Only late in the game did UN officials raise the prospect of violent reactions in East Timor,[14] and while in this case there was a significant response, it came late, after violence had killed thousands of East Timorese and destroyed much of the country's physical infrastructure.

UN managers have two concerns in this context. First, contingency planning for worst-case scenarios can become a self-fulfilling prophecy.[15] If the parties to a conflict see the United Nations planning for a negative outcome, such a perception can sway the parties' own expectations to detrimental effect. Second, if the UN Secretariat is seen by the Security Council to be planning for a negative outcome, this raises concerns that the Security Council will have to expend financial resources and absorb serious risks associated with large-scale peace enforcement operations. But these justifications are insufficient.

Contingency planning is a necessary part of any rational planning process for military or humanitarian operations, a routine process in military establishments the world over. Planning for worst-case scenarios does not necessarily mean that you believe they will occur. Indeed, planning for negative outcomes can actually help forestall them. To deploy missions to complex field operations without proper contingency planning is likely to lead to failures, generating a need for even further responses. This was one of the conclusions of the UN's independent investigation into Rwanda: no UN peacekeeping operation should be deployed without sufficient capacity and proper authorization to use force if confronted with hostile opposition. The UN Secretariat and Security Council are responsible for ensuring that this lesson is implemented. Thus, there remains a need for policy efforts by the Secretariat and Security Council members to ensure that minimum contingency planning and response capacities become a routine part of peacekeeping operations.

Comparing Rwanda with two recent cases, East Timor and Sierra Leone, suggests that half of this lesson has been learned. While there were clearly planning failures in East Timor, both there and in Sierra Leone three critical things were done differently than in Rwanda. First, when faced with violent opposition, the UN firmly stood its ground. In both instances, the UN kept its existing presence in place, and moved swiftly to generate reinforcements. For East Timor, the Secretary-General sent a Security Council mission to Dili to report on the situation; when violence broke in Sierra Leone, the Under-Secretary-General for Peacekeeping Operations went directly to Freetown to bolster the UN force. In both cases, the Secretary-General and his senior lieutenants made concerted and consistent calls on the Security Council and other states to respond. Second, critically, these calls for reinforcements were met by member states within short periods of time. In the case of East Timor, this was aided by the presence, in Australia, of a strong regional power with significant interests in the outcome of the situation. In Sierra Leone, the British government showed impressive leadership despite fairly limited national interests in West Africa. Finally, and critically, when faced with one party clearly in violation of peace agreements and/or international laws, the UN did not attempt to maintain neutrality but rather targeted its efforts to containing the hostile party.

For these three reasons, the death tolls from Sierra Leone and East Timor are counted in the hundreds or low thousands, not in the hundreds of thousands. Nevertheless, the fact that in both cases reinforcements had to be generated at the last minute meant that significant violence occurred in the interim period, especially in East Timor. Moreover, the fact that there was no stand-by capacity for response, and no contingency plans for facing hostile opposition, means that the UN's ability to contain such threats depends on *ad hoc* and therefore unreliable factors. This shows that there is still significant progress to be made to reform UN peacekeeping on the basis of the lessons of Rwanda and other cases. There remains a need for further policy efforts by the Secretariat and by Security Council members to ensure that minimum contingency planning and response capacities become a routine part of peacekeeping operations.

Spoilers and Losers

The need to plan for opposition is a sine qua non of effective peacemaking in cases characterized by the presence of spoilers. The case of Rwanda illustrates the kinds of obstacles that can be posed by spoilers. But it also suggests two other things. First, the presence of spoilers in and of itself does not explain the collapse of the peace process. Second, an additional factor is the creation of *losers* in peace processes, that is, persons and groups who are not hostile to compromise but who lose out in peace agreements and therefore oppose their implementation. The relationship between spoilers and losers is a fertile issue for exploration, and Rwanda demonstrates that losers can be mobilized into hostile opposition by spoilers, adding depth and strength to the foes of peace.

A comparative study of losers in peace processes would shed further light on the dynamics of conflict and its resolution. Additionally, it would be useful to explore the relationship between spoilers and losers in a variety of cases. Strategies for tackling spoilers could be mapped against a spectrum defined by strategies of bringing them into the tent at one extreme and strategies of containing them through military force at the other. A range of such approaches had been used in past cases: in South Africa, where some parties opposed to the general peace were in effect bought into the process by being given a greater than proportional share of decisionmaking power in a transitional phase; in Haiti, where the military *junta* was both induced and pushed out of the country by a combination of pay-offs and some

20,000 plus U.S. marines; and in East Timor, where opponents of independence where forced out of the country by a UN-authorized peace enforcement mission. In such cases, research could identify the impact of the strategies chosen for containing extremists on the process of creating losers. The dynamics of their subsequent relations could then be studied and the impact on the overall outcomes of the peace process explored. Such a research agenda would provide important insights into policy options available to peacemakers in a range of civil war situations.

One central lesson is already clear: if the mediation process serves to isolate hard-liners and extremists, then the implementation process must have sufficient military clout to contain them and neutralize their opposition. Alternatively, if there are limited military resources to bring to bear, the mediation process should work on the assumption of bringing the hard-liners into the process and ensure that that logic is consistent throughout the process. Whatever the core strategic decision about extremists, the strategy to deal with them must be consistent across all phases. The inconsistency of prenegotiation, mediation, and implementation strategies for dealing with spoilers doomed the overall peace process in Rwanda.

Humanitarian Relief in Conflict

The humanitarian crisis that followed the collapse of the peace process in Rwanda highlights the connections between humanitarian relief and conflict dynamics. Notwithstanding the undoubted life-saving impact of humanitarian assistance following the Rwandan genocide, that assistance also had a negative impact on the cycle of conflict.

This is another area where meaningful developments have occurred since the Rwandan genocide. The humanitarian community learned from Rwanda and similar cases of the need to incorporate a political analysis of the potential impacts of assistance into the design of their activities. If less has been achieved in this realm than desired, it is nevertheless the case that this general lesson is today tantamount to conventional wisdom. What is still vigorously debated, however, is whether and to what extent humanitarian agencies should concede to being a self-conscious part of an overall conflict management process. This raises concerns that neutrality, impartiality, and independence of humanitarian actors will be compromised. These are cardinal principles (or, perhaps, sacred cows) of humanitarian assistance.

When operating in the kind of situation that was present in eastern Zaire following the genocide, humanitarian assistance is not neutral in its outcomes, whatever its intentions or principles.[16] In contexts where political or military actors are seeking to control or attack a civilian population, humanitarian efforts to protect and assist that population will be in direct opposition to the strategies and tactics of warring parties. The Rwanda case is an extreme one, but it highlights the potential for humanitarian assistance to have a significant impact on the political and security dimensions of a conflict—not because of violations of neutrality but because in such conflicts neutrality is *itself* a political position. Rwanda also shows that the real cause of unintended consequences is the security vacuum that can be created by the international failure to act.

Of course, the relationship between humanitarian relief efforts and peacemaking initiatives is yet another dimension of the interconnections between third-party interventions in civil war. It shows that such interconnections exist even at the level of the very principles upon which different interventions are founded. This is an important factor in understanding the ways in which inconsistent strategies emerge, generating overall incoherence. Equally, it constitutes a challenge in terms of efforts to enhance the coherence of conflict management.

Strategic Coordination

Indeed, all of the issues discussed above relate in part to the question of connections—or their absence—among different elements of an overall conflict resolution process. In terms of the concepts outlined in Chapter 1, they relate also to the absence of a coordinating element in overall third-party interventions. And they suggest that the very dynamics of interconnected peacemaking processes themselves can produce obstacles. Complex conflicts are met by complex responses, and the very complexity of those responses undermines their effectiveness.

Thus, the policy problem raised by Rwanda is incoherence among conflict resolution efforts and the importance of coordination of strategy and action. From where might such coordination come? What actor or actors might have been able to generate a coherent strategy and ensure its consistent application across all phases of the process? What factors facilitate effective coordination and mitigate against it?

In thinking about coordination, it is important to note that the Rwandan peace process was marred by incoherence despite being a country to which a UN Special Representative was appointed. One need only note that the Special Representative was appointed only *after* the completion of the mediation process and thus was in no position to deal with one of the most critical failings of the process: the inconsistency between the mediation and implementation strategies. Neither was there another self-evident source of coherent and consistent strategy for the Rwandan process. The shifting locus of efforts from subregional to regional to international actors; the major shift in responsibility from the OAU to the United Nations in the transition from Arusha to UNAMIR; and the absence of any kind of systematic coordination mechanism or the like—all mitigated against the development of a well-coordinated strategy for peacemaking and implementation. There was no single mediator involved throughout the Rwandan peace process, no institution that played a leading role in all the different phases, no state that had a consistent leadership role, no actor that focused on coordination of different efforts.

Rather, each actor had its own relationship to the Rwandan parties, its own analysis of the situation, its own organizational patterns, policies, and learning, and therefore its own strategies. Sometimes these were shared, as between the French and Americans. More commonly they were developed in isolation and deployed individually. Neither was there an effective, collective forum wherein third parties sought to align their efforts. Within the diplomatic sphere, the Five Musketeers made some attempt to coordinate among the main diplomatic players, but these efforts did not extend to the United Nations or to several other actors within the overall process and were limited as a result.

Thus, Rwanda appears to confirm Christopher Mitchell's concern (outlined in the Introduction) that the ad hoc nature of conflict resolution interventions and the general absence of coordinating mechanisms were causes of the failure. If incoherence is an impediment to successful conflict resolution, and coordination structures are weak or difficult to identify, then success in third-party processes becomes problematic.

Summing Up: Complexity and Coordination

Comparing Rwanda to other cases from the late 1980s and early 1990s makes it evident that there are increasing challenges to coordination:

the growth in the number of third parties; the resulting complexity of the overall process; the potential for competition or inconsistency between organizations; the range of different conflict resolution approaches; the likelihood of disjunctures between phases; and the limited extent to which the various actors recognize the coordinating authority of the United Nations or any other actor.[17]

Just coping with the complexity of the international response is a challenge, leaving less time and fewer resources for dealing with the complexity of the crisis itself. Moreover, as has been experienced in Burundi, Bosnia, Sierra Leone, and Kosovo, the very fact of complexity exposes the peace process to manipulation and deliberate division by parties to the conflict, especially those who resist third-party peace efforts.

What Rwanda and other cases suggest is the need for strong strategic coordination within peace processes. Those who are responsible for international conflict resolution must develop strategies for dealing with extremists as well as those who would lose out in a peace deal. An early decision must be taken as to whether the essence of the approach is one of inclusion or one of containment. That decision must be taken in part on the basis of an assessment of the level of international resources available for conflict management in the particular case. This decision must then inform a common strategy that serves as an organizing principle for the whole range of third-party interventions, which must also be coordinated. The strategy and coordination must inform and take into account not only third-party efforts aimed at conflict resolution but also efforts in the development and humanitarian fields. The coordination must ensure that there are sufficient efforts at multiple levels to reduce the space available for extremist rhetoric and tactics and that there are effective interconnections among efforts at these various levels. In turn, this will require major investments in policy and organizational development to ensure that there is sufficient capacity to perform the strategic coordination function required to turn multiple but disconnected third-party efforts into an effective and strategic interconnected process. Only if these elements are in place do third-party efforts have a reasonable chance at contributing to successful conflict resolution in civil wars.

By contrast, the reality of international systems for conflict management is characterized by multiple actors with overlapping mandates, weak histories of collaboration, competitive fund-raising tools, and separate reporting lines—all resulting in variable and inconsistent strategies, lack of communication and collaboration between actors, and an overall incoherence in peacemaking efforts. At best these features may be temporarily abated by the leadership of a powerful state. But this will likely be sporadic and ad hoc, time-bound, and limited to a few cases. Whereas ideally strategy would be driven by the needs of the case, the reality, far too often, is that multiple (and in some sense competing) norms and a diffuse international political system are driving complex, competing, and frequently ineffective organizations to develop responses based principally on their mandates and expertise rather than comparative advantage, serious analysis, and appropriate response strategies. The result is an inefficient and frequently ineffective international system for conflict resolution.

Strengthening the strategic coordination of the international system is a challenge when there is a sustained international debate about the role of the United Nations vis-à-vis regional and subregional organizations. The United Nations itself is embattled and frequently unresponsive, and most efforts are in the nongovernmental world, which by nature is least amenable to strategic coordination. The proliferation of conflict resolution actors, sometimes taken as evidence of progress in conflict management, is perhaps more indicative of the fractured and disparate nature of the international conflict management "system." Strategic coordination is so much at odds with the basic parameters of political and organizational competition that initiatives in this realm must overcome serious obstacles.

Reform of international and regional organizations and NGOs to improve strategic coordination and consistency in intervention depends on the nature of political support for such reforms among member states. But here, dialogue and debate is constrained by the fact that political competition among states operates in part through these very institutions and organizations.

This, then, is an important part of Zartman's gap: not between methods and outcomes but between need and supply. The international systems for conflict management function increasingly like a form of inverted market, where supply, not demand, is the dominant factor. The specific features and dynamics of the conflict in question, the nature and objectives of the competing parties to war—these are secondary to the supply of international peacemaking initiatives. Rather, a volatile cocktail of humane motivation, mandates, organizational pressures, and competing state interests generates an abundant supply of international, regional, and NGOs for conflict resolution, whatever the demand. The resulting complexity and incoherence poses an obstacle to effective peacemaking.

Conclusion: Implications of Failure

Of course, we must keep in mind that the weakness of third-party systems and efforts was not the only obstacle to peacemaking in Rwanda. Rather, the most serious obstacles arose from the dynamics of conflict itself. The existence of spoilers, the use of totalistic rhetoric, the hardening of perceptions through time, the barriers to trust—these and other dynamics mitigate against peaceful outcomes in civil wars.

The two factors are, of course, related. When such dynamics as spoilers and totalistic rhetoric are not present in conflicts, the inefficiencies of international systems for conflict resolution will be less important to the overall outcomes. But when faced with the challenges from spoilers and other opponents, those inefficiencies and weaknesses will leave international peace processes vulnerable to manipulation and attack. The fact that existing systems for conflict management are likely to be least effective in the face of those most willing to act brutally to achieve their political ends augers poorly for the prospects of limiting war.

Moreover, Rwanda provides empirical and theoretical evidence to suggest that its failings are unlikely to be unique. Rather, the limitations of international third-party efforts in Rwanda, arising as they did from the absence of a substantive mechanism or process for strategic coordination, as well as the absence of political attention, seem likely to be common features of such peace processes.

Thus, the Rwanda case stands, first, as a cautionary tale about the limits of existing international systems for successfully mounting third-party conflict resolution efforts or, more broadly, for conflict management in the face of small-scale civil wars. It stands, second, as an argument for systematic reform of the international system for managing third-party interventions. In theoretical and practical work to strengthen international conflict resolution systems, much more attention must be paid to the impact of various peacemaking strategies on the internal dynamics of conflict, especially to the ways in which different international efforts connect with one another, creating an overall impact. The absence of strong policies or processes for ensuring coherence of peacemaking initiatives leaves such efforts open to easy manipulation by opponents.

The theoretical deficit of attention to such issues can be rectified by new research agendas. These agendas should focus on comparative analysis of the dynamics of civil war, set against a backdrop of complex international conflict resolution systems. They should also probe more deeply into the question of complexity and coordination—identifying in more detailed terms the sources of complexity, the obstacles to coordination, and the impact of incoherence on the effectiveness of conflict resolution efforts. Unlike much contemporary theory, new research should link analysis of the recurrent dynamics of civil war to rich understandings of the dynamics of conflict resolution processes. It is in the interaction between the challenge and the response that salient lessons for improved practice will emerge.

The organizational deficits highlighted by Rwanda are more difficult to rectify. However, if further theoretical and empirical work reinforces the argument of this thesis about the importance of interconnected peace efforts, there will be a need for sustained efforts in policy and organizational reform at the international level. Organizations and their political sponsors will have to be held accountable, internationally and domestically, for their performance as part of an overall conflict resolution system. This will require far greater attention on the part of the members of the so-called international community to effective engagement with political systems at the *domestic* level.[18] Until those concerned with conflict and its peaceful resolution make a more concerted effort to engage in the domestic processes where foreign policy is set, it is unlikely that there will be a major change in the current conditions of fracture and competition that hamper effective peacemaking.

Far more troubling than either of these two challenges is the third issue: the selectivity of our international systems for conflict management and peacemaking. The marginal place occupied by Africa and Africans in the international political order meant that peacemaking in Rwanda was accompanied by minimal political will. Although this book has unambiguously identified the failings within the peace process itself, there is no doubt that a more concerted international response to the outbreak of genocide in April 1994 would have saved hundreds of thousands of lives. A model is provided by recent events in East Timor, a much higher profile case in political terms, where the international community organized a humanitarian intervention to halt ethnic cleansing and prevent mass killings even after the collapse of a UN-managed transitional and electoral process that contained many of the same weaknesses exhibited in Rwanda. The cost of minimal international attention to African conflicts can be measured simply by contrasting the thousands dead in East Timor with the horrific body counts from Rwanda.

The fact that our international systems for conflict resolution and management are selective, predicated not on human costs but on political calculations, is neither a theoretical nor a policy problem but a profound moral problem. As long as this remains unchallenged, the prospects of preventing future variants of the Rwandan genocide remain unchanged. Thus, for the international community, the Rwandan genocide stands not only as a moral black mark for past failings but also as an omnipresent reminder of a continuing failure to address the underlying international structures that made it possible. It is therefore incumbent on those concerned with the humanitarian dimensions of international politics to use that reminder as a spur to theoretical, organizational, and, most critically, political reform.

Notes

1. See Kakwenzire and Kamukama, "Development and Consolidation," and Prunier, *The Rwanda Crisis,* chap. 6.

2. See esp. Peter Uvin, *Development, Aid, and Conflict;* Sue Lautze and Bruce Jones with Mark Duffield, *Strategic Humanitarian Coordination in the Great Lakes Region*; Organization for Cooperation and Development in Europe, Development Assistance Committee, Task Force on Development and Conflict, *Guidelines.*

3. See, e.g., *Report of the Secretary-General to the Security Council on the Protection of Civilians in Armed Conflict* (New York: United Nations, September 1999).

4. Mazimpaka, author interview.

5. Charles Tilly, "Contentious Politics," address to a research seminar, Center for International Security and Cooperation, Stanford University, December 1996; for a recent account of his theories of intergroup conflict, see Tilly, *Durable Inequalities* (Berkeley: University of California Press, 1998).

6. See Pauline Baker, "Conflict Resolution Versus Democratic Governance: Divergent Paths to Peace?" in Crocker, Hampson, and Aall (eds.), *Managing Global Chaos,* 563–572.

7. See Savir, *The Process.*

8. Pamela Aall, *NGOs and Conflict Management* (Washington, DC: U.S. Institute for Peace, 1997).

9. See Fabienne Hara, "Burundi: A Case of Parallel Diplomacy," in Crocker et al., *Herding Cats.*

10. Jones and Cater, *Civilians in War.*

11. For an elaboration, see Michele Griffin and Bruce D. Jones, "Building Peace through Transitional Authority: New Directions, Major Challenges" *International Peacekeeping* 7, 4 (Winter 2000).

12. I am grateful to Thant Myint-U for highlighting this problem for me.

13. See Astri Suhrke et al., "An Evaluation of UNHCR's Response to the Kosovo Emergency" (Geneva: UNHCR, March 2000).

14. Author notes, United Nations, September 1999.

15. Suhrke et al., "An Evaluation."

16. Recognizing much of this, groups within the humanitarian world have developed two distinct strategies. One is to seek to minimize the political impacts of humanitarian assistance through a back-to-basics or do-no-harm approach that emphasizes the provision of assistance in ways that do not play into the hands of warring factions (e.g., by restricting the availability of lootable goods that may end up being sold to finance military purchases). The second is to recognize the inherent political consequences of humanitarian assistance and seek to ensure that they have a positive rather than a negative impact on conflict dynamics.

17. This analysis draws on material produced as part of a joint project of Stanford University and the International Peace Academy on the implementation of peace agreements. See Bruce D. Jones, "Containing Opponents: Strategic Co-ordination in Peace Implementation," in Stedman et al., *Peace Implementation.* In this process, I posed strategic coordination questions to authors reviewing evidence from sixteen cases of peace implementation in the 1980s and 1990s. The material for those cases forms a major source for the material at hand. Also, as this chapter was being finalized, the U.S. Institute of Peace published its volume on multiparty mediation, *Herding Cats,* which contains a range of practitioner accounts of issues very relevant to the strategic coordination challenge. I have drawn a great deal on this book. Finally, this section draws on my experience, from 1998 to 2000, as a UN official in charge of strategic coordination policy at the Office for the Coordination of Humanitarian Affairs; as a member of the UN's advance team in Kosovo; and as a member of the UN team involved in the design of the East Timor mission. Needless to say, the views expressed in this section are not necessarily those of OCHA, DPKO, or the United Nations.

18. Ed Luck has emphasized this point. See Edward C. Luck, "The Enforcement of Humanitarian Norms and the Politics of Ambivalence," in *Civilians in War,* ed. Simon Chesterman (Boulder: Lynne Rienner, 2001), 197–218.

Acronyms

ACABQ	Advisory Committee on Activities and Budgetary Questions
ADFL	Alliance of Democratic Forces for the Liberation of Congo-Zaire
APCs	armored personnel carriers
BBTG	Broad-Based Transitional Government
CDR	Coalition pour la Défense de la République
CEDAF	Centre d'Étude et de documentation africaine
CEPGL	Communité Économique des Pays des Grands Lacs
CIA	Central Intelligence Agency
CIIR	Catholic Institute for International Relations
CMI	Chr. Michelsen Institute
CND	Conseil National du Développement
CPSU	Communist Party of the Soviet Union
DANIDA	Danish International Development Assistance
DHA	UN Department of Humanitarian Affairs
DMZ	demilitarized zone
DPA	UN Department of Political Affairs
DPKO	UN Department of Peacekeeping Operations
ENVD	Education for Non-Violence and Democracy
FAR	Forces Armées Rwandaises
GoR	government of Rwanda
ICRC	International Committee of the Red Cross
IDC	International Development Corporation
IMF	International Monetary Fund
IPA	International Peace Academy
IRIN	UN Integrated Regional Information Network

JMPC	Joint Military-Political Commission
LSE	London School of Economics and Political Science
MDR	Mouvement Démocratique Républicain
MNF	Multinational Force
MOG	Military Observer Group
MRND	Mouvement Républicain National pour le Développement
NGOs	nongovernmental organizations
NIF	Neutral International Force
NMOG	Neutral Military Observer Group
NRA	National Revolutionary Army
NRM	National Revolutionary Movement
OAU	Organization of African Unity
OCHA	UN Office for the Coordination of Humanitarian Affairs
OLS	Operation Lifeline Sudan
PCD	Parti Chrétien Démocratique
PL	Parti Libéral
PSD	Parti Socialiste Démocratique
RANU	Rwandan Alliance for National Unity
RPF	Rwandese Patriotic Front
RTLMC	Radio et Television Libre Mille Colines
RUF	Revolutionary United Front
SRSG	Special Representative of the Secretary-General
TNA	Transitional National Assembly
UN	United Nations
UNAHAT	UN Advance Humanitarian Assistance Team
UNAMIR	UN Assistance Mission in Rwanda
UNAR	Union Nationale Rwandaise
UNDP	UN Development Program
UNHCR	UN High Commissioner for Refugees
UNOMUR	UN Observer Mission to Uganda-Rwanda
UNREO	UN Rwanda Emergency Office
UNU	United Nations University
USIP	U.S. Institute for Peace
ZCSC	Zairian Camp Security Contingent
ZCSO	Zairian Camp Security Operation

Bibliography

Articles, Books, and Papers

Abbas, Mahmoud (Abu Mazen). *Through Secret Channels*. Reading, UK: Garnet, 1995.

Abrams, J. S. "Burundi: Anatomy of an Ethnic Conflict." *Survival* 37, 1 (Spring 1995): 144–164.

Adelman, Howard. "The Ethics of Humanitarian Intervention: The Case of the Kurdish Refugees." *Public Affairs Quarterly* 6, 1 (1992): 61–87.

———. "The Phenomonology of Genocide." Stanford University/MacArthur Foundation Conference on State-Sponsored Mass Killing. Stanford, 17 April 1997.

Adelman, Howard, and Astri Suhrke. *The Path of a Genocide: The Rwandan Crisis from Uganda to Zaire*. New Brunswick, NJ: Transaction Publishers, 1999.

Adelman, Howard, and Astri Suhrke with Bruce D. Jones. *Early Warning and Conflict Management in Rwanda: Report of Study II of the Joint Evaluation of Emergency Assistance in Rwanda*. Copenhagen: DANIDA, 1996.

Akashi, Yasushi. "Kabila Should Halt the Killing and Let Relief Agencies In." *International Herald Tribune*, 2 June 1997: 8.

André, Catherine, and Jean-Phillipe Platteau. "Land Relations under Unbearable Stress: Rwanda Caught in the Malthusian Trap." Working Paper, Faculté des sciences économiques et sociales. Namur: FUNDP, January 1996.

Anstee, Margaret J. "The Experience in Angola, February 1992–June 1993." *After Rwanda*. In *After Rwanda: The Co-ordination of United Nations Humanitarian Assistance*. Ed. Jim Whitman Jim and David Pocock. London: Macmillan Press, 1996, 161–178.

Aronson, David. "Kabila's Tutsi Connection: Who Really Controls the New Government in Kinshasa?" *Christian Science Monitor*, 8 July 1997: 19.

Ayoob, Mohammed. "State Making, State Breaking, and State Failure." In *Managing Global Chaos: Sources of and Responses to International*

Conflict. Ed. Chester A. Crocker et al. Washington, DC: U.S. Institute for Peace, 1996, 37–51.
Barnett, Michael. "The Politics of Indifference: The Professionalization of Peacekeeping and the Toleration of Genocide." Unpublished paper. December 1995.
Bartoli, Andrea, "Mediating Peace in Mozambique: The Role of Sant'Egidio." In *Herding Cats: Multiparty Mediation in a Complex World.* Ed. Chester A. Crocker et al. Washington, DC: U.S. Institute for Peace, 1999.
Bercovitch, Jacob, ed. *Social Conflicts and Third Parties: Strategies of Conflict Resolution.* Boulder: Westview, 1984.
———. *Resolving International Conflicts: The Theory and Practice of Mediation.* Boulder: Lynne Rienner Publishers, 1996.
Berdal, Mats, and David M. Malone, eds. *Greed and Grievance: Economic Agendas in Civil Wars.* Boulder: Lynne Rienner Publishers, 2000.
Berger, Iris. *Religion and Resistance: East African Kingdoms in the Precolonial Period.* Butare, Rwanda: Institut National de Recherche Scientifique 20 (1981).
Bihozigara, Jacques, et al. "Analyses de la situation Rwandaise." In *Les crises politiques au Burundi et au Rwanda, 1993–1994,* by André Guichaoua. Lille: Université des Sciences et Technologies de Lille, 1995: 185–210.
Bing, Adotey. "Salim A. Salim on the OAU and the African Agenda." *Review of African Political Economy* 50 (1991): 60–69.
"The Blame Game: Northern Ireland's New Crisis: The Government Has Suspended Northern Ireland's Devolved Government. Let the Recriminations Begin." *The Economist,* 19 February 2000.
Bloomfield, David. *Peacemaking Strategies in Northern Ireland: Building Complementarity in Conflict Management Theory.* Basingstoke, UK: MacMillan Press, 1997.
Borton, John, et al. *Humanitarian Aid and Effects: Report of Study III of the Joint Evaluation of Emergency Assistance in Rwanda.* Copenhagen: DANIDA, 1996.
Boutros-Ghali, Boutros. *An Agenda for Peace, 1995: With the New Supplement and Related UN Documents.* New York: United Nations, 1995.
Bradbury, Mark. *Somaliland.* London: CIIR, 1997.
Braekman, Collette. *Rwanda: Histoire d'un génocide.* Paris: Fayard, 1994.
Brown, Michael, ed. *Ethnic Conflict and International Security.* Princeton: Princeton University Press, 1993.
———. Introduction. *The International Dimensions of Internal Conflict.* Ed. Brown. Cambridge, MA: Center for Science and International Affairs, John F. Kennedy School of Government, Harvard University, 1996, 1–31.
Bryans, Michael, Bruce D. Jones, and Janice Gross Stein. *Mean Times: Humanitarian Action in Complex Political Emergencies—Stark Choices,*

Cruel Dilemmas. Toronto: Programme on Conflict Management and Negotiation, University of Toronto, January 1999.
Carnegie Commission on Preventing Deadly Conflict. *Preventing Deadly Conflict: Final Report*. Washington, DC: Carnegie Commission on Preventing Deadly Conflict, 1997.
Chalk, Frank, and K. Johassohn. *The History and Sociology of Genocide*. New Haven: Yale University Press, 1990.
Chr. Michelsen Institute. "Humanitarian Assistance and Conflict." Report prepared for the Norwegian Ministry of Foreign Affairs, Bergen, Chr. Michelsen Institute, Development Studies and Human Rights, 1997.
Chrétien, Jean-Pierre. "Hutu et Tutsi au Rwanda et au Burundi." In *Au Coeur de l'Ethnie*. Ed. J. L. Amselle and E. M'Bokolo. Paris: La Découverte, 1985, 129–166.
———. "La crise politique rwandaise." *Genève-Afrique* 30, 2 (1992): 121–140.
———. "Burundi: pogroms sur les collines." *Esprit* 203 (July 1994): 16–30.
Collier, Paul, and Anke Hoeffler, "Greed and Grievance as Causes of Civil War." Paper presented at the conference Economics of Political Violence, Center of International Studies, Princeton University, 18–19 March 2000.
Cousens, Elizabeth. "Peace Implementation in Bosnia." In *Peace Implementation: Themes, Issues and Challenges*. Ed. Stephen Stedman et al. Forthcoming, 2001.
Crocker, Chester A. Afterword. In *Making War and Waging Peace: Foreign Intervention in Africa*. Ed. David Smock. Washington, DC: U.S. Institute for Peace, 1993.
Crocker, Chester A., Fen Osler Hampson, and Pamela R. Aall, eds. *Managing Global Chaos: Sources of and Responses to International Conflict*. Washington, DC: U.S. Institute for Peace, 1996.
———. *Herding Cats: Multiparty Mediation in a Complex World*. Washington, DC: U.S. Institute for Peace, 1999.
Cunliffe, S. Alex, and Michael Pugh. "The UNHCR as Lead Agency in the Former Yugoslavia." *Journal of Humanitarian Assistance*, 1 April 1996. <www.jha.sps.cam.ac.uk>.
Dabelstein, N. "Evaluating the International Humanitarian System: Rationale, Process and Management of the Joint Evaluation of the International Response to the Rwanda Genocide." *Disasters* 20, 4 (December 1996): 287–294.
Dallaire, Romeo A. "The Changing Role of UN Peacekeeping Forces: The Relationship Between UN Peacekeepers and NGOs in Rwanda." In *After Rwanda: The Co-ordination of United Nations Humanitarian Assistance*. Ed. Jim Whitman and David Pocock. London: Macmillan Press, 1996, 205–218.
Damrosch, Lori. "Politics Across Borders: Nonintervention and Nonforcible Influence Over Domestic Affairs." *American Journal of International Law* 83 (1989): 1–50.

De Figueiredo Jr., Rui J.P., and Barry R. Weingast, "The Rationality of Fear: Political Opportunism and Ethnic Conflict." In *Civil Wars, Insecurity, and Intervention,* by Barbara F. Walter and Jack Snyder. New York: Columbia University Press, 1999, 261–302.

De Lame, Danielle, and Marcel d'Hertefelt. *Société, culture et histoire du Rwanda: encyclopédie bibliographique.* Tervuren, Belgique: Musée Royal de l'Afrique Centrale, 1987.

De Silva, K. M., and S.W.R. de A. Samarasinghe, eds. *Peace Accords and Ethnic Conflict.* London: Pinter; distributed in the United States and Canada by St. Martin's Press, 1993.

De Soto, Alvaro. "Ending Violent Conflict in El Salvador." In *Herding Cats: Multiparty Mediation in a Complex World.* Ed. Chester A. Crocker et al. Washington, DC: U.S. Institute for Peace, 1999.

De Waal, Alex. "Genocide in Rwanda." *Anthropology Today* 10, 3 (June 1994): 1–2.

———. "The Genocidal State: Hutu Extremism and the Origins of the 'Final Solution' in Rwanda." *Times Literary Supplement,* 1 July 1994.

De Waal, Alex, and Rakiya Omar. "Humanitarianism Unbound?" *African Rights,* Discussion Paper No. 5, November 1994.

———. "The Genocide in Rwanda and the International Response." *Current History* (April 1995): 156–161.

Des Forges, Alison L. "Burundi: A Failed or a Creeping Coup?" *Current History* 93 (May 1994): 203–7.

———. *Leave None to Tell the Story.* New York: Human Rights Watch, 1999.

———. "Shame: Rationalizing Western Apathy on Rwanda." *Foreign Affairs* 79, 3 (May/June 2000): 141–144.

Dedring, Juergen. "Humanitarian Coordination." *After Rwanda.* In *After Rwanda: The Co-ordination of United Nations Humanitarian Assistance.* Ed. Jim Whitman and David Pocock. London: Macmillan Press, 1996, 35–50.

DeHeusch, L. "Rwanda: Responsibilities for a Genocide." *Anthropology Today* 11, 4 (August 1995): 3–7.

Destexhe, A. "The Third Genocide." *Foreign Policy* 97 (Winter 1994–1995): 3–17.

Donini, Antonio, and Norah Niland. *Rwanda: Lessons Learned: A Report on the Co-ordination of Humanitarian Activities.* New York: UN Department of Humanitarian Affairs, November 1994.

Doyle, Michael. *UN Peacekeeping in Cambodia: UNTAC's Civil Mandate.* Boulder: Lynne Rienner Publishers, 1995.

Duffield, Mark. "Complex Emergencies and the Crisis of Developmentalism." *IDS Bulletin* 25, 3 (1994).

———. "The Political Economy of Internal War: Asset Transfer, Complex Emergencies, and International Aid." *War and Hunger.* Eds. Macrae and Zwi. London: Zed Books, 1994, 50–70.

Duffield, Mark, Helen Young, John Ryle, and Ian Henderson. *Sudan Emergency Operations Consortium (SEOC): A Review.* Birmingham, UK: School of Public Policy, 1995.

Durch, William, ed. *UN Peacekeeping, American Politics, and the Uncivil Wars of the 1990s.* New York: St. Martin's Press, 1996.

Eckstein, Harry, ed. *Internal Wars: Problems and Approaches.* New York: Free Press, 1968.

Executive Committee of the Rwandaphone Zaireans Association, "Memorandum on the Tragedy of the Rwandaphone Zaireans with some Proposals and Recommendations" (Nairobi: June 1996).

Fabre, D. "L'Union européenne face à la crise rwandaise." *Afrique contemporaine* 178 (April-June 1996): 3–17.

Fein, Helen. *Genocide Watch.* New Haven: Yale University Press, 1992.

Fisher, Ronald J. *The Social Psychology of Intergroup and International Conflict Resolution.* New York: Springer-Verlag, 1990.

Fisher, Ronald J., and Loraleigh Keashly. "Towards a Contingency Approach to Third-party Intervention in Regional Conflict: A Cyprus Illustration." *International Journal* 45 (Spring 1990): 424–453.

———. "The Potential Complementarity of Mediation and Consultation Within a Contingency Model of Third-party Intervention." *Journal of Peace Research* 28, 1 (1991): 29–42.

Forbes, Ian, and Mark Hoffman, eds. *Political Theory, International Relations, and the Ethics of Intervention.* London: Macmillan Press, 1993.

Fortna, Virginia Page. *Chapter 2: Peace Agreements: The Role of Peace Agreements in Ending Wars.* Ph.D. Diss., Harvard University, 1999.

Front Patriotique Rwandais. "Compte rendu de la réunion du 14–15 janvier 1992 entre la délégation du gouvernement rwandais et celle du F.P.R." RPF Territory, Rwanda, 14–15 January, 1992: 3.

Gasana, James K. "La guerre, la paix et la démocratie au rwanda." In *Les crises politiques au Burundi et au Rwanda 1993–94.* Ed. André Guichaoua. Paris: Karthala, 1995, 211–238.

Goldberg, Jeffrey. "Our Africa." *New York Times Magazine,* 2 March 1997: 34, col. 1.

Gourevitch, Philip. "Zaire's Killer Camps." *New York Times,* 28 October 1996: 19, col 2.

———. "Letter from Rwanda: The Return." *The New Yorker* 72, 43, 20 January 1997: 44.

———. "Letter from Cambodia: Pol Pot's Children." *The New Yorker* 74, 23, 10 August 1998: 40.

———. "The Unimagined." *The New Yorker* 74, 26, 7 September 1998: 41.

———. "The Genocide Fax." *The New Yorker* 74, 11, 5 November 1998: 42.

———. "The Beautiful Land of Death." *The Guardian,* 6 March 1999.

———. "The Psychology of Slaughter." *New York Times,* 7 March 1999: 15, col. 1.

Grosse, Stephen. "The Roots of Conflict and State Failure in Rwanda: The Political Exacerbation of Social Cleavages in a Context of Growing Resources Scarcity." Ann Arbor: Department of Population Planning and International Health, School of Public Health, University of Michigan, 15 November 1994.

Guichaoua, André. "La mise en place des nouvelles autoritées rwandaises." In *Les crises politiques au Burundi et au Rwanda 1993–94*. Ed. André Guichaoua. Paris: Karthala, 1995, 722–730.

Gurr, Ted R., and Barbara Harff. "Toward Empirical Theory of Genocides and Politicides: Identification and Measurement of Cases." *International Studies Quarterly* 32, 3 (September 1988): 359–371.

———. *Ethnic Conflict in World Politics*. Princeton: Princeton University Press, 1993.

Hallam, Alistair. "ODA to Rwanda." *Background Note/Joint Evaluation*. London: Overseas Development Institute, 1995.

———. "Overseas Development Assistance to Rwanda." Background Paper, Study III, *Joint Evaluation*. Copenhagen: DANIDA, 1996.

Halvorsen, Kate. "Refugee Camps in Zaire: Humanitarian Issues." Background Paper, Study II, *Joint Evaluation*. Copenhagen: DANIDA, 1996.

Hara, Fabienne. "Burundi: A Case of Parallel Diplomacy." In *Herding Cats: Multiparty Mediation in a Complex World*. Ed. Chester A. Crocker et al. Washington, DC: U.S. Institute for Peace, 1999.

Herbst, Jeffrey. "The Organisation of Rebellion in Africa." Paper presented at the conference Economics of Political Violence, Center of International Studies, Princeton University, 18–19 March 2000.

Hilsum, Lindsey. "Where is Kigali?" Special issue of *Granta* 51, "Big Men" (Autumn 1995): 145–179.

Hoffman, Mark. "Third-party Mediation and Conflict Resolution in the Post-Cold War World." In *Dilemmas of World Politics: International Issues in a Changing World*. Ed. John Baylis and Nick Rengger. Oxford: Clarendon Press, 1992: 261–286.

———. "Doing No Harm? Rethinking the Role of Aid Agencies." *LSE Magazine* (Summer 1997).

Horowitz, Donald. *Ethnic Groups in Conflict*. London: University of California Press, 1985.

Hume, Cameron. *Ending Mozambique's War: The Role of Mediation and Good Offices*. Washington, DC: U.S. Institute for Peace, 1994.

Jabri, Viviene. *Mediating Conflict: Decision-making and Western Intervention in Namibia*. New York: St. Martin's Press, 1990.

Johnston, Sir Harry. *The Uganda Protectorate*. 2 vols. London: Hutchinson, 1902.

Joint Evaluation of Emergency Assistance to Rwanda. *The International Response to Conflict and Genocide: Lessons from the Rwanda Experience: Synthesis Report*. Copenhagen: DANIDA, March 1996.

Jones, Bruce D. "'Intervention Without Borders': Humanitarian Intervention in Rwanda, 1990–1994." *Millennium: Journal of International Studies* 24, 2 (Summer 1995): 225–249.

———. "NGOs in Complex Emergencies: The Case of Rwanda." Ottawa: CARE Canada, 1996.

———. "Civil War, the Peace Process, and Genocide in Rwanda." In *Civil Wars in Africa: Their Roots and Their Resolution.* Ed. Robert O. Matthews and Taisier Ali. Toronto: McGill-Queens University Press, 1999, 53–86.

———. "Security in the Zaire Refugee Camps." Background Paper, Study II, *Joint Evaluation.*

———. "The Arusha Peace Process: Preventive Diplomacy?" Background Paper, Study II, *Joint Evaluation.*

———. "The Arusha Peace Process." In *The Path of a Genocide: The Rwandan Crisis from Uganda to Zaire.* Ed. Howard Adelman and Astri Suhrke. New Brunswick, NJ: Transaction Publishers, 1999.

———. "Military Intervention in Rwanda's 'Two Wars': Partisanship and Indifference." In *Civil War, Insecurity, and Intervention.* Ed. Jack Snyder and Barbara Walter. New York: Columbia University Press, 1999, 116–145.

———. "Strategic Coordination and Peace Implementation: Assessing the Policy Challenge." In *Peace Implementation: Themes, Issues and Challenges.* Ed. Stephen Stedman at al. Forthcoming, 2001.

Jones, Bruce D., and Charlie Cater. *Civilians in War.* New York: International Peace Academy, September 1999.

Jones, Bruce D., and Janice Gross Stein. "NGOs and Early Warning: The Case of Rwanda." In *Early Warning and Early Response.* Ed. Susanne Schmeidl and Howard Adelman. New York: Columbia International Affairs Online, 1998.

Jones, Bruce D., and Charles Tilly. Stanford University/MacArthur Foundation Conference on State-Sponsored Mass Killing: "Towards a Strategic Theory of State-sponsored Mass Killing: Reviewing the Comparative Genocide Debate." Stanford: Stanford University, 17 April 1997.

Kakwenzire, Joan, and Dixon Kamukama, "The Development and Consolidation of Extremist Forces in Rwanda." In *The Path of a Genocide: The Rwandan Crisis from Uganda to Zaire.* Ed. Howard Adelman and Astri Suhrke. New Brunswick, NJ: Transaction Publishers, 1999.

Karim, Ataul, et al. *Operation Lifeline Sudan (OLS): A Review.* Geneva: UN Department of Humanitarian Affairs, 1996.

Keane, Fergal. *Season of Blood: A Rwandan Journey.* London: Viking, 1995.

Keen, David. *The Privatization of War: A Political Economy of Conflict in Sierra Leone.* London: James Currey, 1997.

Kent, Randolph. "The Integrated Operation Center in Rwanda: Coping with Complexity." In *After Rwanda: The Co-ordination of United Nations Humanitarian Assistance.* Ed. Jim Whitman and David Pocock. London: Macmillan Press, 1996, 63–85.

Kuperman, Alan J. "Rwanda in Retrospect." *Foreign Affairs* 79, 1 (January/February 2000): 94–118.
Lægrid, Turid. "U.N. Peacekeeping in Rwanda." In Adelman and Suhrke, *Path to a Genocide*, 231–252.
Laitin, David D. "Somalia: Civil War and International Intervention." In *Civil Wars, Insecurity, and Intervention*. Ed. Barbara F. Walter and Jack Snyder. New York: Columbia University Press, 1999, 146–180.
Lake, David A., and Daniel Rothschild. "Containing Fear: The Origins and Management of Ethnic Conflict." *International Security* 21 (Fall 1996): 41–75.
LaRose-Edwards, Paul. "The Rwandan Crisis of April 1994: The Lessons Learned." Report for Regional Security and Peacekeeping Division (IDC) International Security, Arms Control, and CSCE Affairs Bureau, Department of Foreign Affairs and International Trade, Ottawa, Canada, November 1994.
Lautze, Sue, and Bruce D. Jones with Mark Duffield. *Strategic Humanitarian Coordination in the Great Lakes Region, 1996–1997: An Independent Study for the Inter-Agency Standing Committee.* New York: Office for the Coordination of Humanitarian Affairs, March 1998.
Lederach, John Paul. *Building Peace: Sustainable Reconciliation in Divided Societies.* Toyko: UN University Press, 1995.
Leitenberg, Milton. "Rwanda, 1994: International Incompetence Produces Genocide." *Peacekeeping and International Relations* 23, 6 (November/December 1994): 6–10.
Lemarchand, René. "Burundi: The Politics of Ethnic Amnesia." In *Genocide Watch*. New Haven: Yale University Press, 1992, 70–86.
———. "Burundi in Comparative Perspective: Dimensions of Ethnic Strife." *The Politics of Ethnic Conflict Regulation: Case Studies of Protracted Ethnic Conflicts.* Ed. John McGarry and Brendan O'Leary. London: Routledge, 1993, 151–171.
———. *Burundi: Ethnic Conflict and Genocide.* New York: Woodrow Wilson Center and Cambridge University Press, 1994.
———. *Burundi: Ethnocide as Discourse and Practice.* Washington, DC: Woodrow Wilson Center Press; New York: Cambridge University Press, 1994.
———. "Managing Transition Anarchies: Rwanda, Burundi, and South Africa in Comparative Perspective." *Journal of Modern African Studies* 32, 4 (December 1994): 581–604.
Leslie, W. J. *Zaire: Continuity and Political Change in an Oppressive State.* Boulder: Westview Press, 1993.
Lewis, Ioan M. *A Pastoral Democracy.* Oxford: Oxford University Press, 1961.
Licklider, Roy E., ed. *Stopping the Killing: How Civil Wars End.* New York: New York University Press, 1995.

"Listening Mode in Ulster: The Participants in Northern Ireland's Peace Process are Running out of Ideas." *The Economist,* 22 April 2000.

Luck, Edward C. "The Enforcement of Humanitarian Norms and the Politics of Ambivalence." In *Civilians in War.* Ed. Simon Chesterman. Boulder: Lynne Rienner, 2001.

Lund, Michael S. *Preventing Violent Conflicts: A Strategy for Preventive Diplomacy.* Washington, DC: U.S. Institute of Peace Press, 1996.

MacDonald, John W., and Diane B. Bendahmane. *Conflict Resolution: Track Two Diplomacy.* Washington, DC: U.S. Department of State, Foreign Service Institute, 1987.

Mamdani, Mahmood. "Why Rwanda Trumpeted Its Zaire Role." *Mail and Guardian,* 8 August 1997.

Matloff, Judith. "The New 'Congo' Tries to Restrain Its Vengeance." *Christian Science Monitor,* 21 May 1997: 6.

———. "The War's End in Congo Ricochets into Neighbors." *Christian Science Monitor,* 8 July 1997: 7.

Matthews, K., S. S. Mushi, and J. K. Nyerere, eds. *Foreign Policy of Tanzania, 1961–1981: A Reader.* Dar-Es-Salaam: Tanzania Publishing House, 1981.

Matthews, Robert O., and Taisier Ali, eds. *Civil Wars in Africa: Their Roots and Their Resolution.* Toronto: McGill-Queens University Press, 1999.

Mayall, James, ed. *The New Interventionism, 1991–1994.* Cambridge, UK: Cambridge University Press, 1996.

Miller, Robert, ed. *Aid as Peacemaker: Canada's Development Assistance and Third World Conflict.* Ottawa: Carleton University Press, 1992.

Minear, Larry, and Thomas G. Weiss. *Mercy Under Fire: War and the Global Humanitarian Community.* Boulder: Westview Press, 1995.

Mitchell, Christopher R. "The Process and Stages of Mediation: Two Sudanese Cases." In *Making War and Waging Peace: Foreign Intervention in Africa.* Ed. David Smock. Washington, DC: U.S. Institute for Peace, 1993, 139–159.

Moisi, Dominique. "Intervention in French Foreign Policy." Ed. Hedley Bull. *Intervention in World Politics.* Oxford: Oxford University Press, 1984, 67–78.

Moisi, Dominique, and Lellouche Moisi. "French Policy in Africa." *International Security* (Spring 1979): 108–133.

Mokoli, M. M. *State Against Development: The Experience of Post-1965 Zaire.* Westport, CT: Greenwood Press, 1992.

Morrison, J. Stephen. "Zaire: Looming Disaster after Preventive Diplomacy." *SAIS review* 15, 2 (Summer-Fall 1995): 39–52.

Museveni, Yoweri K. "Democracy and Good Governance in Africa: An African Perspective." *Mediterranean Quarterly* 5, 4 (Fall 1994): 1–8.

Myers, G., T. Klak, and T. Koehl. "The Inscription of Difference: News Coverage of the Conflicts in Rwanda and Bosnia." *Political Geography* 15, 1 (January 1996): 21–46.

Newbury, Catherine. *The Cohesion of Oppression: Clientship and Ethnicity in Rwanda, 1860–1960*. New York: Columbia University Press, 1988.
———. "Rwanda: Recent Debates over Governance and Rural Development." In *Governance and Politics in Africa*. Ed. Göran Hydén and Michael Bratton. Boulder: Lynne Rienner Publishers, 1992, 193–220.
Newbury, David. *Kings and Clans: Ijwwi Island and the Lake Kivu Rift, 1780–1840*. Madison: University of Wisconsin Press, 1991.
———. "Trick Cyclists? Recontextualizing Rwandan Dynastic Chronology." *History in Africa* 21 (1994): 191–218.
Okoth, P. Godfrey. "The OAU and the Ugandan-Tanzania War, 1978–79." *Journal of African Studies* 14, 3 (Fall 1987): 152–162.
O'Leary, Brendan. *The Politics of Antagonism: Understanding Northern Ireland*. London: Athlone Press, 1993.
Omar, Rakiya. "A Bitter Harvest." *The Guardian*, 30 April 1997: 21.
Ottunnu, Ogenga. "Rwandese Refugees and Immigrants in Uganda" and "An Historical Analysis of the Invasion by the Rwandese Patriotic Army (RPA)." In *The Path of a Genocide: The Rwandan Crisis from Uganda to Zaire*. Ed. Howard Adelman and Astri Suhrke. New Brunswick, NJ: Transaction Publishers, 1999.
Ould-Abdallah, Ahmedou. *Burundi on the Brink: A UN Special Envoy Reflects on Preventive Diplomacy*. Washington, DC: U.S. Institute of Peace Press, 2000.
Pakenham, Thomas. *The Scramble for Africa, 1876 to 1912*. New York: Random House, 1991.
Percival, Valerie, and Thomas Homer-Dixon. "Environmental Scarcity and Violent Conflict: The Case of Rwanda." *Journal of Environment and Development* 5, 3 (September 1996): 270–291.
"Political, Social, and Cultural Series." *Africa Research Bulletin* 23–28. London: Basil Blackwell, 1991–1994.
Pomfret, John. "Rwandans Led Revolt in Congo." *Washington Post*, 9 July 1997: A01.
Posen, Barry. "The Security Dilemma and Ethnic Conflict." *Survival* 35, 1 (Spring 1993): 27–47.
Pottier, Johann. "The 'Self' in Self-Repatriation: Closing Down Mugunga Camp, Eastern Zaire." *The End of the Refugee Cycle*. Ed. R. Black and K. Khoser. Oxford: Berghahn, forthcoming.
———. "Agricultural Rehabilitation and Food Insecurity in Post-war Rwanda: Assessing Needs, Designing Solutions." *IDS bulletin* 27, 3 (July 1996): 56–76.
Prunier, Gérard. *The Rwandan Crisis: History of a Genocide*. New York: Columbia University Press, 1995.
———. "Operation Turquoise and the French Role in Rwanda." Presentation for the Workshop for Study II, *Joint Evaluation*. Washington, DC: U.S. Committee for Refugees, December 1995.
———. "The Great Lakes Crisis." *Current History* 96, 610 (May 1997): 193–199.

Reno, William. "Reinvention of an African Patrimonial State: Charles Taylor's Liberia." *Third World Quarterly* 16, 1 (1995): 109–120.

Reyntjens, Filip. "Les éléctions rwandaises du 26 décembre 1983: considérations juridiques et politiques." *Mois en Afrique* 223–224 (August-September 1984): 18–28.

———. "Pouvoir et droit au Rwanda: Droit public et évolution politique, 1916–1973." Teruven, Belgique: Musée Royal de l'Afrique Centrale, 1985.

———. "The Proof of the Pudding Is in the Eating: The June 1993 Elections in Burundi." *Journal of Modern African Studies* 31, 4 (December 1993): 563–584.

———. *L'Afrique des Grands Lacs en Crise: Rwanda et Burundi, 1990–1994*. Paris: Khartala, 1994.

———. *Trois jours qui ont fait basculer l'histoire*. Bruxelles: CEDAF, 1995.

———. *Burundi*. London: Minority Rights Group, 1996.

Rieff, David. "Realpolitik in Congo: Should Zaire's Fate Have Been Subordinate to the Fate of the Rwandan Refugees?" *The Nation* 265, 1, 7 July 1997: 16.

Rouvez, Alain. "French, British, and Belgian Involvement." In *Making War and Waging Peace: Foreign Intervention in Africa*. Ed. David Smock. Washington, DC: U.S. Institute for Peace, 1993, 27–51.

Rubin, Jeffrey Z., and Jacob Bercovitch, eds. *Mediation in International Relations: Multiple Approaches to Conflict Management*. New York: St. Martin's Press in association with the Society for the Psychological Study of Social Issues, 1992.

Rudasingwa, Theogene. "Open Forum on Rwanda." International Alert, March 1996.

Rupesinghe, Kumar. Address to the State Department Forum on Conflict Resolution. Washington, DC. December 1995.

"Rwanda." Special issue of *Journal of Refugee Studies* 9, 3 (September 1996).

Savir, Uri. *The Process: 1100 Days That Changed the Middle East*. New York: Random House, 1998.

Shaw, Timothy, and Olajide Aluko, eds. *The Political Economy of African Foreign Policy: Comparative Analysis*. Aldershot, UK: Gower, 1985.

Shoumatoff, Alex. "Mobutu's Final Days." *Vanity Fair* 444, August 1997: 92.

Smith, Patrick. "Africa at Trigger-Point." *The Observer*, 18 May 1997: 27.

Smock, David R., ed. *Making War and Waging Peace: Foreign Intervention in Africa*. Washington, DC: U.S. Institute for Peace Press, 1993.

Sommers, Marc. "Representing Refugees: The Role of Elites in Burundi Refugee Society." *Disasters* 19, 1 (March 1995): 19–25.

"Special Report on Rwanda." *Crosslines* 2, 4–5 (October 1994).

Speke, John Hanning. *Journal of the Discovery of the Source of the Nile*. London, 1863.

Stedman, Stephen John, and Thomas Olson, eds. *Peacemaking in Civil War: International Mediation in Zimbabwe, 1974–1980*. Boulder: Lynne Rienner Publishers, 1991.

———. *The New Is Not Yet Born: Conflict in Southern Africa*. Washington, DC: Brookings Institution Press, 1994.

———. "Negotiation and Mediation in Internal Conflict." *The International Dimensions of Internal Conflict*. Ed. Michael E. Brown. Cambridge: MIT Press, 1996, 341–377.

———. "Spoiler Problems in Peace Processes." *International Security* 22, 2 (Fall 1997): 5–53.

———. "The Failure of Preventive Action: The Great Lakes Region of Africa, 1994–1997." Memorandum presented at the Center for Preventive Action's 4th Annual Conference. New York, 11 December 1997.

Stedman, Stephen Don Rothchild, and Elizabeth Cousens, eds. *Peace Implementation: Themes, Issues, and Challenges*. Forthcoming, 2001.

Stein, Janice Gross, ed. *Getting to the Table: The Process of International Prenegotiation*. Baltimore: Johns Hopkins University Press, 1989.

Stockton, Nicholas. "Rwanda: Rights and Racism." Unpublished paper. Oxford, December 1996.

Styan, David. "The Origins of 'le droit d'ingérence' and Its Contradictory Relationship with French African Policy." Paper presented at Brazzaville + 50. Boston University. Boston, 7–8 October 1994.

Suhrke, Astri. "Facing Genocide: The Record of the Belgian Battalion in Rwanda" *Security Dialogue*, 29, 1 (1998): 37–47.

Suhrke, Astri, et al. "An Evaluation of UNHCR's Response to the Kosovo Emergency." Geneva: UN High Commissioner for Refugees, March 2000.

Suhrke, Astri, and Bruce D. Jones. "Preventive Diplomacy in Rwanda: Failure to Act, or Failure of Actions." In *Opportunities Missed, Opportunities Seized*. Lanham, Md.: Rowman and Littlefield, 2000.

Tekle, Amare. "The Organization for African Unity and Conflict Prevention, Management, and Resolution." Study II *Joint Evaluation*. Addis Ababa, Ethiopia, December 1995.

———. "The OAU: Conflict Prevention, Management, and Resolution." In *The Path of a Genocide: The Rwandan Crisis from Uganda to Zaire*. Ed. Howard Adelman and Astri Suhrke. New Brunswick, NJ: Transaction Publishers, 1999, 111–130.

Touval, Saadia. "Biased Intermediaries: Theoretical and Historical Considerations." *Jerusalem Journal of International Relations* 1, 1 (1975): 51–79.

Touval, Saadia, and I. William Zartman. *International Mediation in Theory and Practice*. SAIS Papers: International Affairs 6. Boulder: Westview Press, 1985.

Uvin, Peter. "Tragedy in Rwanda: The Political Ecology of Conflict." *Environment* 38, 3 (April 1996): 7–15.

———. "Development, Aid, and Conflict: Reflections from the Case of Rwanda." Helsinki, Finland: UNU/Wider, December 1996.

———. *Aiding Violence: The Development Enterprise in Rwanda*. West Hartford, CT: Kumarian Press, 1998.

Vaccaro, J. Matthew. "The Politics of Genocide: Peacekeeping and Disaster Relief in Rwanda." In *UN Peacekeeping, American Politics, and the Uncivil Wars of the 1990s.* 1st ed. Ed. William S. Durch. New York: St. Martin's Press, 1996, 367–407.

Vail, Leroy, ed. *The Creation of Tribalism in Southern Africa.* London: James Currey, 1988.

Van der Meeren, Rachel. "Rwanda and Burundi: The Refugee Angle on Long Term Problems." Unpublished paper, 1996.

———. "Three Decades in Exile: Rwandan refugees, 1960–1990." *Journal of Refugee Studies* 9 (1996): 252–267.

Vassall-Adams, Guy. *Rwanda: An Agenda for International Action.* Oxford: Oxfam Publications, 1994.

Verschave, François-Xavier. *Complicite de génocide? La politique de la France au Rwanda.* Paris: La Découverte, 1994.

Verschave, François-Xavier, and Claudine Vidal. "France-Rwanda: l'engrenage d'un génocide." Rapport préparé pour l'observatoire permanent de la coopération française. Paris. 19 septembre 1994.

Waller, David. *Rwanda: Which Way Now.* Oxford: Oxfam, 1993.

Walter, Barbara F. "Why Negotiations Fail." Diss. University of Chicago, 1996.

———. "The Critical Barrier to Civil War Settlement." *International Organization* 51, 3 (1997): 335–369.

———. "Designing Transitions from Civil War: Demobilization, Democratization, and Commitments to Peace." *International Security* 24, 1 (Summer 1999): 127–156.

Wamba, E. "Democracy, Multipartyism, and Emancipative Politics in Africa: The Case of Zaire." *Africa Development* 18, 4 (1993): 95–118.

Watson, Catherine. *Background to an Invasion.* Washington, DC: U.S. Committee for Refugees, 1992.

Weiss, Thomas G. "Overcoming the Somalia Syndrome—'Operation Rekindle Hope'?" *Global Governance* 1 (1995): 171–187.

Whitman, Jim, and David Pocock, eds. *After Rwanda: The Co-ordination of United Nations Humanitarian Assistance.* London: Macmillan Press, 1996.

Woodward, Susan. *Balkan Tragedy: Chaos and Dissolution after the Cold War.* Washington, DC: Brookings Institution, 1995.

Zartman, I. William, ed. *Elusive Peace: Negotiating an End to Civil Wars.* Washington, DC: Brookings Institution, 1995.

Zartman, I. William, and Francis Deng, eds. *Conflict Resolution in Africa.* Washington, DC: Brookings Institution, 1991.

Zartman, I. William, and J. Lewis Rasmussen, eds. *Peacemaking in International Conflict: Methods and Techniques.* Washington, DC: USIP Press, 1997.

Zolberg, Aristide, Astri Suhrke, and Sergio Aguayo. *Escade from Violence: Conflict and the Refugee Crisis in the Developing World.* Oxford: Oxford University Press, 1989.

NGO and Government Documents

ActionAid. "Conference Report: Understanding the Great Lakes Crisis." Nairobi, Kenya, 12 February 1997.
African Rights. "Humanitarianism Unbound? Current Dilemmas Facing Multi-Mandate Relief Operations in Political Emergencies." Discussion Paper No. 5, 1994.
Amnesty International. "Crisis in Eastern Zaire." London, 8 November 1996.
———. "Great Lakes Region Still in Need of Protection: Repatriation, Refoulement, and the Safety of Refugees and the Internally Displaced." London, 24 January 1997.
Appathurai, James, and Ralph Hnatyshyn. "Lessons Learned from the Zaire Mission." Report on Canadian Government [MNF] Mission to Zaire and Briefing on Follow Up Meeting by Martin Griffiths. Ottawa, May 1997.
Bedford, Eleanor. "Site Visit to Eastern Congo/Zaire: Analysis of Humanitarian and Political Issues." U.S. Committee for Refugees. Site Visit Notes. 10 April–10 May 1997.
CARE Canada. Internal Reports, 1992–1994. Ottawa, 1992–1994.
CARE Rwanda. Internal Reports, 1992–1993. Kigali, Rwanda, 1992–1993.
———. *Annual Report.* Ottawa, December 1993.
Commission Internationale d'Enquette sur les Violations des Droits de l'Homme au Burundi depuis le 21 octobre 1993. *Rapport Final.* New York and Paris, July 1994.
Council on Foreign Relations. "A Strategy for the Great Lakes Region of Central Africa." New York, 31 March 1997.
Democratic Party. "Museveni, Buyoya, Mwinyi: Stop Strangling the Sovereign Republic of Rwanda." DP/IR/04/93. Report by John Lusingu, International Relations Secretary. Dar-es-Salaam, Tanzania, 31 March 1993.
European Community Humanitarian Office. Operation Survey of URG/RW/7–93/207: "Humanitarian Aid to Displaced People in Rwanda." Brussels, 20–30 November 1993.
Executive Committee of Rwandaphone Zairians Association. "Memorandum on the Tragedy of the Rwandophone Zairians with Some Proposals and Recommendations." Nairobi, Kenya, June 1996.
Government of France, Ministry of Foreign Affairs. "Terms of Reference, Opération Turquoise." Paris, July 1994.
Government of Holland. "Report of the Zairian Camp Security Contingent." Dutch Police Contingent. Unofficial document. Goma, Zaire, March 1995.
Human Rights Watch Arms Project. "Arming Rwanda: The Arms Trade and Human Rights Abuses in the Rwandan War." 6, 1, New York, January 1994.
Human Rights Watch/Africa. "Rwanda: Talking Peace and Waging War: Human Rights since the October 1990 Invasion." 4, 3, London, 27 February 1992.

———. "Beyond the Rhetoric: Continuing Human Rights Abuses in Rwanda." 5, 7, London, June 1993.
———. "Report of the International Commission of Investigation on Human Rights Violations in Rwanda since October 1, 1990: Final Report." London, March 1993.
———. "Genocide in Rwanda April-May 1994." 6, 4, New York, May 1994.
Médecins sans Frontières. "Forced Flight: A Brutal Strategy of Elimination in Eastern Zaire." Paris, 16 May 1997.
Museveni, Hon. Mr. Y. K. Address to the National Assembly of South Africa. Johannesburg, South Africa, 27 May 1997.
Organization for African Unity. JPMC/RWD/OAU/1 (I) Rev.2, "Rules of Procedure for the Joint Political-Military Commission (JPMC)." Arusha, Tanzania, October 1993.
———. JPMC/RWD/OAU/2 (I), "Terms of Reference of the Neutral Military Observer Group." Arusha, Tanzania, October 1993.
Physicians for Human Rights. "Rwanda 1994: A Report of the Genocide." San Francisco, October 1994.
———. "Investigations in Eastern Congo and Western Rwanda: A Report by Physicians for Human Rights." San Francisco, July 1997.
Refugees International. "The Lost Refugees: Herded and Hunted in Eastern Zaire." Washington, DC, September 1997.
U.S. Committee for Refugees. "From Coup to Coup: Thirty Years of Death, Fear, and Displacement in Burundi." Washington, DC, September 1996.

Peace Accords, Cease-Fires, and Related Documents

17 October 1990, "Mwanza Communiqué." Mwanza, Tanzania.
26 October 1990. "Gbadolite Communiqué." Gbadolite, Zaire.
20 November 1990. "Goma Communiqué." Goma, Zaire.
17 February 1991. "Zanzibar Communiqué." Zanzibar, Tanzania.
19 February 1991. "Dar-es-Salaam Declaration on Rwandese Refugees Problem." Dar-es-Salaam, Tanzania.
22 March 1991. "Cease-fire Agreement between the Government of the Republic of Rwanda and the Rwandese Patriotic Front." N'Sele, Zaire.
7 September 1991. "The Gbadolite Cease-fire Agreement between the Government of the Republic of Rwanda and the Rwandese Patriotic Front." Gbadolite, Zaire.
14–15 January 1992. "Compte rendu de la réunion du 14 -15 janvier 1992 entre la délégation du gouvernement rwandais et celle du F.P.R." RPF Territory, Rwanda.
12 July 1992. "The N'Sele Cease-fire Agreement Between the Government of the Rwandese Republic and the Rwandese Patriotic Front, as

Amended at Gbadolite, 16 September 1991, and at Arusha, 12 July 1992." Arusha, Tanzania.

18 September 1992. "Joint Communiqué issued at the End of the First Part of the Second Round of Political Negotiations between the Government of the Republic of Rwanda and the Rwandese Patriotic Front, held in Arusha, from 7th to 18th September 1992." Arusha, Tanzania.

30 October 1992. "Protocol of Agreement on Power-Sharing within the Framework of a Broad-Based Transitional Government between the Government of the Republic of Rwanda and the Rwandese Patriotic Front." Arusha, Tanzania.

9 January 1993. "Joint Communiqué issued at the End of the Third Round of the Political Negotiations on Power-Sharing between the Government of the Republic of Rwanda and the Rwandese Patriotic Front Held in Arusha from 24 November 1992 to 9 January 1992." Arusha, Tanzania.

7 March 1993. "Communiqué conjoint publié à l'issue de la rencontre de haut niveau entre le gouvernement de la république rwandaise et le front partriotique rwandais, tenue à Dar-es-Salaam du 5 au 7 mars 1993." Dar-es-Salaam, Tanzania.

13 April 1993. "Protocole additionnel au protocols d'entente entre les parties politiques qui participent au governement de transition mis en place le 16 avril 1992." Kigali, Rwanda.

9 June 1993. "Joint Communiqué issued at the End of Negotiations between the Government of the Republic of Rwanda and the Rwandese Patriotic Front on the Repatriation of Rwandese Refugee Problem and the Resettlement of Displaced Persons Held in Arusha, United Republic of Tanzania, from 2-6 June 1993." Arusha, Tanzania.

3 August 1993. "Protocole d'accord entre le gouvernement de la république rwandaise et le front patriotique rwandais portant sur les questions diverses et dispositions finales." Arusha, Tanzania.

4 August 1993. "Declaration Adopted by the Regional Summit on the Occasion of the Signing of the Peace Agreement Between the Government of the Republic of Rwanda and the Rwandese Patriotic Front." Arusha, Tanzania.

4 August 1993. "Peace Agreement Between the Government of the Republic of Rwanda and the Rwandese Patriotic Front." Arusha, Tanzania.

United Nations Documents

Carlsson, Ingvar, Han Sung-Joo, and Rufus M. Kupolati. "Report of the Independent Inquiry into the Actions of the UN During the 1994 Genocide in Rwanda." New York, 15 December 1999.

Department of Humanitarian Affairs. "Integrated Regional Information Network: Mission Report from Masisi, Zaire." Nairobi, Kenya, May 1996.

———. "Practical Approaches to the Crises of the Great Lakes: Key Issues and Proposals (also comments)." March 1997.
———. "The Democratic Republic of Congo and the Wider Region: Issues for the Future." Internal Background Briefing Paper. May 1997.
———. "Humanitarian Space in Eastern Zaire." Position Paper. May 1997.
———. "Activities of the DHA-Geneva Task Force for Eastern Zaire in Support of Humanitarian Operations in the Great Lakes Region." New York, July 1997.
Department of Peacekeeping Operations. Internal Report. New York, 18 November 1994.
———. "Comprehensive Seminar on Lessons Learned from the United Nations Assistance Mission for Rwanda (UNAMIR)." New York, 1 June 1996.
———. "Summary of Contributions to Peacekeeping Operations by Country." New York, 1996.
Department of Political Affairs. "Report of the Reconnaissance Mission." New York, March 1993.
Economic and Social Council. Commission on Human Rights, Fiftieth Session: Item 12 of the Provisional Agenda: "Report by Mr. B. W. Ndiaye, Special Rapporteur, on his Mission to Rwanda from 8 to 17 April 1993." E/CN.4.1994/7/Add.1. Geneva, 11 August 1993.
S/25536. "Letter Dated 2 April 1993 from the Permanent Representative of France to the United Nations Addressed to the Secretary-General." 2 April 1993.
S/25810. "Interim Report of the Secretary-General on Rwanda." 20 May 1993.
S/25951. "Letter Dated 14 June 1993 from the Permanent Representative of Rwanda to the United Nations Addressed to the President of the Security Council." 14 June 1993.
S/26927. "Report of the Secretary-General on the United Nations Assistance Mission to Rwanda." 30 December 1993.
S/1994/470. "Special Report of the Secretary-General on the United Nations Assistance Mission for Rwanda." 20 April 1994.
S/1994/924. "Report of the Secretary-General on the Situation in Rwanda." 3 August 1994.
S/1994/1125. "Letter Dated 1 October 1994 from the Secretary-General Addressed to the President of the Security Council." 1 October 1994.
S/1996/286. "Report of the Secretary-General on the Implementation of Resolution 1050 concerning the United Nations Role in Rwanda Following the Withdrawal of UNAMIR." 15 April 1996.
S/1996/887. "Report of the Secretary-General on the Situation in Burundi." 29 October 1996.
S/1996/993. "Report of the Secretary-General on the Implementation of Resolution 1078." 29 November 1996.

S/1997/547. "Report of the Secretary-General on the Situation in Burundi." 15 July 1997.
S/Res/48/248. "Financing of the United Nations Assistance Mission in Rwanda." 5 April 1994.
S/Res/846. "Resolution to Create United Nations Observer Mission to Uganda-Rwanda." 22 June 1993.
S/Res/872. "Resolution to Create United Nations Assistance Mission in Rwanda." 5 October 1993.
S/Res/891. "Resolution to Integrate UNOMUR into UNAMIR." 20 December 1993.
S/Res/912. 21 April 1994.
S/Res/955. 8 November 1994.
S/Res/1050. "On the Arrangements for the Withdrawal of the UN Assistance Mission for Rwanda and Maintaining of the UN Office in Rwanda." 8 March 1996.
S/Res/1072. "On the Situation in Burundi." 30 August 1996.
S/Res/1078. "On the Situation in the Great Lakes Region." 9 November 1996.
S/Res/1080. "On the Situation in the Great Lakes Region." 15 November 1996.
S/Res/1097. "On the Situation in the Great Lakes Region." 18 February 1997.
Secretary-General. *Annual Report on the Work of the Organization.* New York, December 1999.
UNAMIR. "Force Commander's Directive No. 01: Rules of Engagement." Kigali, Rwanda, October 1993.
UNAMIR Code Cable, Kigali, Rwanda, 11 January 1994.
UNAMIR Daily SitRep. Kigali, Rwanda, 22 January, 1994.
UNAMIR/IC/08. Kigali, Rwanda, 14 December 1993.
UNAMIR 162. Code Cable: Booh-Booh to Annan.
UN Disaster Assessment Committee. "Great Lakes Mission Debrief Workshop." Kigali, Rwanda, February 1997.
UNHCR. "Note on High Commissioner's Mission to the Great Lakes Region of Africa." Geneva, February 1997.
———. "Updated Repatriation Operations Plan: Eastern Zaire." Geneva, April 1997.
———. "Lessons Learned from the Burundi and Rwanda Emergencies: Conclusions of an Internal Review Process." Executive Committee of the High Commissioner's Programme. Geneva, January 1997.
UN Humanitarian Coordinator in Burundi. "Joint Operations Plan for Humanitarian Assistance to Burundi." Bujumbura, Burundi, October 1996.
The United Nations and Rwanda, 1993–1996, with an Introduction by Boutros Boutros-Ghali. New York: Department of Public Information, United Nations, 1996.
"United Nations Convention on the Prevention and Punishment of the Crime of Genocide." Multilateral Treaties Deposited with the Secretary-General, 9 December 1948.

Index

Abanyiginya clan, 18
Abeega clan, 18
Adelman, Howard, 5
Akagera National Park, 31
Akazu, 15, 21–24, 24–28; assassination plans by, 36; creation of militia by, 35; defense of power base, 28; dominance by, 26; domination of Presidential Guard by, 27; erosion of power base, 32; generation of fear by, 36; goals of, 35; isolation of, 34; loss of power in agreement, 93; opposition to peace, 46; plan for genocide, 35–38; propaganda by, 35–36, 40, 46; second-track efforts with, 59; as spoilers, 46
Alliance of Democratic Forces for the Liberation of Congo-Zaire, 147, 148
Amin, Idi, 22, 30
Angola, 8, 70, 148
Arusha II, 80
Arusha III, 80
Arusha IV, 80
Arusha V, 81
Arusha Peace Accords (1993), 34; analysis of, 89–97; assessment of outcome, 96–97; collapse of, 103–129; consequences of failure of, 135–151; content, 92–95; delayed implementation of, 35; depicted as sell-out, 111–112; facilitation of, 69–98; foundations of, 69–79; implementation phase, 96, 103–129; initial efforts, 61; limitation of concessions in, 91; mediation phase of, 69–98; participants in, 69–79; prenegotiation for, 53–66; presidential power under, 80–81; as preventive diplomacy, 89–90, 95; seen as imposed by outsiders, 89–90; signing, 85; as trigger for genocide, 36; as unacceptable settlement, 159
Arusha peace process: adjacent processes, 85–89; analysis of, 89–97; appropriate intermediaries in, 9; changing perceptions during, 71; communicative process in, 70–71, 90; conflict subsequent to, 11; content, 92–95; diplomatic perspective, 89; donor conferences, 10; enforcing contested, 5; facilitator at, 72; failure of, 158–160; formal delegations to, 71–72; groundwork for, 3; hostility toward, 4; implementation phase, 103–129; inclusivity of, 90; initial negotiations, 32; inventory, 10; isolation of government and, 4; issues in, 79–85; mediation/facilitation, 69–98; moderates in, 91; observer delegations in, 71–72, 74–78; opposition to, 32, 113–118; prenegotiation phase, 4, 53–66;

Protocol on the Rule of Law, 80; refugee issue in, 83; role of parties in, 94–95; spoilers and, 13n26; third-party efforts in, 4, 11, 85–89; timelines in, 79–85; as unacceptable settlement, 74, 93, 95; as victory for Rwandese Patriotic Front, 74
Assistance, development: conditionality on, 61, 62; Rwandan reliance on, 61

Bagasora, Théoneste, 33, 38, 72, 92, 94, 99n6
Banyarwanda, 21, 22, 23, 28
Banyingana, Paul, 30
Baril, Maurice, 150
Barnett, Michael, 122–123
Belgium, 116; colonial rule by, 17–19; peacemaking efforts by, 53, 64, 65; peace mission to Rwanda, 53; role in Arusha peace process, 75; warnings to United Nations, 114
Beliard, Jean-Christophe, 77
Bertollo, Monsignor Guiseppe, 60, 86, 87
Bihozagara, Jacques, 59
Bizimungu, Pasteur, 49n34, 57
Booh-Booh, Roger, 114, 117, 119
Boutros-Ghali, Boutros, 121
Britain: military missions from, 139
Broad-Based Transitional Government, 80, 81, 91, 104, 105, 111–114
Bucyana, Martin, 36, 113
Bunyenyezi, Paul, 30
Burundi: collapse of democracy in, 36; coup in, 137; dictatorship in, 25; ethnic relations in, 20; humanitarian operations from, 138; observer role, 74; partial genocide in, 40; political developments in, 147; presidential assassination in, 36, 107, 118; refugees in, 20, 137; support for Rwandese Patriotic Front, 74, 100n24; violence in, 107, 108
Byerly, John, 70, 76
Byumba, 32, 42

Cambodia, 70, 109, 110
Canada: military missions from, 139; Multinational Force and, 148–150
CARE, 146, 152n6
Carnegie Commission on Preventing Deadly Conflict, 127
Castes, 18
Cease-fires, 15, 31, 55, 79; broken by Forces Armées Rwandaises, 55; failure of, 15, 55; Gbadolite arrangement, 56; Kinihira, 137; N'Sele Cease-fire Agreement, 55; observer groups for, 56; policing, 55; violations, 85
Central African Republic, 30
CEPGL. *See* Communité Economique des Pay des Grands Lacs
Cholera, 139, 144, 145
Chrétien, Jean-Pierre, 41
Church: contact with Rwandese Patriotic Front, 60; ethnic tensions in, 60, 88; Justice et Paix, 88; mediation efforts by, 59, 60, 86; role in genocide, 102n54
Civil war: complexities of, 6; contingencies of, 6; death toll in, 2; genocide as escalation of, 2; life-cycles of, 6; organizational responses to, 6; subjective nature of, 7
Claes, Willy, 121
Class mobility, 18
Clinton, Bill, 123
Coalition pour la Défense de la République, 32, 34, 36, 50n47, 95, 111–114, 117, 135, 159; demonstrations against peace talks, 82; exclusion from transition government, 82, 94, 96; extreme positions of, 33; formation of militias by, 35; genocide involvement, 39; goals of, 32; membership, 32; in new government, 81; representation in negotiations, 72; seats in Transitional National Assembly, 82
Cohen, Herman, 29, 57, 58, 66, 67n14, 70

Colonialism: Belgian, 17–19; boundaries and, 16; German, 17; Hamitic thesis and, 17, 18; impact on state formation, 16; oppression under, 18; social change and, 20; Tutsis domination under, 19

Communication: facilitation of, 9, 70–71, 90; between parties, 9

Communité Economique des Pay des Grands Lacs (CEPGL), 54, 57; convenor role, 64, 65; credibility issues, 65; monitor role, 64

Competition: electoral, 20; political, 16–20, 34

Conflict: collections of constituencies in, 6; coordination of strategy and action in, 171–172; dynamics, 5, 170; inflammatory rhetoric in, 8, 113, 157, 158; internal, 3; management, 3, 5, 54; methods of, 5; monitoring, 2; obstacles to peaceful resolution of, 157–158; political competition and, 16–20; prevention, 5; renewal of, 144–150; settlement, 69; social, 70; societal levels and, 7

Conflict resolution, 2, 5, 69–71, 86, 96, 128, 163; appropriate intermediaries in, 9; connections between initiatives and, 7; processes of, 9

Conseil National du Développement (CND), 81

Dallaire, Romeo, 105, 108
Dar-es-Salaam Declaration on Rwandese Refugees Problem, 55, 83
D'Aviola, Michel, 75
Decolonization, 19; control of, 20
Demilitarized zone, 33, 86, 104
Demobilization, 7
Democracy: premature, 164–165; pressure for, 19, 21, 28, 32, 61, 63; transition to, 4
Des Forges, Alison, 44
Diouf, Abdou, 74
Disarmament, 7
Dusaidi, Claude, 59

East Timor, 126, 167–169
Economic: collapse, 21, 24, 27, 32, 45; decline, 27
Economic Community of Countries of the Great Lakes Region, 54
Economy: parallel, 13$n22$; political, 13$n22$, 24
Education for Non-Violence and Democracy, 88, 98
Ethnic: hatreds, 39; identity, 19, 20; relations, 88; tensions, 60
Ethnicity, 16; clan and, 18; constructivist accounts of, 48$n10$; creation of, 16–20; identity cards and, 19; primordialist version of, 48$n10$; as social feature, 48$n10$
Exports, 27

Fall, Louis "Papa," 74
Famine, 27
FAR. See Forces Armées Rwandaises
59ers, 21, 22, 23; in National Revolutionary Army, 22; in opposition movement, 22
First Rwandan Republic, 24, 25
Five Musketeers, 87
Forces Armées Rwandaises (FAR), 26–27, 118, 155$n52$, 162; attacks on Rwandese Patriotic Front, 31, 32; breaking of cease-fires, 55; genocide involvement, 38, 39, 41; lack of effectiveness of, 33; military capabilities, 50$n49$; rearmament of, 31; regrouping, 146; reliability of, 38; retreat of, 42, 43; Rwandese Patriotic Front's victories against, 28, 29; in summer offensive, 42; support from France for, 30; use of refugees as human shield, 140; in Zaire, 140, 144, 147
France: African policy, 76–78; enskiller role, 64; explorer role, 64; intervention in Rwanda, 29, 30, 43, 77, 83, 123–127; mediation efforts, 57, 61; Operation Turquoise and, 3, 123–127; pressure on Rwanda for democracy, 61; reassurer role, 64; role in Arusha peace process, 70, 75–77; support for Forces Armées

Rwandaises, 30; support for government of Rwanda, 77
Franco-African Summit (1989), 61
Fuller, Carol, 57

Gabiro Highway, 28, 30, 49n35
Galinie, Lieutenant-Colonel, 61, 63
Gasana, James, 33, 99n2
Gatabazi, Felicien, 36, 112
Gatsinzi, Marcel, 119
Gbadolite talks, 56
Genocide: Arusha Peace Accords as trigger for, 36; causes of, 47n1; coerced participation in, 39–41; coordinated aspects of, 39; death toll from, 2, 43–44, 51n64; escalation toward, 35–38; examples of, 51n70; execution of, 36–39; implications for research, 163–175; internal displacement and, 137; lack of understanding of, 116, 117; misinterpretation of impending signs of, 116; noncoerced participation in, 39–41; NGOs and, 137, 138; nonresponse to, 121–127; perception of opportunity in, 40; plan for, 35–38; poverty and, 39; role of fear in, 40; roots of, 15–47; by Rwandan government forces, 16; scale of, 1; sources of, 21–24; support for, 39; survival of, 135; Tutsis as target, 16
Genocide Convention (1948), 6
Germany: colonial rule by, 17; role in Arusha peace process, 75
Groupe de Contact, 86, 87

Habyarimana, Juvénal, 15, 24, 28, 58, 117, 162, 164; assassination of, 36, 118; assistance from France for, 30; call for refugee return by, 54; in clan-based Hutu regime, 26; in coalition government, 63, 64; initial rule by, 25; international pressure on, 91; in peace negotiations, 36, 54–55, 72; pressures on, 32, 61, 102n57, 161; rejection of accords, 84; successful regime of, 25

Haiti, 109, 110
Hamitic thesis, 17, 18
Hartley, Aidan, 34, 49n35
Herbst, Jeff, 8
Hicks, Irvin, 56
Hoffman, Mark, 9–10
Humanitarian aid: during conflicts, 170–171; control of, 144, 145; costs of, 139; distribution, 144, 145; during genocide, 136–140; in postgenocide period, 150; resuscitation of genocide and, 146, 170–171
Humanitarian crises, 124; displacement in, 136, 137; international community and, 14n39, 136; political response to, 140–144; relief response to, 136–140; renewed conflict and, 136, 170–171
Humanitarian Safe Zone, 138
Human Rights Watch Arms Project, 24
Hutus: discrimination from other Hutus, 26; domination of government, 16; elites, 19; generation of fear by *akazu*, 36; oligarchy, 15; political mobilization by, 16, 19; preferential treatment of, 25, 26; in pre-independence Rwanda, 18

Identity: cards, 19; clan, 16; ethnic, 19, 20; national, 16
Implementation phase, 103–129, 166; demonization in, 111–113; early warnings in, 113–118; mistrust and, 157; mobilization in, 111–113; Neutral International Force in, 104–105; polarization in, 111–113
Impuzamuganbi, 35, 41, 112
Integration: military, 7, 79, 83, 84, 91, 93, 94
Interahamwe, 35, 38, 39, 41, 112
International Committee of the Red Cross, 137
International community: failure to act, 2; pregenocide efforts of, 2–3
Interventions: military, 83; third-party, 47, 85–89
Ireland: military missions from, 139

INDEX

Israel: military missions from, 139

Japan: military missions from, 139
Joint Military-Political Commission (JMPC), 85, 91, 95, 100n27, 101n34; creation of, 79; design of, 71; role, 79, 80; as second channel, 79, 80
Juppé, Alain, 43

Kabila, Laurent, 147
Kagame, Paul, 22, 23, 28, 30, 31, 36, 57, 59, 72, 75, 79, 147, 154n45
Kanyarengwe, Alexis, 119
Kanyarushoke, Ambassador, 57, 92
Kayibanda, Gregoire, 25, 49n28
Kenya: peace talks in, 53
Kibungo, 42
Kigali: fighting in, 42; politics in, 45, 46; Rwandese Patriotic Front victory in, 42
Kuperman, Alan, 126

Land: arable, 39; availability, 27; crises, 39; declining productivity, 27; density, 45; pressure, 21
League of Nations, 19
Lemarchand, René, 20, 89, 90, 91, 95
Les évenements, 20
Les génocidaires, 118, 121, 135, 138, 140, 162

Mackintosh, Anne, 88
Mai-Mai forces, 147
Marchal, Luc, 119
Marley, Anthony, 77, 87
Mazimpaka, Patrick, 34, 72, 95, 164
MDR. *See* Mouvement Démocratique Républicain
Médecins sans Frontières, 137
Mediation, 165; adjacent processes to, 58–64; community-based, 88, 166; international efforts, 57–58; nonregional participation in, 57; official summit meetings, 54; process, 4; regional, 54–57
"Memorandum on the Tragedy of the Rwandaphone Zaireans with some Proposals," 154n44

Military: integration, 79, 83, 84, 91, 93, 94; interventions, 83; leadership, 7; positions held by Habyarima's clan in, 26
Military Observer Group, 54–56; deployment, 64; poor performance of, 65
Militias: formation of, 35; genocide involvement, 38
Mitchell, Christopher, 9, 10, 58, 61, 64
Mitterand, Francois, 29, 76
Mitterand, Jean-Christophe, 76
Mobutu Sese Seko, 24, 30, 54, 56, 118, 148
Moussali, Michel, 36, 113, 116
Mouvement Démocratique Républicain (MDR), 63, 111; in new assembly, 82; in new government, 81; representation in negotiations, 72; seats in Transitional National Assembly, 82
Mouvement Révolutionnarie National pour le Développement (MRND), 25, 32, 50n47, 111–113, 118, 162; demonstrations against peace talks, 82; formation of militias by, 35; government as subset of, 26; membership, 32; moderates in, 59; in new assembly, 82; in new government, 81, 93; relationship to state, 26; second-track efforts with, 59; in Transitional National Assembly, 82
Mozambique, 70, 108
Mpungwe, Ami, 70, 71, 77, 78, 90
MRND. *See* Mouvement Révolutionnarie National pour le Développement
Mugambage, Frank, 147
Multinational Force, 148, 155n52
Munyaneza, Ambassador, 119
Museveni, Yoweri, 22–24, 29–31, 43, 54, 55, 57, 58, 100n24
Mwanza Communiqué, 53–55
Mwinyi, Ali Hassan, 54, 55, 71, 78, 118

National Revolutionary Army (NRA), 22, 24; desertions from, 29; support for Rwandese Patriotic Front, 29

National Revolutionary Movement, 23
Ndadaye, Melchior, 36, 107
Ndasingwa, Landoald, 72
Neutral International Force, 83, 97, 104–105, 107, 108
Neutral Military Observer Group, 34, 75, 79, 80, 85, 86, 99$n13$, 102$n47$, 104
Newbury, Catherine, 18, 25
Newbury, David, 18
Ngulinzira, Boniface, 60, 61, 65, 72, 80, 92
Nigeria, 121–124; cease-fire observation by, 56; observer role, 74
Nilotic peoples, 18
Nongovernmental organizations (NGOs), 124; during genocide, 137–139; indigenous, 7; mediation efforts by, 88; in refugee operations, 146
Northern Ireland, 7, 8
NRA. *See* National Revolutionary Army
N'Sele Cease-fire Agreement (1991), 55, 79
Nsengiyaremye, Dismas, 72
Nsengiyumva, Archbishop Vincent, 63, 86, 102$n54$
Nsengiyumva, Bishop Thadée, 59, 60
Ntagerura, André, 119
Ntambyauro, Agnes, 119
Ntaryamira, Cyprien, 118

Obote, Milton, 22
October War, 28–30
Operation Support Hope, 139
Operation Turquoise, 43, 122–127, 138; humanitarian objectives of, 3, 124; as public-relations exercise, 125; purpose of, 124; sanctuary for *les génocidaires*, 125
Opposition: assassination of members of, 36; in coalition government, 63, 64; factionalization of, 35; fragmentation of, 111, 112; planning for, 166–169

Organization of African Unity, 104, 167; convenor role, 64, 65; cooperation with United Nations, 75, 86; credibility issues, 65; diminishment of role, 34; lack of trust in, 74; Liberation Committee, 54; military deployment by, 3; Military Observer Group, 34, 75, 79, 80, 85, 86; monitor role, 33, 64; opposition from United Nations, 104; peacemaking efforts, 53, 54; in peace process, 56
Organizations: aid, 88; coordination between, 129; expertise in, 167; international, 5; interstate, 54; lack of awareness in, 167; lobby, 23; regional, 54. *See also* Nongovernmental organizations
Oslo process, 7
OXFAM, 88, 102$n53$, 146; Education for Non-Violence and Democracy, 88

Parmehutu, 19, 20, 25. *See also* Parti Socialiste Démocratique
Parti Chrétien Démocratique (PCD), 63; in new assembly, 82; in new government, 82; seats in Transitional National Assembly, 82
Parti Libéral (PL), 63, 111; in new assembly, 82; in new government, 82; representation in negotiations, 72; seats in Transitional National Assembly, 82
Parti Socialiste Démocratique, 63, 111, 112; in new assembly, 82; in new government, 81; seats in Transitional National Assembly, 82
PCD. *See* Parti Chrétien Démocratique
Peacekeeping, 103–129; consequences of failure in, 135–151; dynamics of, 157–177; failure in, 127–129; integration of military units and, 7; obstacles to, 157–158; resistance to, 109; risks of, 105; trust issues and, 7; United Nations Assistance Mission in Rwanda, 103–111

Peacemaking, 3; adjacent processes, 58–64; complexities of, 9, 64–66, 127–129; conncections between initiatives, 64–65; coordination element, 10; diminishment of interest in, 13*n22;* early efforts at, 53–66; failure of, 3–6; implementation phase, 103–129; international efforts, 61–64; multitrack negotiations, 58, 61–64; obstacles to, 157–158; prenegotiation, 53–66; regional efforts, 53–57; resistance to, 8; second-track negotiations, 58–61; security fears and, 7; third-party roles, 64, 85–89; United Nations involvement in, 34; unofficial iniatives for, 59–61; Vatican efforts, 59, 60, 86

PL. *See* Parti Libéral

Political: activism, 63; competition, 16–20, 34, 124; cooperation, 80; decay, 24; decisionmaking, 128; economy, 13*n22,* 24; escalation, 45; fragmentation, 45; of indifference, 122–123; leadership, 7; mediation, 4; mobilization, 8, 16, 19, 36, 44, 45; negotiations, 32, 34, 58, 65; opposition, 1, 35; patronage, 35; stability, 27; tension, 27

Politics: multiparty, 61–64; polarization of, 103; of war, 32–35

Pottier, Johan, 18

Power: circles of, 63; domination by Habyarimana's clan, 26; hierarchy of, 18; structures, 24

Prenegotiation phase, 159, 164; adjacent processes during, 58–64; connections to later difficulties, 66; international efforts during, 57–58; political mediation process in, 4, 53–66; regional efforts during, 53–57

Presidential Guard, 27, 111, 118, 140, 162; domination by *akazu,* 27; genocide involvement, 38, 41

Protocol on the Repatriation of Rwandese Refugees and Resettlement of Displaced Persons, 83

Protocol on the Rule of Law, 80

Prunier, Gérard, 27, 41, 43, 44, 51*n64,* 125

PSD. *See* Parti Socialiste Démocratique

Radio et Television Libre Mille Colines, 36, 117

Radio Rwanda, 30

Refugees: humanitarian corridors for, 155*n52;* in peace talks, 83; political control over, 144, 145; rights of return for, 23, 28, 92; Rwandese Patriotic Front and, 23; separation of soldiers from, 140, 141; in Tanzania, 78; in Uganda, 66*n6;* in Zaire, 43

Repnik, Hans Peter, 75

Reyntjens, Filip, 36, 39, 82

Rhetoric: inflammatory, 8, 113; as strategy, 8; totalistic, 8, 157, 158

Rights: human, 61–64, 88, 102*n53,* 102*n57;* of refugees, 92

RPF. *See* Rwandese Patriotic Front

Rudasingwa, Théogène, 72, 79, 119

Ruhengiri, 31, 42

Rutaremara, Tito, 31

Rwabugiri (King of Rwanda), 17

Rwanda: alternative history of, 160–163; church role in mediation, 59, 60, 86; consistency of borders, 17; coup in, 24; domestic pressure for change in, 73; economic collapse in, 21, 24, 27, 28, 32, 45; environmental issues in, 27, 47*n1;* ethnicity in, 48*n10;* evolution of politics in, 24–28; export earnings, 27; extremists in, 4; famine in, 27; French intervention in, 29, 30; French policy in, 76–78, 100*n19;* internal discrimination system, 19; international pressure on, 28; military interventions in, 3; moderates in, 4; multiparty government in, 61; political stability in, 27; population density in, 27; postindependence, 24;

precolonial state, 17–18; quota system in, 25; refugees from Burundi, 108, 137; refugees from Zaire, 138; reliance on international assistance, 61; renewal of conflict in, 144–150; "salami approach" in, 142, 143; Second Republic, 25; social stresses in, 21; structural adjustment program in, 27; United States policy toward, 61, 75, 78

Rwanda, government of: in Arusha peace process, 34, 71–74; assassination plans, 36; coalition formation, 50$n45$; divisions during negotiations, 72; French support for, 77; Hutu domination of, 16; lack of commitment to process, 73; in mediation efforts, 57, 58; moderate members in, 34; power sharing in, 33; refusal to allow refugees to return, 23; reservations about Organization of African Unity, 104; Second Republic, 25

Rwandan Alliance for National Unity (RANU), 23

Rwandan Revolution, 20

Rwandese Patriotic Front (RPF), 21–24, 159; activities during negotiations, 34; advantageous position of, 92–95; in Arusha peace process, 34, 71–74; attacks by Forces Armées Rwandaises, 31, 32; bargaining strength, 94; commitment to process, 73; conflict with Rwandan army, 15; contact with Church, 60; demonization of, 36, 46, 111–113; diaspora support network, 59; effectiveness at negotiations, 72, 73; fear of, 40; formation of, 23; French intervention and, 43; guerrilla campaigns of, 31, 54; initial invasion of, 15; invasion at Kagitumba, 28; in mediation efforts, 57, 58; membership, 16; military superiority of, 33, 50$n49$, 85, 147; mobilization against, 112; in new assembly, 82; in new government, 93; offensives launched, 33; propaganda against, 36; as rebel movement, 15; refugees and, 23; resistance to United Nations support, 104–105; retreat into Uganda, 30; seats in Transitional National Assembly, 82; in summer offensive, 42–43; support from Burundi, 100$n24$; support from National Revolutionary Army, 29; Tanzanian support for, 85, 100$n23$; Ugandan support for, 24, 31, 58, 74, 100$n24$; victory against Forces Armées Rwandaises, 28, 29

Rwigyema, Fred, 22, 23, 29, 49$n36$

Sadaam Hussein, 8
Safe Humanitarian Zone, 43, 124
Sankoh, Fodeh, 8
Savimbi, Joseph, 8
Security: failure to address, 96; fears, 46, 157, 158; guarantee, 166; needs, 71; private sector, 142; in refugee camps, 141
Senegal: cease-fire observation by, 56; as honest broker, 74; observer role, 74
Sierra Leone, 8, 126, 168, 169
Snyder, Charles, 70, 76
Social: categories, 44; change, 20; cleavages, 16; collapse, 24; conditions, 45; conflict, 70; history, 16; manipulation, 44; relations, 17, 18; services, 27; status, 18; tension, 27
Society: civil, 88; conflict and, 7
Somalia, 109, 120
Spoilers, 8, 10, 46, 158, 169–170; existence of, 13$n26$
State: access to, 19, 25; colonialism and, 16; concessions by, 26; employment, 25; formation, 16
Stedman, Stephen, 8
Stockholm International Peace Research Institute, 2
Structural adjustment program, 27
Student protests, 27
Suhrke, Astri, 119

Tanzania, 3, 50*n49*; attempts to implement accord, 118, 119; economic issues in, 25; as honest broker, 78, 85; invasion of Uganda, 22, 30; as mediator to talks, 58; neutrality of, 78; peace talks in, 53; refugees in, 20, 78, 137; role in Arusha peace process, 70, 71, 78; support for Rwandese Patriotic Front, 85, 100*n23*

Third parties: lack of coordination between, 4–5; peacemaking efforts by, 9–10, 85–89; resources of, 11

Tilly, Charles, 164

Transitional National Assembly, 81

Tutsis: demonization of, 36; dominance by, 18–20, 45; in exile, 15; outflux to other countries, 20; political mobilization by, 16; in pre-independence Rwanda, 18; privileges for, 19; propaganda against, 36; in Rwandese Patriotic Front, 16

Twagiramungu, Faustin, 111, 112

Twa peoples, 16

Uganda: economic tensions in, 22; 59ers in, 22; genocide in, 25; invasion by Tanzania, 22, 30; National Ruling Council in, 23, 24; observer role, 74; peace talks in, 53, 54; refugees in, 20, 21, 23, 24, 66*n6*; and Rwandese Patriotic Front, 30, 31, 58, 74, 100*n24*

Ugandan People's Defence Forces, 154*n46*

UNAMIR. *See* United Nations Assistance Mission in Rwanda

Unemployment, 27

Union Nationale Rwandaise (UNAR), 20

United Nations: Advance Humanitarian Assistance Team, 137; Civilian Liaison Unit, 144; contingency planning at, 167, 168; cooperation with Organization of African Unity, 75, 86; Department of Peacekeeping Operations, 34, 105, 110, 133*n75*, 141–143; Department of Political Affairs, 34, 75; Development Programme, 75; failure to provide support, 104; Fifth Committee, 107; impact of organizational dynamics on peacemaking, 128; lack of trust in, 74; monitoring function, 33; Neutral International Force, 83, 97; peacekeeping operations, 3–5, 109; peacemaking operations, 34; poor administrative systems in, 167; Secretariat, 110, 115, 121, 146, 160, 166, 167; Security Council, 43, 105, 107, 109–111, 115, 121–123, 142, 146, 160, 167; Special Representatives, 10; United States hostility toward, 109; warnings, 113–115

United Nations Assistance Mission in Rwanda (UNAMIR), 34, 103–111, 122–123, 126, 160, 162, 166; attacks on, 119, 120, 131*n52*; budget, 107; challenges to, 107; deployment, 105–108; extremist response to, 111–113; lack of defensive equipment, 108; lack of intelligence capacity, 108; lack of relevance of, 116; management of, 108–111; mandate, 106, 107; opposition to, 111; planning for, 105–108; role as guarantor, 108; target of genocide, 119; troop contingents, 108; United Nations politics and, 108–111; withdrawal of, 111–121

United Nations Assistance Mission in Rwanda II, 122–123, 126

United Nations High Commissioner for Refugees, 36, 54, 75, 122–123, 139, 141, 154*n36*, 167

United Nations Observer Mission to Uganda-Rwanda (UNOMUR), 34, 75, 86, 99*n13*

United States: assistance to Uganda, 58; Central Intelligence Agency, 29, 115, 116; delinker role, 64; Department of State, 29, 57, 59, 61, 67*n14*; enskiller role, 64, 76; explorer role, 64; hostility to

United Nations, 109; intelligence by, 29; mediation efforts, 57, 67$n14$; military missions from, 139; Multinational Force and, 148–150; Operation Support Hope and, 139; policy toward Rwanda, 61, 75, 78; reassurer role, 64; role in Arusha peace process, 70, 75, 76; slow response to genocide, 123; technical assistance from, 57–58
UNOMUR. *See* United Nations Observer Mission to Uganda-Rwanda

Vaccaro, J. Matthew, 109–111, 121, 126
Van der Meeren, Rachel, 24
Vatican: neutral messenger role, 64; peacemaking efforts by, 59, 60, 86
Virunga National Park, 31, 42, 50$n44$

War: international, 12$n7$; parallel economies during, 13$n22$; perpetuation of, 13$n22$; political economy of, 13$n22$; themes of, 45–46; tools of, 46
War, civil, 12$n7$; history of, 15–47; resolution of, 69

Weapons: import violations, 35
Weiss, Thomas, 2
Wiengast, Barry, 40
Woodward, Susan, 136

Young Turk movement, 15, 21–24

Zaire, 24, 118; assistance to Habyarimana, 30; camps in, 141, 143; cease-fire observation by, 56; corruption in, 25; Forces Armées Rwandaises in, 43, 140, 144, 147; *les génocidaires* in, 125; observer role, 74; Operation Turquoise in, 43; peace talks in, 54; refugees in, 43, 137; support for government, 100$n24$; Ugandan troops in, 147; war for control of, 136, 147, 148
Zairian Camp Security Contingent, 144
Zairian Camp Security Operation (ZCSO), 144
Zanzibar Communiqué, 55
Zartman, I. William, 5, 163
Zimbabwe: cease-fire observation by, 56; observer role, 74
Zizimungu, Pasteur, 28
Zone Turquoise, 43, 138, 140

About the Book

Bruce Jones investigates why the wide-ranging efforts to forestall genocidal violence in Rwanda in 1994 failed so miserably.

Jones traces the individual and collective impact of both official and unofficial mediation efforts, peacekeeping missions, and humanitarian aid. Providing theoretical and empirical evidence, he shows that the failure of the peace process was not the result of lack of effort, or even the weakness of any particular effort. Rather, it was due to a combination of factors: the lack of connections among the various attempts at conflict resolution; the intransigence of the warring parties; the lack of a coherent strategy for managing spoilers in the peace process; and weak international support.

Peacemaking in Rwanda generates critical insights into the limits of our contemporary systems for conflict prevention and management, serving as a sobering argument for reform of the international conflict management system.

Bruce D. Jones is currently special assistant to the UN's special coordinator for the Middle East peace process, based in Gaza. Previously, he was responsible for strategic coordination and postconflict policy issues at the UN's Office for the Coordination of Humanitarian Affairs. He has published widely on Rwanda, the Great Lakes region, and complex emergencies.